OVERRIDE

OVER RIDE

Discover Your Brain Type,
Why You Do What You Do,
and How to Do It Better

CONNELL COWAN, PhD
DAVID KIPPER, MD

CITADEL PRESS
Kensington Publishing Corp.
www.kensingtonbooks.com

CITADEL PRESS BOOKS are published by

Kensington Publishing Corp.
119 West 40th Street
New York, NY 10018

Copyright © 2022 by Connell Cowan, PhD, and David Kipper, MD

PUBLISHER'S NOTE
This book is sold to readers with the understanding that while the publisher aims to inform, enlighten, and provide accurate general information regarding the subject matter covered, the publisher is not engaged in providing medical, psychological, financial, legal, or other professional services. If the reader needs or wants professional advice or assistance, the services of an appropriate professional should be sought. Case studies featured in this book are composites based on the author's years of practice and do not reflect the experiences of any individual person.

All Kensington titles, imprints, and distributed lines are available at special quantity discounts for bulk purchases for sales promotions, premiums, fund-raising, educational, or institutional use. Special book excerpts or customized printings can also be created to fit specific needs. For details, write or phone the office of the Kensington sales manager: Kensington Publishing Corp., 119 West 40th Street, New York, NY 10018, attn: Sales Department; phone 1-800-221-2647.

CITADEL PRESS and the Citadel logo are Reg. U.S. Pat. & TM Off.

ISBN: 978-0-8065-4119-8

First Citadel hardcover printing: October 2022

10 9 8 7 6 5 4 3 2 1

Printed in the United States of America

Library of Congress Control Number: 2022938545

ISBN: 978-0-8065-4121-1 (e-book)

For Susan, Sean, and Coby
My love always,
C.C.

For Sam and Chanel, the Shields who forever
protect me from falling on my Sword,
D.K.

Contents

OVERRIDE

Comfort—Too Much of a Good Thing

Why Do I Keep Doing Things I Know Don't Serve My Best Interests? Answer: An Unconscious Addiction to Comfort

"WHY *DO I DO* THINGS I know take away from the quality of my life and why *don't I do* the things that would be helpful and constructive for me?" These are the questions most of us have some ongoing struggle with.

"Why do I sabotage myself and let my diet fall apart?" "Why when I plan to go to the gym do I find myself heading for home instead?" "Why do I blow up at my kids when I know a more measured approach would be more effective?" "Why do I find myself holding back when I'd like to be less cautious?" "Why when I can only afford to pay the minimum on my credit card do I find myself online ordering still another something I really don't need?" "Why when I need to be studying do I find myself lost again scrolling through social media?" "Why do I worry about my health when nobody else seems to be so focused on theirs?" "Why is taking the edge off with that drink or two when I get home from work so compelling?" "Why do I worry so much?" "Why do I tend to see the bright side when my husband, looking at the same facts in our life, comes up with more pessimistic views?" "Why do I have to find myself avoiding things I'd like to be able to do? Indulging in things I shouldn't?"

Why? Why? Why?

A new theory we've been validating for years provides some clear and practical answers to these questions. In its most stripped-down form the theory posits that human beings, over the millennia, have developed two different coping styles, rooted in their genetics, based upon their brain chemistry, and activated by stress. These "styles" provide some valuable attributes to us as well as some predictable challenges. As a species, we are uniquely primed to possess foresight and an ability to project into the future in highly complex ways. We use this capacity of ours to guide our decisions. Picture this: in each of our minds, we have a stage upon which we run through a variety of scenarios. Studies show that around the age of four or five we begin to understand an important aspect of reality: that events can play out in very different ways and we interact with and actively shape these outcomes. In essence, we are fortune-tellers, contingency generators. If we do this or that, then this or that might happen. These scenarios, designed to model possible outcomes, provide the basic calculus for our actions. On these stages in our minds, we apply different "filters" to the scenarios we envision, each generating information, the accumulation of which shapes our behavior. These filters are comprised of the memories of past experiences, the connection to the culture we live in, family influences and traditions, values and attitudes, feelings for others around us, the ability to imagine, our needs and desires, the physical constraints of the situation, and *the deeply hidden influence of our unique brain chemistry*. It is that last filter influencing our behavior that is the one we've struggled to understand for many years and is the core of our theory and subject of this book.

How We Got Together

We first met decades ago through mutual friends and almost immediately dived into discussing the overlaps in our respective fields. As a physician, David had his hands more than full dealing with the "what" of the ailing human body, while Connell, as a psychologist, sorted out the "why and how" of things. David knew, of course, that many of his patients' symptoms were psychological in origin, and Connell saw patients who, irrespective of their personal issues, experienced the effects of their distress in all-too-real physical terms. Sometimes we argued and other times agreed, but always we learned from each other. And we both knew that the "what" and the "why" of illness were intimately connected.

What we both agreed upon was that the joker in the deck was stress. Good stress, bad stress; it didn't matter. This wild card would surface and upset the applecart. One of our first go-rounds centered on whether peptic ulcers were caused primarily by stress. David said, "You're going to give me an ulcer with your undocumented stress theory." He of course had the last laugh when, in 1982, a bacterium called *H. pylori* was found to be a major cause of ulcers.

Our writing interests took us in different directions for some time. David explored the dynamics of addiction and brain chemistry, while Connell published books on relationship issues. But always our talks returned to the complex intersection of stress and illness.

We have now shared forty years of dialogue and collaboration. Our friendship has deepened. We've seen each other through times that were trying and painful and those that were celebratory— shared birthdays, the deaths of our parents, and Dodger games on hot summer nights, not to mention a few beers along the way. We also share several traits. Our interest in our work intersects with our interests in life; we both have an insatiable curiosity about why things are the way they are, and we care deeply about our friends and families and those we've treated. That's about where our similarities end. David is much more gregarious and outgoing, while Connell is more reticent and contemplative. If David looks on the bright side, Connell peers into the shadows. Up sprang a sort of Jack Sprat partnership between the two of us in which we each serve an essential function.

Over the years, we've witnessed the country experience an exponential rise in competition, productivity, and stress. And increasingly, we saw how the emotional issues of our patients complicated their physical complaints and vice versa. By sharing patients, we undertook a deep exploration of the links between these two spheres, the emotional and the physical. It became increasingly clear that stress—and how our patients handled it—was the biggest single factor in determining both overall contentment or good mental health and length of life. Some patients developed strategies to recognize and deal with stress, while others were resistant to this fix, not recognizing the enormity of the issue. We traced the impact of stress on our own lives as well. We learned that stress was actually not our problem; instead, it's *our reaction* to the discomfort created by the stressors—good and bad—that was the key. This was a celebrated missing piece of our puzzle.

As we (and our patients) aged, we became fascinated by the exciting and emerging science of biogerontology. More specifically, we turned our attention to the core causes of aging and the ways in which our lifestyles and attitudes either speed up or slowdown that process. Everyday stress and pressure affect everything from our organs, our microbiome, and our risk for illnesses to our sleep patterns, our willingness to exercise, our eating habits, and our emotional state. Stress and longevity were clearly comingled factors. We set out to try to understand how they related to each other.

We constructed an elaborate way to measure aging speed. In essence, we developed an in-depth questionnaire from which we could calculate what we referred to as a longevity quotient, or LQ (with LQ inversely correlated to aging speed—the higher the LQ, the slower the aging speed). The questionnaire was scaled in a way similar to an intelligence test, with the average LQ set at 100. We called this instrument the LongevityScan. Unfortunately, the test had built-in shortcomings. It was comprised of nearly four hundred items that required information patients had to get from their doctors, making it a cumbersome exercise. Still, it gave us valuable data on how patients compared to others of their age and gender. But what it didn't do was explain, beyond having good or bad genes, why some people had higher scores than others or how best to help people with low scores raise them in a sustainable way. We had plenty of clear and useful information to share with patients. Understanding the healthful changes they could make in their lives was never the obstacle. The stubborn hurdle was their resistance to using the information and actually making the changes.

We plowed through a mountain of studies on stress and its damaging effects on our bodies and sense of well-being. But in truth, we were stuck. Even though we'd left the door of possibilities ajar, there were no deeper discoveries in sight. What we had was unwieldy, with too many permutations and combinations, and we continued to scratch our heads, unable to gain insight into the durability of someone's inability to make and sustain healthy changes.

Then bingo! We had an epiphany. It had been right under our noses all along. What we had been looking for were predictable clusters of behavior that correlated with age-related illness and accelerated or slowed aging damage. What we found was much deeper. The clusters of behavior we saw weren't related directly to aging but rather to arousal. Or, more precisely, the level of excitation in the central nervous system. People who were understimulated behaved in predictable ways that were very different from those who felt overstimulated. Our behavior is related to the distribution of our neurotransmitters and these behaviors are expressions of stress coping. *The patterned strategies people use to manage stress are hardwired, embedded in our inherited neurochemistry.* Getting our noses out of studies and papers we suddenly recognized these patterns in our family, friends, patients, and, yes, ourselves. So simple and elegant: when stressed, we will behave in a certain way, and the roots of that behavior are coded in the build-ing blocks of the autonomic nervous system.

Our autonomic nervous system, which should be called the "automatic" nervous system, is the branch of our physiology that controls those life-sustaining systems that we unconsciously take for granted: the beating of our heart, how we breathe, how our blood pressure adapts to changing positions, how our brain cleanses itself and deletes or stores the day's memories when we sleep, and *the reflexive behaviors that appear when we are stressed.* Why did some of our patients struggle with symptoms connected to how they calm themselves (smoking that cigarette, eating that chocolate cake, having another glass of wine), while others had is-sues that stemmed from a need to increase nervous system stimulation in order to self-soothe (making that unnecessary ex-travagant purchase, blowing up at their colleague, spending hours playing action-packed video games). The answer astounded us. All of them, some more neatly than others, fell generally along one side or the other from a need to either calm or stimulate them-selves to get comfortable. The wiring of our autonomic nervous system is inherited; we get the distribution of our various brain chemicals from good old mom and dad. Then we structure our lives, our personalities, our habits in reaction to the coursing of those chemicals. For much of the time, these patterned tendencies remain in the background, largely unnoticed. They come to the foreground and exert their influence during stressful events or calls for decision-making.

This nascent understanding became the lodestar for a novel theory of stress management that we have documented and con-firmed over the years with scientific data. Using sets of slightly unbalanced neurotransmitters, Mother Nature has given us two very different stress-coping styles. Could this be some sort of accident? We think not. We believe that these different styles con-ferred important survival advantages depending upon the presenting circumstances of the stressor. Had one style proved more successful across the centuries, natural selection would have given us one style, instead of two, possessing very different strengths and weaknesses.

We found something else that was particularly striking: we humans aren't the only creatures who deploy these divergent stress-coping strategies; these offensive/defensive, bold/cautious responses are expressed across the animal kingdom. Let's explore a couple of examples.

Two monkeys, placed in side-by-side see-through cages, were given slices of cucumber as treats along with their usual fare. Both monkeys were quite content receiving the cucumber treats until one monkey got the regular slice of cucumber while the other got a big, plump grape. This is where the story gets interesting. It turns out we are not the only species that has a sense of fairness. In this study of induced stress, it didn't take long for the cucumber monkey to note that his pal next door was being treated very differently, was getting something better. This blatant inequality caused unease in both monkeys (but not enough for the grape-getting monkey to share his treats), with the cucumber monkey experiencing the greater stress. In fact, monkeys receiving the veggie treat got angry and either threw the cucumber slice back at the experimenter or turned away and refused to accept it (monkey pout). This pattern with different monkey pairs was repeated multiple times with the same behavioral results. Non–grape-getting monkeys dealt with this induced stress by either becoming aggressive or behaving as if they didn't care. Let's call this the sword-or-shield defense—the aggrieved monkey either whipped out a sword or put up a shield in response to the injustice. The stress induced in these monkeys revealed two distinct coping styles.

Another example of how stress-coping styles sort out into two types can be seen in the behavior of the great tit. The great tit is a small but fierce bird making its home in woodlands, parks, and gardens from Europe to Asia. It is powerful and formidable for its size, with a bill capable of breaking open hazelnuts, acorns, and even the occasional heads of smaller prey. But as tough as these little birds are, they are no match for their nemesis, the stronger sparrow hawk. Studying stress in this species, researchers exposed twelve great tit populations to the recorded call of the hunting sparrow hawk during the great tits' normal breeding season from early April to late June. Normally, the majority of these birds breed late in the season, but faced with the clear threat of a hunting predator, some undaunted great tit pairs bred earlier than they normally would. Their less courageous brethren did exactly the opposite, choosing to breed very late in the season. There were no differences in the breeding success regardless of whether they bred earlier or later than normal. Hearing the call of their mortal enemy the sparrow hawk resulted in some taking their chances and breeding very early in their season, while others, stressed by the same calls, chose to wait and breed much later in the cycle. Two different coping styles, just like what was observed in the grape-deprived monkeys. Cole Porter was way ahead of the science when he wrote: "Birds do it, bees do it..." assuming his "it" was a reference to how animals manage their stress in two very different behavioral patterns. And yes, we humans do "it!" as well. We were thinking about calling our book *Monkeys, Great Tits, and You* but thought the title might be misunderstood.

So what about you? Before we go any further, we'd like you to take a short test. Follow the simple instructions, score your answers as directed, and don't overthink your responses. This test predicts which of these great tribes you are likely to align with, particularly when responding to stressful situations. Are you more likely to counter adversity with aggression, or is your nature to be more cautious? Are you a monkey pouter or a great tit with premature procreation? Let's find out.

Personal Brain Type Questionnaire

1. I worry more than other people I know.   T   F
2. I sometimes act before taking the time to con-   T   F
   sider all the issues.

3. I enjoy a good adrenaline rush.   T   F
4. I look at all the angles before taking action.   T   F
5. By nature, I think of myself as being outwardly   T   F
   expressive.
6. If I want something, I want it right now.   T   F
7. I seem to worry a lot about my health.   T   F
8. I'm not known for being aggressive.   T   F
9. I'm pretty easily distracted.   T   F
10. I prefer to lead rather than follow.   T   F
11. I often begin new projects before I finish the ones   T   F
    I've started.
12. Social situations can make me nervous.   T   F
13. I'm willing to wait, sacrifice, and plan for things I   T   F
    want.
14. I'm always on the hunt for something new.   T   F
15. Fairly often, I find myself worrying to excess.   T   F
16. It's hard for me to express my anger and I often   T   F
    hold it in.
17. I hate having to do the same old things over and   T   F
    over.
18. When things go wrong, I tend to blame myself.   T   F
19. I'm pretty assertive most of the time.   T   F
20. People know when I'm mad.   T   F
21. I sometimes find myself saying yes when I really   T   F
    mean no.
22. I look at the big picture instead of paying   T   F
    attention to the small details.
23. I'm not easily thrown by uncertainty.   T   F
24. Being flexible is one of my strong suits.   T   F
25. It's often difficult for me to focus.   T   F
26. When it comes to risk, I'm very cautious.   T   F
27. I'm good at paying attention to detail.   T   F
28. I tend to keep many of my feelings hidden.   T   F
29. I'm at my best early in the morning.   T   F
30. I think slowly, but I'm pretty accurate.   T   F

Scoring

For every answer marked as true, fill in the circle corresponding to the question number on the graphics of the brain below. Whichever brain has more circles filled represents your brain type—Shield or Sword. You will likely have circles filled on both images. That's because there are no pure brain types. As you can see, Swords tend to have some Shield tendencies within them and vice versa.

However, your "predominant" brain type will predict both how you are *likely* to respond to stress and the ways in which you will manage discomfort.

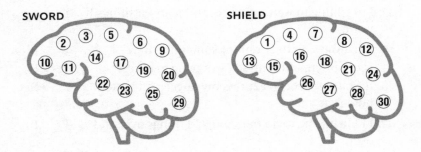

Congratulations. You have now identified yourself as a Sword or Shield in terms of how you're likely to react and cope with stress. If you have more circles filled in on the Shield brain, you are likely to be less aggressive and carry a shield into your battle with stress, but if you filled in more on the Sword brain, then pick up your blade and understand how you wield it!

As you may now surmise, one of humanity's tribes, the Swords, is coded to be particularly sensitive to stimulation, novelty, and reward, while the Shields of the world are coded to be more sensitive to avoiding harm and danger. Each coping style possesses strengths as well as an array of behavioral shortcomings. See how your Sword or Shield behaviors line up with the following list. And as we've indicated, you may recognize some of your behaviors on both sides of this chart and this is consistent with our knowledge that we all share some behaviors on our nondominant brain type side of the equation.

Brain Type Behaviors

SHIELDS	SWORDS
Contemplative in nature—tends toward introversion	Expressive in nature—tends toward extroversion
Parasympathetic reactivity	Sympathetic reactivity
Seeks to avoid stimulation	Seeks out stimulation
Easily aroused	Difficult to arouse
Motivated by avoiding punishment	Motivated by anticipating reward
Likely to imprint more memories of negative outcomes	Likely to imprint more memories of positive outcomes
Tends to think before acting	Tends to act before thinking
Able to delay gratification	Finds it difficult to delay gratification
Controls impulses easily	Controls impulses poorly
Low need for novelty	Seeks out novelty
Tends to be risk averse	Tends to be risk tolerant
Holds anger in	Lets anger out
Tends toward pessimism	Tends toward optimism
Thinking style is slow but accurate	Thinking style is fast but often inaccurate
High attention to detail	Low attention to detail
Avoids routines	Depends on routines
Flexible and adaptive to change	Rigid, doesn't do well with change

Brain Type Behaviors, *continued*

SHIELDS	SWORDS
Tendency toward hypochon-driasis	Tendency toward symptom denial
Sexual problems	Sexual addictions
Addictions likely to alcohol and sedatives	Addictions likely to cocaine and other stimulants
High pain tolerance	Low pain tolerance

The understanding of these two distinctive patterns that humans deploy to manage stress provides an explanation for a variety of behaviors whose origins have remained poorly understood. More important, it points the way to type-specific interventions that have proved effective when stress-coping styles go awry in the lives of our patients.

Two Kinds of People

This idea of two personality types is not a novel one. Remember Type A and B personalities? Popularized by a 1974 best seller, *Type A Behavior and Your Heart*, this theory posited that hard-driving Type A patients were significantly more prone to heart attacks than the more easygoing Type Bs. The science behind the theory was ultimately discredited; the authors, cardiologists Meyer Friedman and Ray H. Rosenman, had failed to account for other Type A habits, such as a penchant for drinking, smoking, and eating rich foods. But since everyone knew someone who fit the description of the Type A personality—the boss who screams, the easily angered father, or the workaholic exercise junkie—and since the theory carried so much commonsense validity, the term persisted, for it seemed to tell us something profound about the way we were racing around, letting stress drive us to an unhealthy, even deadly degree.

For his part, Meyer Friedman grew to resist the way people spoke of his theory as one of personality types, which seemed to imply you were born being one or the other and couldn't interact very effectively with your own health outcome. He attempted to put the emphasis back onto behavior, and he developed a program through which Type As could reduce their risk of heart attack. Friedman said that, with work, he himself had evolved from a Type A to a Type B. The science has come a long way since Friedman's Type A and B descriptions, but his notion that there are two broad kinds of people was spot-on.

Deepening the Story: Neurotransmitter Type Imbalances

One challenge we all face from the day of our birth onward is the stress of simply being alive over the passage of time. How we deal with this inevitable force determines lifelong success, fulfilling intimate relationships, and vitality—or their opposites: failure and ineffectiveness at work, unhappy family lives, and poor health. Why do some of us take totally unnecessary chances, while others are more prudent and cautious? Why are some of us so aggressive with our anger, while others seem to suffer silently or blame themselves? Why are some able to defer gratification so easily, while others experience that kind of waiting for the reward as excruciating? Why are some of us rigid and others more adaptable and flexible? Why is establishing healthy routines easy for some and much more difficult for others? Why are some of us prone to anxiety, while others seem so undaunted by life? Why?

We don't will these things; we notice them. These underlying tendencies are the manifestation of our neurochemistry. They are translated into our everyday behavior and approach to life, written in the blueprint of our DNA.

Where in our body we are sorted into one of these two teams may surprise you. No, it's not in our brains, as you may have guessed. The story starts deep in our gut in a strange little neighborhood located in the small intestine. It is the code written within a humble batch of cells there that governs the distribution of chemicals (neurotransmitters) that stream throughout our nervous system and profoundly influence our behavior. The orchestration of these neurotransmitters plays out through the instruments of our autonomic nervous system and creates our very personalized brain type.

The autonomic nervous system operates with two powerful branches. The first component is the sympathetic system, designed to excite, arouse, and motivate us. The second, the parasympathetic system, is oppositely programmed to relax, inhibit, and calm us. As a species, we wouldn't have survived without these two competing arms of our nervous system. The neurotransmitters that fire these two systems are in a constant and dynamic drive for homeostasis or balance, to restore *comfort—the perception of safety*. If the sympathetic system is activated, the parasympathetic system responds to calm things down and reestablish balance. The sensory signal we recognize for "stabilization" in the brain is comfort—whether or not it's in our best interests to feel comfortable at that exact moment or with that particular decision!

Unfortunately, none of us possesses the perfect balance of arousing and calming neurotransmitters. Due to a variety of genetic, epigenetic (the circuits that tell a gene to turn on or to remain silent), and environmental influences, the distribution of our neurotransmitters tends to be more imbalanced in one of two directions. We believe these subtle imbalances to be a by-product of evolutionary forces and to have conferred upon us modern humans an important tool for survival.

This translates into a nervous system that is driven by neurotransmitter imbalances (primarily deficiencies of these brain chemicals) that are on either the excitatory (stimulating) side or inhibitory (calming) side. One or the other of these imbalances predominates, has the controls, and is singularly focused on an effort to maintain the perception of *comfort*. These two neurochemical imbalances are shaped by either dopamine (boss of the excitatory system) or serotonin (the inhibitory system chief).

Dopamine with its team members adrenaline, noradrenaline, glutamate, and acetylcholine all act to excite the nervous system and are at the heart of the fight-or-flight response to a perceived threat (it's no accident that this most basic response to stress mirrors these two brain type tendencies). The neurotransmitter dopamine also controls our motivation, pleasure, and reward circuitry. Every love letter ever written is drenched in dopamine, as is every blackjack chip laid down on the table, every ambition, every adventure embarked on.

The serotonin system with its neurotransmitter cousin GABA act to calm an over-amped brain and is in the driver's seat in the areas of anxiety, mood, and obsessions, or their more pleasant opposites—openness and a sense of well-being. Every caution felt, impulse controlled, gratification deferred, every action withheld or avoided, is related to the influence of serotonin.

Our big brains translate these neurotransmitter-driven styles into both conscious and unconscious behavior. This is where our Shield or Sword style comes into play. The decisions and behavioral leanings influenced by brain chemical imbalances are put in place and maintained by how much cortical activation or arousal there is in the system. Swords usually function with a bit too little arousal and Shields with a bit too much. These relatively stable and consistent imbalances in arousal are the drivers of different patterns and tendencies. But there are exceptions. Can we identify primarily as a Shield or a Sword but also see aspects of our decisions and actions that are more associated with the other side? The short answer is absolutely. We all do at certain times or under certain circumstances.

Cortical arousal has not only typical set points or levels within individuals but also fluctuations. Context and situation are powerful determinants in shaping these changes in arousal levels. For example, Shields are not always cautious and protective; they can be much bolder and more expressive when they feel safe. Signals of safety have the effect of reducing (only temporarily) arousal and releasing less cautious decisions. Make any Shield feel really safe and you'll see them flash their hidden blades.

Any heightened emotionality causes a rise in cortical arousal. Swords don't like too much arousal in the system any more than do Shields. Anger fits that mold. Anger is pent-up arousal and Swords are more likely to seek a release (reduction) through blame and externalizing anger. Having the same surfeit of arousal, Shields are more likely to reduce the discomfort by directing that negative energy inward.

So, feeling safe is a releaser of Sword tendencies in Shields and feeling unsafe is a releaser of Shield-like behaviors in Swords. Why? Again, it's all about arousal. Take, for example, a health scare where a person is waiting to get the results of a potentially devastating diagnosis. During these times, Swords can exhibit distinctly Shield-like behaviors. Anxiety, obsessive-compulsive disorder (OCD), and depression are more on the Shield side, but not necessarily when a Sword's level of arousal is elevated by feeling threatened. Because they are deficient in the calming brain chemical serotonin, Shields rarely feel too little arousal. But due to circumstances and situational events, Swords can and do experience too much arousal. Threats, be they emotional or physical, cause jolts of arousing brain chemicals, leaving Swords feeling hurt, anxious, and unsafe. During these moments of heightened arousal, Swords, too, look for ways to reduce it. If the threat is emotional, they seek external ways to release the arousal, chiefly by the expression of anger. But if the threat is physical, as in our example of possibly getting a bad diagnosis, Swords can exhibit the same internal compensatory behaviors as do Shields—anxious spinning and catastrophizing.

Bottom line: too much or too little arousal is odious and uncomfortable for both Shields and Swords. Clearly, there is a Goldilocks effect to cortical arousal—not too little and not too much but just the right amount is what we all like.

Understanding Stress and
Its Relationship with Comfort

Stress, of course, is unavoidable; no one lives a life without having to deal with it. What exactly is stress? Most simply put, it is any disturbance to our internal sense of balance. As a species, we were built to handle distressful threats and plenty of them. But our first-line armor against this assault was designed to deal with short-term events where the disturbance to balance was resolved quickly. Out of the corners of our eyes we see a car bearing down on us, and we step out of the way. Without waiting for us to fully process the event, our amygdala sends a message to the hypothalamus, the command center in our brain, causing a cascade of chemical releases and activating the sympathetic nervous system. This component of our autonomic nervous system then broadcasts signals to the adrenal glands that begin pumping adrenaline into the bloodstream. You know that feeling—sweaty palms, rapidly beating heart. Airways in our lungs open to provide more oxygen, our senses sharpen, and blood sugar and stored fats flood the vascular system to provide immediate energy. Next, the hypothalamus triggers the other component of the stress response system, the HPA axis (the hypothalamus, the pituitary and adrenal glands). This network is designed to keep the sympathetic nervous system fired up. Then, if our brain still registers a threat, the stress hormone cortisol is released, keeping the body on high-alert status. However, once we know we're safe, we pause for a moment on the sidewalk, breathing a sigh of relief as the braking part of the nervous system kicks in to calm the chemical storm in our body, sending out an all-clear signal. The event has ended. We all handle that kind of distressful event pretty easily and it doesn't cause any long-term damage to our bodies.

Chronic, low-lying stress is a whole other matter. Perhaps the most relatable example of the subtle drip, drip, drip of stress is what we've all gone through during the pandemic, causing increases in domestic violence, alcohol intake, and mental health events. This kind of stress can be so subtle and omnipresent that we adapt to the signals of its presence. But our bodies don't. Stress is not only uncomfortable emotionally: it also is, in its increasingly prevalent chronic form, harmful to the body. If soon-to-be mothers are stressed, their babies are dosed with their stress as they slide along the birth canal and get smeared with mom's microbiome. This early exposure to stress hormones can cause permanent negative changes to the immune system and this may explain why there is so much variance in how well people ward off infections and even some chronic diseases. Stress even possesses the capacity to remodel the brain. Studies show that the stress hormone norepinephrine (activated during a stressful event) creates long-lasting structural effects upon our neurons and other brain cells. These physical changes alter brain function and can lead to anxiety, depression, and drug addiction. Stress, and how we cope with its sinister impact on our health, plays a pivotal role in all the age-related illnesses: cancer, diabetes, heart disease, and dementia. It shortens telomeres and shortens lives.

Despite the remarkable advances in medical technology, life expectancy in the United States is going down. This sad downward trajectory is largely attributable to but one factor: our inability to deal with stress in healthy ways. The increases in liver disease, drug overdoses, and suicides are primarily stress-related outcomes. And, as if simply living in our competitive, sped-up world wasn't stressful enough, the trauma of the coronavirus pandemic landed, causing even greater distress to an already-divided country.

How We've Learned to Cope with Stress

Without much thought, we all do battle with the myriad stressors in our lives. Instinctively, we know stress is dangerous for us. We know this because stress feels uncomfortable. Stress creates an emotional disequilibrium and our natural tendency is to try to return to a state of balance and homeostasis. Whether we're Swords or Shields, we use our internal balance/comfort barometer to ward off these unpleasant experiences. As humans, we've been doing this since we spread across the globe. And the truth is that the strategies we use have been successful if maintaining some relative state of comfort is the criterion.

The problem is that while comfort is a powerful motivational spur, it doesn't always lead us in healthy directions. In many ways, our instinctive, comfort-driven coping strategies have led us astray. Often the smarter coping strategy would be to override the siren of comfort and toughen up a bit. But we've all gotten soft and our indulgence in comfort is hurting us. It's not smart to trade short-term comfort for long-term hurt.

As described, chronic stress carries along with it HPA activation and a production of the hormone cortisol. A nervous system redolent with cortisol is a system on high alert. Sword and Shield brains deal with the presence of this hormone in different ways. Shields, deficient in the calming brain chemical serotonin, are left in a state of heightened vigilance that reads as potential threat and anxiety. The net effect of this low-lying stress is to accentuate Shields' innate tendency to go into protection mode and avoid any circumstances or activities associated with signals of potential distress. Sword brains process the drip of cortisol as aggravation or irritation. Their response to this uncomfortable situation is to look for some way to discharge the tension (usually some expression of anger). And remember, Swords are deficient in the brain chemical dopamine that fires the reward center of the brain. Instead of being harm sensitive like Shields are, Swords are reward sensitive. The presence of cortisol has a muting effect on natural feelings of ease and pleasure, leaving Swords hungry for some sort of dopamine hit and making it more difficult for them to delay gratification and making impulse control more difficult.

What's important to understand here is your relationship with arousal. There is no easy measure of arousal, no thermometer or blood pressure cuff, no lab test. We each sense our level of arousal in subjective ways. For Swords, where arousal is typically on the low side, the experience of that sensation is often described as feeling bored, distractible, edgy, or irritable. And for Shields, the sensation of feeling overly aroused is most often described as subtle distress, nervousness, and anxiety. Were we able to have some magical rheostat to dial arousal up or down, we would feel more comfortable and not have to employ strategies to raise or lower our levels.

It comes down to this: we unconsciously look for a way either to tamp down stimulation or to ramp it up. Swords and Shields have different thresholds for getting comfortable. Shields tend to feel overstimulated pretty easily. Because of those feelings, they unconsciously regulate their discomfort by engaging in behaviors that reduce arousal, trying to get back to a feeling of comfort or normality. Swords, deficient in dopamine, tend to feel understimulated and unconsciously correct by looking for ways to create sensation and increase arousal.

Stress is demanding. It packs the power of a two-year-old squalling on the department store floor after you pried loose the toy grabbed along the way. Everyone's eyes are on you. You have to do something. That's where habit kicks in. Habit is what we know, the comfort of the familiar, what's worked for us in the past. And these habitual reactions are governed by our brain chemical imbalances.

We are all creatures of habit and our habits can have as much good judgment and intelligence as the moon has cheese. How many of us walk in the door after work, pour ourselves a martini, put our feet up on the coffee table, and watch the evening news? "What happened to that bag of chips? I couldn't have eaten the whole thing!" Or we may find ourselves screaming at the kids or losing our temper with our spouse over some perceived transgression. Or maybe we close our eyes for a few minutes, attempting to meditate, until our cell phone chirps out a notification, demanding our attention. So much for meditation. And then there's the temptation of prying open a pint of peppermint chocolate chip ice cream, telling ourselves we deserve it after a day like we had today. All of these behaviors are designed to regain an acceptable level of arousal, which becomes synonymous with being comfortable.

Habit is blind and all about immediacy. As the stressor is processed, a demand for "normalcy" is experienced, setting in motion the deployment of our unique bag of habitual tricks. Relief is just a reflexive habit away.

Agency is important to the design of an organized life. We all strive to control our experiences and pretend as though we are behind the wheel. But instead of really being in charge, much of the time we act blindly and out of habit. Sure, stress is distinctly unpleasant; life is filled with annoyances and the anticipation of pressure and discomfort. But until you learn how you've been set up to respond to stress by your brain chemistry, stress will continue to grab you by the back of the neck and push you around.

Our mission here is to drill down into how our two tribes are set up to cope with stress and show you how these dynamics operate both for and against you. But this book goes beyond the observational and into the potential. We believe that there are healthier and more constructive ways to cope with the stress and we are going to show you how to learn to incorporate them into your lives. By understanding your personal reflexive tendencies you will be able to leverage motivation and make difficult but healthy changes easier and more lasting.

CHAPTER ONE

The Irresistible Push and Pull of Arousal

*How Brain Activation, or Arousal, Unconsciously
Shapes Whether We Are Focused More
Internally or Externally*

RICHARD DREYFUSS WAS INTERVIEWED ON CNN in 2014 after winning the Academy Award and was asked if he planned to write an autobiography. His response gives us a distinct peak into his brain chemistry. "I don't know, but if I do, it will be called *The Hunt* because I'm much more comfortable on the hunt." He flashed his brain type in 1982 when he was arrested for cocaine possession after crashing his Mercedes into a palm tree along a winding canyon road in Los Angeles. See if you can find the clues and identify our beloved actor as Sword or Shield.

If your analysis revealed a thrill for the "hunt" to be more meaningful than the prize (his Academy Award) and the risk-taking of driving recklessly, you've only one clue to go. That would be the cocaine. What all these clues have in common is their association with an imbalanced dopamine system.

We can be pretty confident that Richard Dreyfuss is a Sword. A Shield's autobiography might be titled *Overcoming Stage Fright*. A Shield might be arrested after crashing his Mercedes, but more likely with alcohol on his breath.

While the choices Shields make can be starkly different from those of Swords, their central motivational engine is the same: they are trying to modulate their level of emotional discomfort. But there is a difference in the way that these two tribes experience that discomfort and it all spins around how they tolerate and process cortical activation or arousal. Yes, *it's all about arousal*. As we've described, arousal is the amount of stimulation or excitation in the nervous system and it is the propellant of motivation and the reason we do all of the things we do. Swords are drawn to it and Shields will go out of their way to avoid it. How do you relate to arousal? Any thoughts as to how it pushes you around in small ways in your life? Do you see things you do that are in service of reducing arousal or increasing it? These are a few of the questions to keep in mind as you read the pages ahead.

There are another couple of differences between these brain types we should get right out in the open. Because of their relationship to arousal, Swords tend to have a whole lot more fun, while the Shields tend to be more comfortable covering their backsides. A recent story covered by CNN illustrates this point. On a freeway leaving Ogden, Utah, an SUV was spotted weaving between the lanes and police pulled it over. The officer walked up to the driver's side of the car, peered in incredulously, and asked, "How old are you?" "Five," the young boy behind the wheel told him. He then spilled out the rest of the story. He'd asked his mother to buy him a Lamborghini and gotten angry when she said no. He collected the three dollars he'd saved, along with the keys to the family car, and set off to California to make his dream come true. Let's be really clear here: this little boy is not a Shield.

A Shield example would be decidedly less dramatic but certainly no less intricate. Had that audacious little boy been a Shield instead of a sword, the story might have gone more like the following: a boy dreams of having an exotic sports car. That's probably where the story would stop because a Shield would likely play the "ask mom" out, imagine her no, and the dream would be internalized. That boy would likely feel the same sting of anger, but it would go unexpressed and instead of finding the car keys, driving off, and getting pulled over by the police, that child would likely run a series of thought scenarios. One scenario might be something like, What if I get lost and can't find the highway? Another version might be finding the highway and getting far enough away from home only to get stopped by the police. Yet another imagined action might be making it all the way to California successfully and trading those dollars for the car. But all these versions would be played out in his head, all the while he is sitting in his room.

Have you ever thought about how controlling you are in your life? How you're most comfortable when you are doing things the way you like to do them? It is that same controlling impulse that pulls the levers in our brain type. Shields do much of their work under the hood, in their minds, while Swords wield their controlling needs more through action in the real world. Take a moment and think back. Which kid were you a little more like? Not that you ever borrowed the family car when you were five, but did you do adventuresome things that surprise you looking back on them now, or were you more restrained and cautious?

Nature has given us an amazing gift of these slightly imbalanced teams of brain chemicals. Had we all been born without these imbalances, all of our ways of dealing with the challenges and pressures of living would be similar. Nature appears to favor diversity and somewhat of a heightened response to stress over a more nuanced one. To expand our degrees of freedom, nature selected two sets of responses that are mirror images of each other, each hardwired and reflexive. Life over the millennia threw a complex mix of existential threats at our ancestors; had we not had such oppositional decision-making approaches and had these coping styles not been built-in or had required a lot of calorie-crunching thought, modern human beings may not have survived.

Infant Swords and Shields:
Trust and Sensory Stimulation

Sword and Shield traits are evident very early in a child's life and dictate their development. Let us remind you of Swords' relationship to arousal. Being short on the cortical activation side leaves Swords ever on the lookout for ways to increase it. We all look to feel some subjective version of "good," and for Swords that feeling is achieved by engaging a rich stimulus environment. As infants, not only are they tolerant of sensory excitement; they are also comforted by these external inputs. Stimulation is welcome because it raises the level of arousal they are naturally in short supply of.

Trust is more easily established in Sword babies because of their comfort with stimulation. When you are looking for arousal, the world seems to be a pretty friendly and safe place. Establishing trust always requires a leap of faith, opening up some gap, however small. If you don't open up a gap, no trust is established. If you do, and that gap is filled in a positive way, you've laid down one increment of trust. Drawn to stimulation, social and otherwise, Sword children are gap creators, more open to new experiences, social and otherwise. And that easy willingness translates, more often than not, into trust—trust in themselves as well as others. Swords' attraction to stimulation requires a target, and novelty becomes an easy bull's-eye, capturing attention. This penchant for novelty cuts in two directions. It widens the aperture in a positive way for early social learning, but the same comfort with novel stimulation can lead to mild or sometimes moderate distractibility. The circuits in our brain that control concentration and attention are the same as those that control impulsivity. Being set up to consume novelty is also a setup for poor attentional control.

Our Shield brothers and sisters have a very different relationship with arousal. Bottom line is that Shields have a distinct distaste for arousal and that dislike forms the spine of their patterned reactions. Their dislike of arousal is no accident. As we've mentioned, having an imbalance on the calming side of their nervous system, they have too little in the way of serotonin available in the right places at the right moment. From the time Shields are infants, their experience in the world is a subtle, or sometimes not-so-subtle, feeling of being overstimulated. And feeling overstimulated is experienced as vaguely dangerous. Given the rude awakening of suddenly having to exit the birth canal, a baby's first emotional hurdle is trust. Still lacking the capacity to regulate their own emotions and inner world, Shields are particularly vulnerable to the ways in which they are related to by their mothers.

Much has been written about a child's early emotional experiences, from Harry Harlow and his monkeys to Jean Piaget to John Bowlby's seminal work on attachment. While this important literature is beyond the purview of this book, suffice it to say Shield babies are especially in need of a calm, attentive, and nurturing mother. Born without the sufficient brain chemicals to wind themselves down naturally, they need caretakers to demonstrate on a real-time basis that the world and their place in the family are safe. These demonstrations of safety can go a long way toward creating the earliest building blocks of trust. The reason we say "demonstrate" is because trust can't simply be intended; it is earned and learned over time by consistent trustworthy and safe behavior. But despite having a really good mom or dad, Shield babies are left with a bit too much arousal for them to feel totally at peace in their own skin for very long. So, to you parents out there, don't despair. You can give your Shield baby love, but you can't give them serotonin. Their inherited deficiency in this important brain chemical is no one's fault. In fact, it is nature's way to give your Shield baby a very potent way to relate to the world.

The potency of the built-in coping style of Shield babies carries some predictable and sometimes-painful struggles, but it also confers upon them some wonderful strengths and attributes as we will describe. Early on, Warren Buffett signed up for a Dale Carnegie course to try to overcome his dread of public speaking. Donald Trump put his name on everything from buildings to beef. He made a fortune selling his dreams even as he presided over the debris of high-risk ventures, many of which went belly-up. While both of these men have been immensely successful, we'll leave it to your surmise which is the Shield and which the Sword.

Pleasure and Pain

Marking the role of pleasure in human motivation has its roots in the ancient world and was first proposed by Epicurus. In more modern times, Freud's pleasure principle was used to describe a kind of infantile quest for immediate gratification in the instinctive seeking of pleasure and avoidance of pain. From our perspective, we see this two-sided dynamic a little differently. Pleasure and pain represent the motivational engine for each of our stress-coping styles. Swords and Shields are dominated by or more sensitive to different parts of the brain: Shields are most affected by the brain's threat detection circuitry and Swords by its reward circuits. For Swords, the default motivational strategy is approach, looking to get some sort of pleasurable experience (reward), while Shields' motivational spur is the avoidance of pain (punishment). In fact, a Shield's most instinctual motivation is harm avoidance. The signal that something may be amiss or that threat or danger may be lurking out there is, of course, cortical arousal, broadcast by way of the amygdala. That's why we gave them their name. Shields are built to have a defensive and protective posture. And this most primitive and unconscious way to respond subtly colors everything they do throughout their lives.

Let's take a closer look at Shields' defensive posture. One way that Shields seek to protect themselves is through the process of worry. Shields can be notorious worriers. Give them the slightest of reasons and they are all in. Even though worrying is painful, a recent study illuminates how it is rewarded over time. Instead of worrying being linked to the possibility of a bad outcome as simply observational, researchers found something much more surprising. What they discovered was that for worriers, their worrying behavior actually became causal. Here is how it works: The worrier becomes aware of the possibility of a bad outcome and begins the worrying process. Then, lo and behold, the bad outcome doesn't come to pass and they experience relief. But they don't stop there. They don't simply think, Well, I worried needlessly. Worriers actually unconsciously link their worrying to the outcome. In other words, they worried, nothing bad happened, and it was their worrying that did the trick; the worrying prevented the bad outcome. And so, you can see how natural-born worriers get their worrying tendencies rewarded over time. What they are left with is not "I worry even when I don't have to," but some unconscious version of "If I worry, I can control my outcomes." It's little wonder that Shields spend so much time in their heads.

Their brother and sister Swords have a muted response to the potential for threat and are more animated by the possibility of pleasure and getting some sort of reward. Our connection to pleasure has obvious survival value; it's not an accident that food tastes good to us or that sexual activity is rewarded with a dramatic and pleasurable finish. But Swords, born shy on the arousal side, are inherently drawn to possibilities on the upside of the equation. Instead of being cautious and pain-avoidant, they tend to be pleasure oriented and assertive, providing them with a more offensive posture in the world.

Swords inherit their sunnier, outgoing nature in some interesting ways. As you know, Swords are sensitive to arousal and look to increase it by stimulating dopamine. To better understand how this comes about, let's take a brief weed dive and look at the DRD2 A1 allele. This genetic variant from mom or dad dampens the expression of the dopamine receptors in the brain reward sites, muting dopamine's ability to activate the reward pathway, dulling feelings of joy, pleasure, and aliveness. In its more exaggerated version, this condition is referred to as reward deficiency syndrome. This genetic variant, among others, explains why Swords seek out dopamine to normalize the brain's reward system. While Shields will go to great lengths to avoid the sensory effect of arousal, Swords expend time and energy cobbling together experiences they've learned that jack arousal up.

Approach and Avoidance

"Approach and avoidance" is a phrase frequently used to describe conflicts where movement toward a goal has both positive and negative anticipations, leaving it both desirable and undesirable at the same time. It's like one of those moments when you're having a hard time making up your mind about whether to do something or not. Here's the way it works for Swords: faced with the same list of pros and cons, they are more likely to focus on the pros and say yes. Shields, with the same basic information, will tend to emphasize the cons and say no. These oppositional tendencies that characterize Swords' and Shields' decision-making are approach and avoidance, respectively.

Imagine two guys in a singles bar having a beer. A good-looking woman glances in their direction, getting the attention of both. Each of these men feels equally attracted to her. Which do you think will walk over and say hello, and which is more likely to sit on the stool as if his pants are glued to it? That's right; the Sword gets up and introduces himself to the woman with a smile, while the Shield sits enviously by as the glue sets. Both men ran a series of if/then possibilities through their minds, and each added them up and acted on their assessment of those possibilities in different ways.

The dynamics of approach and avoidance, of course, play out in all the dimensions of our lives. These tendencies are emotional regulation tools, self-soothing strategies. Swords tend to approach to excite and Shields tend to avoid to calm themselves, and sometimes not in the best interests of either.

Let us be clear. Shields don't always say no. In fact, they are often just as likely to say yes, but their yeses tend to satisfy different motivations than the yeses of Swords. As an example of this, let's look at overeating. As you know, obesity in this country is at epidemic proportions. Irrespective of our particular brain type, we are all susceptible to overeating and its damage to our health. A donut is a donut. Right? Well, not exactly. Shields and Swords are at equal risk for excessive weight gain and both "approach" the donut but have different strategic goals for biting into that delectable sweet. Swords overeat to stimulate and increase arousal and Shields eat to self-soothe and avoid it. In fact, it is these differing arousal-regulating motivations that allow us to create leveraged strategies for sustained weight loss, described later in the book.

Because of our relationship with arousal, our brain chemicals can lead us to identical behaviors serving goals in direct opposition to one another. And other times, those same chemicals exert their hidden influence on dissimilar decisions and outcomes. Have you ever thought about how you relate to the dimension of uncertainty/certainty? Do you gather together whatever facts you have and quickly come to a conclusion and decision about the event or issue? Or do you tend to stew and worry about the paucity of information at hand, continue poking around trying to tease out more, and defer your decision until more facts become apparent? If you are a Sword you're more in the first category and if you are a Shield more in the second.

Everyone loves certainty, a sure thing, and no one is particularly drawn to uncertainty. But Swords tend to be less bothered by uncertainty than are Shields because of their differing relationships with arousal. The neurotransmitter dopamine codes for *certainty*, while serotonin codes for *uncertainty*. So, what does that mean? When we feel certain about the circumstances surrounding an action or decision, our dopamine neurons fire at a higher rate. This sensory signal carries along with it a "go" sign that says yes to the experience. And this experience is circular. We like certainty and saying yes because it feels good. Swords, who tend to be oriented toward external sensory cues, are drawn to actions because they stimulate the dopamine-firing reward cycle. They are rewarded by the feedback they receive from their outgoing natures, gain greater confidence over time and experience, and repeat the cycle. Remember the example of the two guys in the bar? Let's say the sensory information they both receive is identical and let's say it's neutral—they both find the woman attractive but aren't receiving any signals from her. Let's also say they both have the same wish for companionship. Both of these men have to make a decision and both make a mental and emotional risk/reward assessment. Both face an uncertain outcome. Here's the separation: Shields will sacrifice the possibility of a reward to satisfy their greater need for certainty information. The reason he sits there on the stool is that he's waiting for a "go" signal that's muted by the uncertainty in the situation and the perceived threat (possible rejection) embedded in chance-taking. The Sword man is less concerned about any downside consequences and goes over and says hello. This orientation toward the world is the very definition of what is known as "approach." Shields, as you know, have a different orientation to the world and that is "avoidance."

Now let's take a closer look at avoidance. Avoidance doesn't happen in a vacuum. It happens in the context of possibilities. There are some possibilities that are categorically bad (drowning) and some that are good (breathing), but there is a much more nuanced group of possibilities in between. Stripped away of its good and bad crusts, the loaf of bread is evaluated by Shields in a very different way than it is by Swords. Shields tend to see its more harmful possibilities, while Swords tend to see that same mixed bag of possibilities as potentially beneficial. That range of possibilities, of course, is the same, only the reaction is different. Could this be, in part, because of the size of the amygdala? Studies show that children born with larger amygdalae (our Shields) are more prone to having anxiety disorders. Swords, as you know, are not as entangled with their amygdala and are more in thrall to their reward system.

In fact, Swords' innate infatuation with the workings of their reward circuitry makes them vulnerable to addiction. Addictions are simply repetitive actions that provide the pleasurable hit of a reward. Bad habits are those that lead to cheap rewards that are destructive. The brain is a bit like a thick forest. Habits are made by the paths we follow. That first instance, as we walk along, doesn't leave much of an imprint (create neuronal connections in brain language), but repeated travels down that path carve a distinct groove in the forest floor (lay down neural connections). And pretty soon, that's where we find ourselves walking, despite our knowing that the destination may lead to self-defeating effects. Much more about the formation of bad habits, their addictive nature, and their relationship to faulty self-soothing later.

As we've said, Swords' approach style—seeking arousal—has its benefits and its liabilities. And Shields' aversion to arousal comes with its own strengths and weaknesses.

A heightened signal of arousal is like a magnet; it always looks for something to attach itself to—a cause that can be understood and possibly controlled. For Shields, "controlled" is the operative word. As the signal strength of arousal rises, Shields feel anxious, and if it rises too quickly and too high they can have anxiety attacks.

Setting aside anxiety attacks for the moment, Shields learn to control moderate levels of cortical activity by using their default strategy: avoidance. Shields search for an explanation for the arousal, evoking the question: "What's causing this uncomfortable feeling I'm having?" Their second question is: "How can I avoid this thing?"

Some definitions here may be helpful. Fear is seeing a bear stepping through the door and gnashing his teeth at you. Anxiety is having a similar feeling with no bear in sight. It's not just uncomfortable; it's disconcerting. The bear isn't there but the feeling is. Arousal feels dangerous even though the circumstance connected to it isn't. Some Shields unfortunately live with these heightened emotional states much of the time.

Shields' primary motivational impulse is to avoid harm. Harm, of course, is loosely defined as most anything the arousal gets attached to. Lucy, a woman in her thirties, recalled an experience from her childhood. After school one day, she saw a small knot of children squealing and making noises of shock and excitement.

She pushed in to see what they were all looking at. Glancing down, she saw an injured mouse missing one of its legs. She recoiled in horror and disgust, beginning a lifelong fear of rodents. From that moment on, Lucy avoided any and all situations where rodents could be present and was afraid to enter her son's kindergarten class because they had a hamster as a class pet.

Mice are pretty easy to avoid most of the time. Dealing with other people is not. When the arousal is attached to interacting with others, social anxiety can become a problem. Mason, a loving and thoughtful father, had a hard time understanding why his five-year-old son got sick to his stomach the morning of his birthday party and barely managed to participate. Shields come into social interactions already feeling overstimulated. Add in a bunch of rambunctious kids acting like kids do, and it's easy to get completely overwhelmed.

Avoidance gets attached to as many things as it does because it works. It works because avoidant behavior reduces arousal and makes us a little less uncomfortable. At least for the moment. What's important to understand, however, is that avoidance is not simply about a reaction to an event; it is also about *anticipation*. Shields anticipate an uptick in arousal and it is that anticipation of discomfort that triggers the avoidant behavior.

As humans, we learn behavior that works. Sadly, "works" is a relative word. We all want to be comfortable, whether comfort at that moment is healthy and constructive or not. Much of human learning requires repetitive actions that are systematically rewarded. Avoidant behavior is no exception; it is learned over time because it is rewarded by the brain. Each avoided action is rewarded by a little nugget of, at least, temporary relief, the building block of habit.

Directed from Within or Without

Over the years, much has been written about the push and pull of the inner and outer forces that shape behavior. Are we validated more by self-appraisals or the reactions and approval of others? Are we motivated more by our inner fears or by the prospect of getting something pleasingly rewarding? Obviously, the family and social values we learn when we are young lay down an indelible core that follows us through our lives in our decision-making. But overlaid upon those experiences are the behaviors shaped by our brain chemical imbalances that emphasize either the internal or the external world. No one relates strictly to one or the other, but the predominant style for Shields is guided more by internal factors, whereas the external world holds greater sway for our Sword sisters and brothers.

David Riesman, an American sociologist, introduced the terms "inner-directed" and "other-directed" in his analysis of those who are guided more by either their own internal values or those values they recognize among their peers. Finding enjoyment and comfort in a variety of social activities, Swords tend to fit Riesman's description of other-directed. More recently, in his book *Outliers*, Malcolm Gladwell described how inner-directed people were particularly adept at being able to deal with circumstances beyond their control. From our perspective, the tendency to direct thought, feeling, and emphasis on one's inner world describes the Shield's essential orientation, and the reciprocal energy generated by focusing on the external world forms how Swords are oriented.

More than eighty years ago, Carl Jung popularized the notion of introversion/extroversion as a dimension of personality. We all have our own ideas and pictures of ourselves and those around us that place us and our friends somewhere on that spectrum. But Jung was very specific. He saw this dimension as a person's unconscious tendencies that directed and received energy either from within (introverts) or from without (extroverts). Picture the young hard-drinking and hard-living "bad boy" George W. Bush pairing up with the modest and soft-spoken librarian Laura. George was energized by crowds and social experiences and Laura animated more by solitary moments. So, who feasts upon social interactions and energy? You know who. Swords sop it up because it creates a sense of normalcy and aliveness that they are unable to feel as fully when engaged in more contemplative activities.

Much has changed over the years in terms of how this dimension has been understood and studied. We've described to you how Freud's notion of the pleasure principle actually has biological roots with Swords being reward sensitive and Shields being harm or punishment sensitive. The British psychologist Hans Eysenck theorized a biological model for introversion/extroversion. He linked the associated behaviors to differences in cortical arousal, with extroverts preferring a more stimulating environmental experience and introverts preferring less stimulation. Now we understand why. We believe that the tendencies described by both of these theorists are related to specific deficiencies in the brain chemicals dopamine and serotonin. Introversion has long been thought of as an inherited personality trait. As we've discussed, there is a genetic link to the distribution of our important brain chemicals. Those of us born with too little available serotonin tend to focus on internal feelings and sensations and those of us who come into the world with too little dopamine focus upon external events. This split into our two great tribes, the Shields and Swords, is the perfect explanation and definition for introversion and extroversion.

Sword babies calm themselves with their external engagement, comfort with sensory stimulation and a more welcoming social outlook. Why? It works. They crave social and sensory engagement. Focusing on the outer world increases central nervous system excitation and this higher level of arousal brings the system into better balance and feels good. On the other side of the spectrum, not being able to calm yourself naturally because serotonin isn't available to tamp down the excess arousal leads to feelings of anxiety and the perception of danger (whether it's there or not). And having that condition from birth leaves Shield babies focused internally, if for no other reason than there is so much noise in the system caused by a surfeit of arousal. It's not an easy task for baby Shields to begin to make sense of the world outside them when what's going on within them demands so much attention. These are the children who like to be swaddled and held close and sleep best in a dark and quiet room.

Years ago, Jerome Kagan, an American psychologist, began studying how infants related to stimulation in a series of studies that still go on today. Kagan put together five hundred four-month-old infants looking to see if, in a forty-five-minute session, they could identify which children would develop into introverts and which into extroverts. He constructed a stimulus-rich experience of strong scents using alcohol swabs, had colorful mobiles that danced and moved above the infants' heads, and played a recording of balloons popping and loud unfamiliar voices. About 20 percent of these infants showed severe distress, cried, and waved their hands and kicked their legs. Approximately 40 percent of these children were quiet and exhibited very little in the way of movement and showed no distress. And another 40 percent were somewhere in between. We think this "in-between" 40 percent represented those "hybrids" we know to be in the middle of our bell-shaped curve of Shield and Sword behaviors, but all with a predominant leaning even if their reactions were not clear-cut.

Kagan went on to study these children as they grew up. What he found was that the high-reactive, jittery children were those most likely to have developed as they matured into quiet, serious, and cautious personalities. The low-reactive infants (the quiet ones in the experiment) turned into children who were more relaxed and confident. These jittery infants in Kagan's experiments were clearly our Shields and those who sailed through those stimulus overload experiences unperturbed were the Swords. The Sword babies were energized by the experience (it balanced their brain chemistry and stimulated their reward circuitry), where the same experience, because of the high stimulus value, set off the threat circuits in Shield babies.

We all, in real time, try to make sense of our waking experiences. Picture this: a woman sitting down eating her lunch. Suddenly, she feels herself wobble a bit on her chair, a very disquieting experience. A Sword would likely in those first seconds identify what was going on correctly: a mild earthquake. A Shield might very well think there must be something wrong internally, that she was going to faint, before then recognizing that it was the earth shaking, not her.

Swords' more outward-directed orientation creates a tendency toward finding others and circumstances as the agents and explanations for events. This tendency to focus on "you or it" is magnified during times of stress, particularly when things don't go their way. Their hunt for an explanation as to the why of an event doesn't typically begin with an examination of what they might have done to contribute to the situation. Instead, they tend to look to the outer world for the answer or, often, the culprit.

Shields are sensitized to cause and effect a little differently. Because of their itchy, overstimulated nervous systems, they are focused more on "I and me," rather than on "you or it." Because of their internally directed focus, they tend to see themselves as responsible for their experiences whether they are or not. This orientation combines great power as well as some predictable emotional burdens. It is a strength to see and acknowledge the role you play in an interpersonal conflict but an emotional weight when you direct blame inward when a more balanced attribution of responsibility might be more appropriate.

In the midst of a conflict, do you first think about your contribution or responsibility or is your first line of defense often an accusation?

Julian Rotter, observing directionality in personality styles, developed the concept of locus of control. His thoughts about what people believe, in terms of the control they have over situations and experiences, have been widely studied. Those of us who have an internal locus of control tend to put themselves closer to the causal center of their experiences, while those with an external locus of control tend to attribute external factors as the controlling agents in the important events in their lives. Having an external locus of control is associated with greater levels of perceived stress, greater interpersonal conflict, poor job satisfaction, and poor physical and mental health. We believe imbalances in brain chemistry are the biological basis for how we relate to the role we play in the unfolding experiences in our lives. Shields definitely land upon having an internal locus of control, while Swords land more often upon an external one.

How do you value inner satisfactions, secret victories, the small accomplishments no one but you may see? How do you look at the degree of control you feel you have in your life? Are you quick to find others at fault when things go awry or more inclined to blame yourself?

So, jittery babies turn out to be more quiet and serious adults and the quiet babies become the more assertive and gregarious grown-ups. How can this possibly make sense? As you may know, children diagnosed with attention problems and/or hyperactivity are often prescribed stimulants by their doctors. A stimulant for a kid who is easily distracted and can't sit still in his chair? Counter-intuitive! Here's the way it works: Picture a vertical line measuring cortical arousal in the system. And midway a horizontal line that stands for just the right amount of stimulation to feel normal, safe, at peace. When there is too little natural arousal, kids have to do something to stay awake and engaged, anything to stimulate them-selves. This self-stimulating behavior is what is identified as hyperactivity. And when these children are given a stimulant that raises the level of arousal in the system pharmaceutically, they can give up the compensatory restless behavior they used in their at-tempts to try to feel normal.

Shields, to feel normal, have a different compensatory task. On that arousal scale, they are above that horizontal line that feels safe. Growing up with more buzz in the system, they tend to turn inward for two reasons. First, they are naturally less sensitive to the reward circuitry in their brains than are Swords. And second, Shields prefer the lower-stimulus environment of privacy and hav-ing alone time. Instead of soaking up and needing the energy sparking around the room in social interactions the way Swords do, they are often worn out by the experience. As one of our patients, Ruth, put it, "My husband comes to life with friends in crowded, noisy restaurants. Rather than competing with that wall of noise, I find myself pulling inside, making quiet observations of some of the people around me, and finding some of my own thoughts more interesting than trying to follow the din around me. I can see that Ted is reluctant to say that last goodbye. I'm relieved and pretty much exhausted. When he asks me the inevitable question, if I had fun, I'm never quite sure how to answer. I know it's a different kind of fun than Ted has. It's not that I don't like these people—I do. But I prefer more intimate one-on-one gatherings or just us with another couple. I know if I say that he'll tell me he wishes I'd just relax, that if I could I'd enjoy these times more. It's not that I don't enjoy them in some ways, but certainly not how Ted does. And, to be honest, those nights can feel like work."

Does Ruth have more negative emotions than Ted? Not necessarily. It's that Ruth prizes and prioritizes moments when she is free to get into the flow of her mind over times that involve a heavier stimulus and social demand. On the other side, Ted, very much a Sword, is invigorated by stimulating social interactions and draws necessary energy from them.

Contemplative versus Expressive Natures

Because of our slight brain chemical imbalances, we are sensitive to very different brain areas and circuits. Babies born with too little available dopamine are nurtured by sensory stimulation and made more comfortable by its presence. It is precisely this comfort with experiences that increase arousal that sensitizes Swords particularly to the brain's reward circuits. We learn very quickly which circumstances lead to comfort and which do not. It is the comfort derived from the stimulating outer world that reinforces a more external orientation.

Being more contemplative begins very early on and has to do with the loud signaling of the amygdala. As you know, the brain has two hemispheres and we have an amygdala that sits inside our skulls right above our left and right ears. The amygdala is part of the limbic system, a network of the "reptilian" or "emotional" brain that controls instinctual behaviors like hunger and thirst, sexual impulses, and fear. The amygdala rapidly processes sensory information and sends out orders for us to respond. This is particularly true when it comes to signals of danger. If out of the corner of an eye we detect a baseball sailing our way, we duck. We don't wait to check in with the cortex to ask if that's a smart thing to do; we just get out of the way. The amygdala registers a threat and we react, even before the message of an incoming ball reaches the cortex. In fact, we react first and think later. When our amygdala fires, it creates an instantaneous reaction throughout our nervous system. Our blood vessels constrict, our blood pressure rises, our heart beats faster, and we dump stress hormones into our system.

While we all possess two amygdalae, some are more easily activated and busier than others. Shields have these more active little brain bodies that churn out all too frequent false alarms leading to a state of heightened arousal and vigilance. As children, Shields learn they can dial down their level of unpleasant arousal and the threat signals it activates by placing their focus inward. These learned tendencies are designed to reduce the noise in the system and create feelings of calm and safety.

What we are talking about here is quite simply a tendency, not an either-or. We all like to feel in control and adopt behaviors that foster that feeling. And these tendencies aren't "good" or "bad," just different. Shields' contemplative leanings are associated with many benefits, such as the potential for creativity and the sometimes-deeper thinking that goes along with moments of solitude. The opposite of contemplative tendencies is expressiveness, a Sword trait, which has its own benefits such as a more optimistic disposition and greater social self-confidence.

Our tendencies often categorize us as introverts or extroverts and direct how we navigate our world and our experiences. Extroverts and introverts shown a series of photographs of objects and faces exhibit very different brain activity. Extroverts (our Swords) when looking at pictures of faces, exhibit much higher levels of brain activity than do introverts. It's not that Shields don't prize intimacy, love, and abiding friendships as much as do Swords. In fact, they may value human connection even more deeply in that those few who are chosen represent a much smaller swath of people. In contrast, Swords' outward focus spins around interaction with others, experiences that they find particularly rewarding.

Another directional dichotomy that reflects how Shields and Swords behave is in how they tend to deal with negative emotions. Think of these differences as vectors of energy pointing either inward, toward the person, or away. Shields are more likely to be on the receptive side of these arrows, internalizing these emotions, while Swords tend to fall on the more expressive side, broadcasting these emotions out to others.

Let's take a look at anger. There is no more primary a human emotion than anger, and our experience of it requires a lot of energy. That energy is linked to an increase in stimulation and arousal. Even though Swords are more sanguine with heightened arousal than are Shields, in truth it's uncomfortable for both when arousal rises too high. We all look for some way to discharge this awful feeling. Shields, in an attempt to modulate that uncomfortable cortical activation, tend to turn that energy inward and against themselves. Swords have a distinctly different technique to discharge that energy; they tend to express it in an outward direction.

We all get angry. Anger is the emotion we use to protect our sense of self—our integrity and dignity. Aggression is another thing entirely; it is a reaction to a more central and dire threat. Violence is the exaggerated form of aggression. New techniques using fiber-optic cameras have been able to identify the neural circuits that control rage and aggression in the brain. To better understand the complexities of how this works, a brief description of the neuroanatomy of aggression may help. Each of us possesses a powerful system in our brain: the limbic system. This ancient system connects emotion, threat detection, learning, memory, and decision-making. The amygdala is linked to threat detection, the hippocampus is linked to memory and learning, the hypothalamus is linked to aggression and reward, and the prefrontal cortex is linked to decision-making.

Obviously, Shields and Swords both have all of the same neural circuits that comprise the limbic system. As we described, Swords tend to express their angry feelings in an external way, while Shields internalize anger. During an angry event (let's say some kind of interpersonal conflict), Swords are frequently coded to think or say something that begins with the word "you" and Shields are chemically programmed to say or think something that begins with the word "I." Shields often look for relief from the arousal of anger by taking blame for the event and Swords are more prone to spewing blame and accusation on the other person.

But what if we jump it up a bit? Let's talk about rage—anger on steroids—for a moment. First, we are all capable of it, for all animals are. Across the range of species, animals express their violent instincts to protect their young, obtain food, and defend themselves when threatened with injury. While such experiments are no longer permitted to be performed for ethical reasons, in the 1960s Spanish neuroscientist Jose Rodriguez placed an electrode on a woman's right amygdala. As she was sitting on a chair, playing her guitar and singing, he stimulated the electrode. She stopped playing and singing, stood, threw the guitar across the room, and began attacking a nearby wall. The woman's amygdala broadcast a threat message to a small cluster of neurons in the hypothalamus known as the hypothalamus attack center and triggered blind rage.

Here is how all of this relates to Swords and Shields: Anger is processed from the bottom up (the reflexive behavior of that woman's rage) or from the top down. By "top down," we are referring to getting the prefrontal cortex involved in the decision-making. Being more externally oriented, Swords' anger operates bottom up. Their first order of defense against too-high arousal levels (remember, not even Swords like arousal that is too high) is to look for something or someone "out there" as both the cause and the solution to regulating the discomfort. Discharge, typically in the form of blame and accusation, is the go-to strategy.

Conversely, Shields tend to be a little less volatile than Swords in their dealings with most situations that involve angry disputes. But this advantage comes with costs: anxiety, self-blame, and depression. This is the sequence: The Shield's amygdala detects a threat and signals both the hypothalamus and the prefrontal cortex. Shields, at that moment, are likely to take a moment or two to run the situation by the prefrontal cortex. That judging and decision-making part of the Shield's brain typically says, Whoa, this is causing way too much arousal in the system. What can I do to tamp it down? To control that uncomfortable arousal, Shields turn it on themselves, being much more prone to self-blame and looking for what part they played in the conflict—a kind of, What did I do to get myself in this bad situation?

Looking at how Swords and Shields relate to arousal through the lens of either an internal or external focus lets us understand a lot about why they do what they do. What could be more important than to discover a deeper understanding of why we do what we do? You might take a moment here to examine your own focus. There is great value in understanding the levers that set your decisions and actions in motion. Where do your comforts lie? How busy is your amygdala? How dominant is the reward center in your brain? How comfortable are you with contemplative moments? How restless and distracted? In moments of conflict, are you more prone to accusation or self-blame and self-recrimination?

In the next chapter, we are going to switch the lens a bit and dig deeper into some of the important ways our imbalanced brain chemicals impact our emotional world, how we process our feelings and learn to express them.

CHAPTER TWO

The Roller Coaster of Emotional Regulation

How Our Brain Chemical Imbalances Influence Our Feelings as Well as All of the Myriad Decisions They Shape

DEPENDING ON YOUR BRAIN TYPE, having too little or too much arousal drives oppositional emotional strategies designed to compensate for those imbalances. Shields counteract the arousal they feel by holding that buzzing world a bit at arm's length. That singular strategic impulse impacts the quality and diversity of their choices and decision-making. Swords' central strategy is, essentially, "bring it on." These hardwired tendencies have far-reaching consequences.

Shield and Sword Emotional Vulnerabilities

Being a Shield carries with it a certain risk of anxiety, depression, and OCD, all of which are associated with having a deficiency on the calming side of the nervous system. Depression and anxiety are really two sides of the same coin. It makes us anxious feeling depressed, and it's depressing to feel anxious. It's no wonder that many people experiencing significant depression or anxiety are prescribed drugs known as selective serotonin reuptake inhibitors (SSRIs) to increase their level of available serotonin.

But aside from taking an SSRI or serotonin and norepinephrine reuptake inhibitors (SNRIs), there are some other ways to rebalance your neurochemistry and build up diminished levels of serotonin. Vitamin B_6 supports production of serotonin in the brain and B complex can be helpful for stress reduction, as is 5-HTP (5-Hydroxytryptophan), Saint-John's-Wort, ginseng, and nutmeg. And do you know what else increases serotonin? Good old-fashioned exercise, an activity that also bumps up pleasant-feeling endorphins as well. Even sunshine interacts positively with serotonin levels.

Shields are not just natural worriers; they score high on the control freak scale as well. Sure, we all like to feel in control, but it's that highly developed control element that makes Shields vulnerable to developing OCD. Shields scan for things they can attach to their itchy arousal. Usually these attachments are random thoughts, not totally out of the realm of possibility. You get into your car and you think, Wait a second; did I lock the front door? Pull the plug on the coffee machine? Turn off the burner on the stove? So, you go back in and check. As a one-off experience, that may be a very reasonable and prudent task. But if you have to run back in to check time after time, that's OCD.

Compulsive behavior—the C in "OCD"—is the Shield's method of avoiding the arousal caused by the uncertainty. One patient spoke about how he'd run out of gas circling the block near his house, wondering if, by some terrible chance, he'd hit a pedestrian inadvertently. He was so tormented he had to make the loop again and again, each time mistrusting his memory.

The fix here is easy to describe, but not so easy to do. It's not easy because it requires dropping out the C part, the going back to check. And that requires something very hard for Shields because it means learning to tolerate the arousal that they have controlled with their compulsive actions.

As we described to you, Shields are those people who have an imbalance of serotonin on the shy side. While the details are beyond the purview of this book, it is possible to have too much serotonin. Having an excess of serotonin creates what is known as serotonin syndrome. A mild version is characterized by agitation and restlessness and its more extreme version is marked by seizures, high fever, and unconsciousness. Serotonin syndrome is caused by combining serotonin-enhancing medications and by MDMA, the recreational drug known as Ecstasy.

Having too much or too little dopamine can also have negative health consequences. Having a serious deficit in dopamine is the root cause of Parkinson's disease. And on the other side, having a surfeit of dopamine is connected to schizophrenia. But most Swords have only small dopamine imbalances. While science has yet to firmly pin down the causes of bipolar disorder or attention deficit hyperactivity disorder (ADHD), being a Sword is a risk factor for both. Each of these conditions is chronic, but treatable with a combination of medication and therapy. Like serotonin, dopamine can also be enhanced. Exercise, sleep, and relaxation (listening to music and meditation) all increase dopamine signaling. Saturated fats act to suppress dopamine, while dairy and protein, as well as foods high in tyrosine—particularly bananas and almonds—all enhance production of dopamine.

Hypochondriasis and Its Opposite: Symptom Denial

Russell, fifty-eight, has had heartburn for two weeks. He is a sales manager at a Toyota dealership and keenly aware that he is not going to meet his monthly quota. Being quick-tempered, he blames two of his salesmen, the loan specialist, and the Covid virus for decimating his showroom traffic. His sometimes-uneven managerial skills have been on display lately, and he seems to be in a chronic state of annoyance and anger. So of course he has heartburn. He barely notices how many Tums he has been popping or the extra cigarettes he's been starting but not finishing. He won't, however, go to the doctor. Why? He's a Sword! And Swords see the world through an external lens; what's happening in the showroom is far more relevant than what's happening in his esophagus. It's not that he's unaware of the discomfort in his chest or he wouldn't be reaching so often for another Tums. It's that he interprets the cause as the stress he's under as situational and denies the possibility of an important underlying issue. When he finally did go to the doctor, it was only because of a comment his brother made, watching Russell pop another Tums: "You going to wait for this to happen to you to check out what those pains are about?" Russell was visiting his brother in the hospital where he was recovering from a mild heart attack.

Shields relate to somatic symptoms and concerns in a whole different way.

"If this is soap I'm smelling in my salad, please tell me and I will throw it out."

Adam looked sheepishly across the table at his wife and replied, "Guess I didn't rinse it well enough."

He was relieved when, in the early days of the pandemic, he was allowed to work from home. But as the weeks passed, his anxiety only escalated. Unopened boxes he ordered online piled up outside his door as he waited the forty-eight hours he'd been told the virus stayed alive on the cardboard. As the weeks turned to months, he'd gotten more and more distressed, and tonight he took things to another level. Not only had he done the usual wipe down of the food packaging with sanitary wipes, but this night he found himself peeling the head of lettuce, putting it in a bowl, and washing each leaf with soap.

Adam suffers from hypochondria. Technically speaking, hypochondria is characterized by the fear or belief that one is ill based on physical symptoms that either are medically unexplained or, if present, cause disproportionate distress. A newly discovered skin blemish is worried into a cancer and a headache suddenly becomes a brain tumor. Hypochondria doesn't just cause mental anguish; the constant worrying of hypochondriacs stimulates the release of harmful stress hormones that actually do cause real physical damage. True hypochondria affects about 2 to 5 percent of the population and these obsessive worriers are fairly equally distributed between men and women. Hypochondria doesn't appear to be related in any significant way to a history of serious childhood illness or trauma. In fact, no one knows exactly what causes these debilitating worries in some people, but we have some cogent thoughts. But first, keep in mind that not every Shield focuses excessively on bodily symptoms; it's simply that because of their distribution of brain chemicals they are at a higher risk of doing so.

Shields tend to be more vulnerable to somatic worrying than their Sword cousins. Why? Let's take a closer look at Adam. He has no history of any unusual childhood sicknesses or trauma, but during late adolescence he started washing his hands so often that his skin cracked and, around the same time, he began googling every symptom he had, real and imagined. Like Adam, hypochondriacs are sensory amplifiers and hypothesis generators. It's as if Adam made a contract with himself to be perpetually vigilant about anything that might relate to his physical health and well-being. He knows the unwritten rules that too frequently dominate his thinking are decidedly different from those of his wife, Jill, who is generally pretty good-natured about his bodily concerns and his need to talk about them.

Because of Adam's slight calming side chemical imbalance, his hypervigilance is no accident; it is set in motion and maintained by his naturally higher level of cortical activation: our old friend arousal. Even as a child, he recalls asking himself, "Why am I feeling nervous or weird when there doesn't seem to be anything to worry about or anything to be afraid of?" The source of his low-level fear was only his perception of the heightened signal strength of arousal.

Here's the way it works:

Arousal $\rightarrow$ sensory amplification $\rightarrow$ a sense of danger $\rightarrow$ the hypothesis generating of why questions

Adam remembers a moment in his childhood as he waited at home for his mother, who had gone in for a doctor's appointment and was late in getting back. He sat at the window looking for her car to turn into the driveway. As it slowly got dark, he kept checking the clock over the mantle and with each passing minute his sense of dread rose. Adam's dread was a by-product of heightened arousal and hypothesis generating. He started with thoughts of a potential flat tire and running out of gas. These explanations quickly spun into thinking the doctor had found something very wrong with his mother, that they had taken her to the hospital, and then quickly on to the conviction that she had some sort of terrible accident.

Adam also remembered that by the time his mother pulled into the driveway he was so dry mouthed that he couldn't swallow. In the next few days, he found himself focused on swallowing and spinning out a slew of explanations, each more worrisome. Even after he was reassured by the doctor his mother took him to and despite the tests done and being told his throat was normal, his worries remained. Adam was off to the races.

Hypochondria is a sibling of OCD. The compulsion here is the talking about the latest symptom, the googling of the symptom, the doctor visits, the trips to the ER. Overriding these compulsive strategies to modulate and reduce arousal can present a daunting challenge.

The best start is to recognize these tendencies as your own, talk to your doctor about them, ask the doctor to restrict the frequency of your visits, and limit the doctor's reassurance to only one per visit. As you will recall, worrying gets rewarded by the brain and "I worry about getting cancer" can become "I don't get cancer because I worry about it." And none of this activity is particularly conscious thought. It is for these reasons that an excessive bodily focus is so durable.

It's not easy or comfortable being labeled a hypochondriac. If you find yourself with a heightened focus on somatic symptoms, remember this: You're not crazy. What you are is an imaginative hypothesis creator. Anyone struggling with too much arousal is prone to questioning why. The reason for this is that it is normal and natural to want to make sense of the discomfort, to attach it to some source—the reason I'm feeling *this* is because of *that*. Connecting an abstract feeling to a physical symptom brings a sense of relief, some modicum of control. What symptom worriers can do is recognize these tendencies and relate to them with understanding and compassion. Some people find it calming to remind themselves that the probability is that they are just fine and that they are only looking around for something to attribute the natural buzz of arousal in their system to. Others find it helpful to apply the three-day rule: "If I'm still feeling this way three days from now, I'll call the doctor." (Of course, this shouldn't include acute abdominal or chest pain or stroke symptoms, which should be checked out immediately.) Or best yet, having the understanding that you tend to regulate your natural arousal in this way, try instead to address it by engaging in an active internal dialogue that is soothing, encouraging, and reassuring. Here is a drill one of our patients found useful: "I've been here before, had these same worries even if the content is different. These worries turned out to be needless. I have choices. I can do something different this time. I don't have to travel that same anxious path. I'm giving myself a leap of faith. I'm assuming this is just what I do, how I've learned to interpret the signals of arousal. I'm assuming that's what is going on and that I'm not sick. I have a tendency to assume illness until proven otherwise. I'm choosing to do something different: I'm assuming wellness. But what if this time is different and there really is something wrong? I'll know soon enough. This time I'm telling myself that I am just fine, that these worries I'm having are only that, simply worries, not signs of illness. And every time I find myself going back to these thoughts, I'm going to land still another time on being calming and reassuring. Going through this exercise again and again until it becomes the habit and replaces my worri-some spinning."

Try, for a change, going to the best-case scenario instead of the worst and reminding yourself that this current symptom is likely magnified by natural arousal. You could also commit to building in regularly scheduled mindfulness meditation. This is a powerful way of dealing with the real source of these tendencies, your dis-comfort with arousal.

A thought for those of you who are close to someone with hypo-chondriacal tendencies: shaming them is counterproductive. They are already embarrassed by these recurrent worries. It's best to re-late to them with kindness and understanding.

And for those of you who might identify with a tendency to no-tice something amiss and tell yourself, "Oh, it's probably nothing and will just go away," symptom denial and wishful thinking is a Sword trait. Swords' essentially optimistic natures can lead them to ignore or discount sometimes even important physical issues. Now might be a good time to schedule some of those things you may have put off, like that overdue colonoscopy or mammogram.

Reactivity, Flexibility, and Adaptation to Change

Remember the studies done by Harvard psychologist Jerome Kagan that observed infants and their reaction to external stimula-tion? About 40 percent of the children responded to those strange visuals and popping balloons with little or no reaction. These were the kids with the calm amygdalae, the ones who grow into more social, confident, and outgoing adults—our Swords. During sub-sequent interviews with these children as they grew up, the low-reactive children tended to relate to the much older inter-viewers more as peers rather than as authority figures. They weren't scanning the field for potential dangers, seeming to be com-fortable with themselves. In possession of enough available serotonin, Sword children tend to grow into confident, self-assured adults. Shields, on the other hand, tend to have a reactive amygdalae. This tends to focus them more on potential downsides, mistakes, and the possible faux pas. This dynamic unfortunately detracts from the experience of pleasure, particularly in social situations. As children, Swords are social doers and experimenters, whereas Shield children lean in the direction of being social watchers or observers. Of course, these dynamics orbit around which brain circuits (fear or reward) are more dominant. Comfort with (or attraction to) arousal frees up bolder social interactions for Swords who, from early on, learn a lot about themselves through trial and error. Less afraid of making mistakes than their Shield cousins, they experiment with themselves socially, sometimes getting smacked down for their blunders, but learning quickly nevertheless.

From infancy on, those with too little serotonin tend to be reactive by nature. As young children, they are the ones who have a harder time with separation, feeling more comfortable with a parent by their side. Preschool and kindergarten can be challenging early on in that they combine uncertainty, unfamiliarity, and separation, a powerful mix of demands that stimulate uncomfortable levels of arousal. Shield children sometimes deal with such situations by developing stomachaches, negativity, and protests designed to avoid the experience. The volume on their invisible arousal antenna is set to high and they don't have the chemical reserve to calm it down. Fortunately, this kind of reactivity fades over time with a reassuring mom or dad's voice and the gradual backfill of real experiences that reduce uncertainty and the unfamiliar.

Emotional reactivity can be an unpleasant experience. The best antidote for this discomfort is more than the passage of time and experience; it is learning how to self-soothe. Trying to soothe ourselves is natural and reflexive, but unfortunately we don't instinctively know how to do it in healthy ways. We see a lot of adults who never learned how to soothe themselves constructively and instead turn to self-defeating and unhealthy behaviors. For instance, a pint of chocolate chip ice cream and a vodka tonic are among Shields' favorite self-soothing strategies, which in excess are detrimental to their health. Because a Sword's resting state tends to be the experience of too little arousal, they are not particularly reactive to their fear circuitry. Instead, in their hunt for stimulation they can be distractible and vulnerable to their own dysfunctional self-soothing techniques. Because of this, Swords are prone to a variety of addictions, the goal of which is self-stimulation, be it with cocaine or that same pint of ice cream.

It may seem surprising, but because of their nervous systems Shields are highly sensitive reactors to the new and unexpected. While they can be eminently capable at following a plan, they really shine when a change of circumstance or unanticipated snag occurs. Swords are often excellent at laying out complex logical sequences, but they can draw blanks when things go wrong.

To explain why, let's step back for a moment and fill in something a little more fully. We've described the function of dopamine and serotonin because they're the primary brain chemicals that animate our autonomic nervous system, but certainly they are not the only ones. The sympathetic nervous system, with dopamine and its team members adrenaline, noradrenaline, glutamate, and acetylcholine, all act to excite the nervous system. The parasympathetic nervous system, with serotonin and its neurotransmitter cousins acetylcholine (yes, it's a player on both teams) and GABA, act to calm an over-amped brain. It is likely that Swords' entire team of brain chemicals on the excitatory side of the nervous system (sympathetic) is a little on the shy side, not simply in dopamine levels. And likewise, Shields end up on the short side in terms of not only serotonin but also its teammates on the calming side of the nervous system.

We bring this up to describe a critical role that noradrenaline (like dopamine, a chemical on the stimulating side) plays in our responses to uncertain situations, helping us to adapt to changing circumstances and learn. When the tasks at hand seem stable, we tend to rely on our previous experiences to help us anticipate what will happen in the future. But when the situation becomes volatile, our brain needs to let go of expectations and allow for the rapid learning that is required for the adaptation to change. Shifting between these approaches is a function of the brain chemical noradrenaline.

A recent study is relevant here. Study participants initially listened to sounds that were followed by an image of either a house or a face. Pretty quickly, they learned to predict the image they saw based upon the sound that they heard before the image appeared. Then the researchers began to mix things up a bit. The sounds and images started to change, increasing uncertainty and making it necessary to learn new associations quickly. Half the group was then given a placebo drug and the other half the beta-blocker and antianxiety drug propranolol (it should be noted that none of the participants suffered from anxiety). Propranolol blocks the neurotransmitter noradrenaline. The researchers found that the propranolol group was slower than the placebo group when they were required to learn to use new information to adjust their expectations as to which image might come next in the changing situation. The propranolol group relied more on their prior experience to make their predictions when faced with uncertainty rather than quickly learning new associations.

What does this mean in the real world? This may be why Swords (who tend to be on the shy side of stimulating brain chemicals such as noradrenaline) tend to rely more heavily on the past than do their Shield cousins, who as you know have plenty of brain chemicals on the stimulating side and tend to have greater flexibility in rapidly changing circumstances. Swords, then, tend to focus a bit more on the past to predict the future, while Shields tend to focus a bit more on the present for their prediction of the future.

So, what's the primary takeaway here? Having to deal with a noisy nervous system makes Shields more flexible and that kind of lifelong learning is a positive skill set, especially when dealing with change. Being able to dance more nimbly with rapidly changing demands and circumstances is a very functional side effect of a Shield's brain chemical imbalance. The absence of that kind of learning leads to the opposite: a more rigid stance in the world that makes Swords a bit more routine bound and resistant to change. When, from childhood onward, you have to look for ways to stimulate yourself (create a feeling of normal arousal), you tend to develop reliable and predictable strategies to accomplish that goal. These patterns become ingrained and we don't like to have to give them up, even if the ground has shifted a bit. These tendencies can make change a more difficult process for Swords.

If you identify with being a Sword, you might ask yourself to review the old and reliable patterns that define your daily existence and make sure that they still are healthy and work for you. What we are referring to here are lifestyle issues: how we eat, move, rest, and manage stress. Are the ways you eat, exercise, sleep, and self-soothe constructive or are they simply familiar? How do you handle new and changing situations and demands? Are you able to engage in the new learning that's required, or do you find yourself resisting, however subtly? Can you identify one area of your resistance to newness where you know you are dragging your feet but that might be helpful to master? If you can, why not take a swing at conquering it? Whatever it is, break it up into manageable chunks and commit to a begin date. And here's the good news: change and doing something new creates uncertainty and, yes, arousal! Use that small bump as an indication of something positive, as the marker of a challenge. And remember, getting used to doing anything new takes time and patience (time Swords have, but patience can be a test of their commitment to a learning process). It's best to remind yourself of the small steps rule: steps that are directionally correct, however small, will lead to mastery.

And for you Shields, don't be too smug here. Sure, you're pretty good at being flexible to changing demands, but you may not be so good at changing patterns attached to avoidant behavior. Take a look at the habits you revert to in order to avoid arousal. Anything unhealthy you notice about the way you eat? Drink? How about maintaining a consistent exercise routine? That can be uncomfortable. Are you going to sleep too late? Getting up too late?

Avoiding any social or work challenges that if engaged would make you feel stronger and more confident? Can you identify any behaviors that don't serve your best interests but you have been resistant to change? And here's a hard one: What could you do simply because it's enjoyable, because it brings you pleasure? There's nothing like today. Right now. Risk making some change you know will serve you better in the long run. The same small steps rule applies. Confronting avoidant tendencies is difficult. It requires learning to tolerate very real moments of emotional discomfort. But remember this: only good things come from toughening up.

A reminder: Identifying yourself as a Sword or a Shield doesn't mean that you identify with the magnitude or direction of all Shield or Sword behaviors that we describe. These are leanings or tendencies, not absolutes.

Impulse Control and the Delay of Gratification

Shields typically have very good impulse control. Unlike their Sword siblings, they have so much arousal buzzing around that not only are they not sensation seekers; they are sensation avoiders. Novelty, risk, and sensation are the bright shiny objects that can trigger impulsive behavior. Swords are prone to indulging in impulses because they are tied to the emotional expectations of a reward (loading a drop of dopamine into the reward circuits). As we've described, Swords do this because it's stimulating and dials up arousal.

The last thing Karen needed was another purse, but there she was, finding herself once again on eBay bidding for one more bag that she didn't need. Even with her credit card bills blinking bright red in her brain, she pressed the "place bid" button. As she often did, Karen felt a surge of guilt and remorse seeing the UPS truck pull up outside. She hid the new purse deep in her closet, knowing her husband would question her about it had he seen it. "No more," she promised herself. But that very night, despite her intentions, she found herself cracking open her laptop and in a few keystrokes was again trolling eBay. The impulse was irresistible.

Indulging in these kinds of impulses is simply not among the experiences that animate those with more protective natures (Shields). Interestingly, the science of impulse control is not only associated with a dopamine deficiency; studies show that it also is an issue of elevated levels of serotonin. That's right, with an excess of the calming neurotransmitter serotonin, impulsive behavior accelerates.

An excess of serotonin is never a Shield's problem. In fact, for many impulse suppression is the issue. While a Sword's impulse is associated with the anticipation of a reward, Shields often pair the anticipation of an impulse with some negative outcome. Remember, harm avoidance is the central motivational spur for those with deficient levels of serotonin. In some cases, this protective instinct can be helpful and a strength, but in others an obstacle.

Sandy is seventeen and a studious high school senior. Shy, slender, and blue-eyed, she is much more attractive than she feels. Sandy suffers from social anxiety. As a healthy young teenager, she worked very hard to squelch any kind of impulse attached to sexual attraction. Sandy avoided any situation where she would have to deal with boys. Going to a public school made this difficult, but clever girl that she is, Sandy developed some pretty effective strategies. When we first saw Sandy, she had neatly convinced herself that she had no particular sexual feelings, even though her dreams told a different story. She dressed in purposefully frumpy clothes with the explanation that they made her invisible to all the "oversexed" boys. She said, "I think I'm probably destined to be a nun or something, except that I'm not a Catholic."

Sandy was a secret fan of the talent shows on television, which she watched in the privacy of her bedroom. She would sing along to certain singers, but only when there was no one home. She was not technically anorexic, but she followed a Spartan eating plan that made carrots fixed any which way sound interesting. And while she got frequent invitations to social events, she always managed to demur.

Sometimes Shields can exert such a tight lid on healthy feelings and desires (yes, impulses) that they become submerged. The first glimmer of change with Sandy came when she related a dream she had, in which she found herself walking along a wooded trail in the hills behind her house. Suddenly, the trail was cut by a fast-moving stream. She wanted to get to the other side but was afraid to cross. About to turn around, she saw a boy standing just downstream, watching her with a grin. What she remembered next was that her hand was in his and they walked through the water to the other bank. When she was asked if she recognized the boy, her face turned bright red and she replied, "He's a really cute guy in my English class."

One day recently, Sandy came in with a couple of chocolate chip cookies to share. "Gluten-free," she announced, "but they're still pretty good." Then her face turned that bright red again as she said, "I remember you saying that some impulses are good to express. Right? Well, a boy asked me to the prom and I accepted." Sandy was starting to get to know herself as a developing young woman.

Knowing when to say yes or no to an impulse is important. Impulses are thoughts attached to feelings that call for some decision to be made. They are neither good nor bad in and of themselves, and whether they are good for us or not depends upon context. Swords' most basic engagement orientation increases the likelihood of them saying yes to an experience even when a no might be safer and more prudent. It took Karen some time to understand that her shopping addiction was really related to her dopamine deficiency and learn to override the impulse. What we had Karen do was line up all of her purses on her bed and put a Post-it on each one. We had her write the last time she had used the purse. Of the forty-one purses that were almost spilling off her bed, Karen had used only three in the last six months. The rest were simply stashed away in a corner of her attic. This exercise confirmed for Karen that her purchases were really unnecessary and purely impulsive. We explained to her the chemical aspect of behavior. This takes away some of the guilt and shame and ties the compelling feeling of the impulse to a simple chemical reaction. Then we pointed to the unused bags to illustrate the disconnect between the impulse (anticipation and purchase) and the result (the appreciation of the purse itself). Dopamine is all about the looking, dreaming, and planning about an activity or an object and has nothing to do with its appreciation. It's all about the motivation "to do" something, but totally independent of the enjoyment of the fruits of the action. Tearing apart the impulse and the pleasure (or lack thereof) of the purchase allowed Karen to understand that the dopamine reward was all front-loaded, that it was all in the excitement of the fantasy. We knew she had really gained control of the situation when she came in and told us, "I can go on my computer and look and imagine what it would feel like to own one of those purses I see there, but I don't have to actually buy it. I remind myself that I probably won't ever use it."

Anyone who's ever stayed up late studying for an exam knows everything there is to know about the decision-making and experience of delaying gratification. Keeping your nose in a book comes at the expense of many things you might rather be doing at the moment, not the least of which is getting your much-needed rest. Of course, both Swords and Shields can delay gratification, but Shields tend to do it a little more easily and are a bit better at it. Why?

Most certainly, impulse control is a critical part of that calculus. But that's not the whole story. Swords and Shields both focus on what they are missing, what the delay is costing them. For Swords, the cost of studying for that test might be a couple of hours of gaming, a hot date, or a few hours spread out on the couch streaming some new Netflix series. And coming along with whatever the delay costs happen to be is the absence of some sort of rewarding experience.

When it comes to Shields, instead of focusing on having to give up a reward, they tend to focus more on the consequences attached to *not* giving it up. Instead of focusing on missing out on hours of playing video games, they focus on how poorly they will do on the test if they don't study. For Swords, sometimes the loss of the reward breaks the willpower chain and the television might get turned on. But for Shields, the dynamics are different. As they are less reward sensitive and more harm avoidant, dodging the possibility of getting a poor test score is actually an internally rewarded experience. So, for Swords having to delay gratification is often experienced as a net loss, while for Shields delay is seen as a net gain. Let's dig a little deeper into self-control and the ability to delay that gold ring.

Many of you will remember the famous Stanford marshmallow experiments, led by psychologist Walter Mischel. Five-year-old children were led into a room and seated at a table. A marshmallow was placed on the table and the children were told that if they could wait fifteen minutes before eating it, they would receive a second treat. The experimenter then left the room, coming back in after the fifteen minutes had elapsed. Some of the children gobbled down the marshmallow as soon as the door closed, while others found strategies to curb the impulse to eat it and waited out the time to get the second treat.

What the experimenters found were some strong correlations between the ability to delay gratification and later life successes such as higher SAT scores and fewer behavior problems. Later attempts to replicate Mischel's study brought his findings into question. Controlling for family income, for example, made those strong correlations vanish. If you have a couple of hungry siblings and a bare pantry to begin with, you're likely to grab that treat when you see it for fear that it won't be there the next time you look around.

But irrespective of the complications in studying self-control and the ability to delay gratification, these are important skills to have. Because of their imbalanced brain chemicals, Swords have a more difficult time putting off getting a reward than do Shields. Shields, you will remember, are less sensitive to reward and because of this may actually experience fewer temptations. Temptations by their very nature can carry with them the fear of getting carried away and losing control of the ability to modulate emotional comfort—things Shields strive to avoid.

Because Swords are sensitized to reward and the possibility of an arousal bump, they have a difficult time delaying gratification. That delay is associated with a state of decreased arousal and its anticipation is uncomfortable.

Shields sometimes conflate the constructive ability to delay gratification with simply putting off dealing with something attached to the anticipation of discomfort. It's best not to kid yourself here. It can be all too easy for Shields to lend credence to their excuses when all they're doing is avoiding feeling uncomfortable. Look for something you'd like to have and find some way to give it to yourself. Don't think object here; think process. A patient of ours said he had always wanted to be able to ask a woman to dance. At school dances he would see a girl he liked but could never get up the courage to ask her to dance. Later in life, at weddings and other social events, even when he was with a date, he would steer clear of the dance floor. He said it was because he didn't want to stumble through a few steps but wanted to feel confident and to take lessons. He always found some excuse to put off doing that, but the real excuse was that he felt too shy and uncomfortable to sign up for a class. When finally he did, he gave himself a gift that paid off far beyond the dance floor. He won back a meaningful swath of confidence and belief that he actually could do something he believed he couldn't.

A Sword's journey here is a little different. They can find that they occasionally sabotage themselves by indulging in impulses or by abandoning a process before it's completed because they get bored, lose patience, or become distracted by something else that seems more interesting or compelling at the moment. This could be anything from moving from hobby to hobby to hobby to never finding a reason for having a third date. When novelty fades, it's possible to end up with a garage filled with uncompleted projects or, worse, alone because you were always looking for someone new to excite you.

Optimism and Pessimism

Possessing a sunny and outgoing countenance is one of Swords' greatest strengths. Optimism, a common core Sword characteristic, is linked to pretty much all the good things in life from resilience to satisfaction. Being reward oriented and risk tolerant is a formula that increases adventuresome experiences from very early on in a child's life. And being less sensitive to punishment and the possibility of bad outcomes allows Swords to be less daunted by the prospect of the necessary little failures we all endure. Having a mental set that predicts positive outcomes can go a long way to bringing those very outcomes to fulfillment. Swords are fortunate, for an upbeat outlook feels better experientially. In fact, one of the most consistent findings that relate to optimistic people is that they are overall happier than their less positive cousins and that increased happiness is durable and lasting over the decades. Studies suggest that this happiness may be related to a person's sensitivity to rewarding social situations, their subsequent engagement in more social activities, or more effective emotional regulation. These descriptors are all within a Sword's ken. The only danger can be decisions based more on hope or wish that overvalue upside potential and undervalue downside risk.

We assume by now you can see how being a Shield is not always easy or even pleasant. Their tendency toward being pessimistic is a simple outgrowth of their protective nature. While Swords look for reasons to say yes to a decision, Shields tend to look for reasons why they should say no. Sadly, pessimism is one of Shields' greatest potholes.

Based upon new research, repetitive negative thinking is linked to cognitive decline. Researchers at the University of London studied 292 people all above the age of fifty-five using a number of tests measuring language and spatial skills, attention, memory, and cognitive functioning. A little less than half the group allowed their brains to be scanned to look for measures of tau and amyloid proteins—deposits that are biological markers for Alzheimer's disease. Participants were asked about how they thought of and dealt with negative experiences, how often they found themselves dwelling in the past, and worries they had for the future.

Over a four-year period, those who engaged in the most repetitive negative thought patterns exhibited more memory problems and greater cognitive decline than those with more positive thought patterns. And perhaps most telling, these same participants also showed the greatest buildup of tau and amyloid deposits in their brains.

So negative thinking leads to dementia? Well, not so fast. Before you jump to conclusions, let's look at the study more closely. As important as this research is, this kind of study shows associations or correlations, not necessarily cause and effect. There may be some third element related to both negative thinking and cognitive decline. We believe that this might just be the case.

It may not be Shields' penchant toward negative thought patterns that is the culprit, but instead their tendency over a lifetime to avoid new challenges, new social situations, and new experiences calling for unfamiliar skill development. Shields' brains are used to their chronic distaste for heightened arousal and the obstacles to new experience their reactions confer. But our brains are plastic and constantly being physically remodeled by the new experiences we have. The emphasis here is on novelty, the newness of the experience and its unfamiliar stimulation that remodels our brains. It may very well be that keeping memory and cognition intact longer and warding off the damaging deposits of tau and amyloid plaque can be accomplished by embracing the new challenges and stimulating experiences that remodel our brains.

The task for you Shields (and it's never too early or too late to begin this) isn't to start running around thinking positive thoughts suddenly; the critical task is to challenge your reflexive no to new experiences and find ways to say yes to them more often. To begin this process of override, you might want fill out an Avoidance Log (see chapter 4).

And how about you Swords? Being open and optimistic is a wonderful trait and way to be in the world. We encourage you to hang on to it, for it serves you well. The only downside is the possibility of missing something on the minus side that shouldn't be missed. Optimism should never take the place of realism. During the pandemic, there were those who weren't as careful as they might have been and got sick. This won't happen to me may very well be an optimistic thought, but it offers little in the way of needed protection. You might take a moment here and ask yourself what things you do that are supported more by wish, hope, and trusting belief than by anything more substantial. When you are confronted with a decision, it's not being pessimistic to cover your backside when that's the more realistic and appropriate choice.

Risk Tolerance

The last emotional element shaping our behavior is risk tolerance. Our willingness to accept risk is largely dependent upon our relationship with arousal. Those of us with too little natural systemic arousal are more risk tolerant than those with a bit too much. Let's take a quick look at something as ancient and consequential as migration. Looking back at the voluntary migrant flows that have shaped our world, we can ask: Who got restless when plentiful game thinned and hunters returned home empty-handed too often? Or when overharvesting or microclimate changes caused roots and seeds to become harder to find, who stayed and who left? Their names have been lost in the dust of time, but we do know something about their neurochemistry and this chemical soup tells us a lot. During times of uncertainty and hardship, Shields would have been busy building a case for saying something like, "Yes, these are challenging times, but we may be safer managing to get along with what we have than moving into an unknown that could be worse." Their Sword cousins would be less daunted by whatever possible dangers they might find over that far hill and more inclined to make a move. Familiarity, in and of itself, provides a certain amount of comfort for Shields, even when what's familiar is unpleasant or has its downside (the devil you know sort of thing). Not so for Swords. It's not that they don't prize comfort; it's just that they tend to discount the value of familiarity just as they underestimate danger.

Shields tend to be risk averse. Stepping into anything novel, anything out of their circle of emotional comfort, means having to deal with an unpleasant bump up in arousal. We are all comfort driven and, for most Shields, taking risks is an uncomfortable endeavor. If you are an investor, being a little risk averse can be a real asset. Because of this, they make fewer false positive errors and don't bet the house on a penny stock someone touts as being the next Amazon. But these same decision-making tendencies can have a downside. Shields are vulnerable to making false negative errors. They are more likely, for example, on the day of a big dip in a stock they've been following, to wait it out. Afraid the stock will slip even further, they hesitate and watch, helplessly gritting their teeth, as buyers sweep in and drive the stock higher once again.

Swords tend to read uncertainty a little differently than do Shields. The bump up of arousal it creates isn't seen as odious and a danger, but as exciting and a step toward a possible reward. Put a Sword and a Shield on a white-water raft together for the first time. They have exactly the same experience, but one might breathe a sigh of relief to be off the water and the other clamber to do it all over again.

This might be a good time to take a moment to think about the ways in which you relate to risk. Which side do you typically fall upon? How has your tolerance for risk affected the decisions in your life? How do you see it operating in your social relationships? Have you been the one to choose your friends or are you chosen by them? How do you see risk operating in your decisions around money? Are there elements of risk that have had an impact on your work and career? What are the influences of your tolerance for risk that get expressed in your health? Indulging in too much alcohol? Still smoking? Spending too much time sitting around when you, at the least, could be spending a few minutes walking every day? Too anxious to schedule appropriate screening tests, maybe pretending you don't need them? On balance, do you think you take too little risk or too much? You get the idea. All of these questions can be illuminating. Remember, based upon your brain chemical imbalance, you are set up unconsciously to respond a bit in one direction or the other. This shaping influence is, of course, independent of logical, deductive thinking. If you are a Sword, it might be helpful for you to tone down your exuberance for engaging in a decision or action that contains important risk. It may not be a rational thought process that beckons, but just a sly and potentially self-defeating ploy to create a needed dopamine hit. And conversely, for you Shields fanning the hesitations and cautions around a decision, the danger you face may not be in the real world but only in the noisy buzz of your brain chemistry. Be bold; challenge some of your decisions; lead a life with more degrees of freedom.

So, what's the big picture here? The takeaway? Our emotions shape our decisions and the habits they turn into. The vast majority of these decisions are on a micro level and the habits they create are expressed unconsciously. The value of learning more about the influence your particular brain chemistry plays in your life is to be better able to bring these hidden levers out into the open, to honor those that work for you and to challenge and override those that don't. Take a close look at the things you *do* as well as some of those things you *don't but would like to* in the best of all worlds. Do you see the fingerprints of your brain type at work here?

Not only is your brain type a major player in the workings of your emotions; it also has its silent but busy fingers in how you think, explored next.

CHAPTER THREE

The Tug-of-War That Drives How You Think

How Our Relationship with Arousal Determines the Basic Elements That Make Up Our Cognitive Style

HOW WE THINK, REACH CONCLUSIONS, and make decisions has many cofactors, from early family experiences to education and friends to religious and party preference, to mention only a few. But in addition to such obvious influences of how we digest and use information is something much more subtle: the imperceptible ways in which our brain chemistry exerts its powerful sway. Unbidden, it pulls and shapes us with little in the way of conscious awareness. There are some things we notice more by effect than by direct observation, like the invisible force of gravity in a high fly ball at a baseball game. The workings of our brain chemistry are best explored by examining the fingerprints they leave behind on our behavior.

Reward Processing: At the Mercy of Our Errors

How we behave, of course, is entangled with how we learn. We learn by watching and doing things that our brain keeps track of. Our old friend dopamine is a big player in how the brain encodes what it has learned. In the lingo of those who study this phenomenon, the brain accomplishes its complex learning process by tracking what are known as "reward predictions errors." What does this mean exactly?

In order to gain some sense of agency in the world, we cobble together our observations and experiences and begin a series of trial-and-error experiments. Whether it be trying out a motor task like crawling across the floor or making our first mutterings in an attempt to approximate words, we make a stab in the direction of our goal. These "experiments" are predictions of what we hope might prove to be successful. Dopamine helps the brain code how accurate our predictions are. Reward prediction errors essentially are the *differences between the reward we predicted (the success of our experiment) and the reward we actually received (how close we came to being successful).*

Here's how it works: If we are more successful than we predicted, we get a big dopamine hit, encoding a *positive prediction error*. If we are about as successful as we thought we would be, dopamine signaling stays at baseline levels. And if we are less successful than we thought we would be, dopamine signaling dries up (a *negative prediction error*). Based upon the accretion of these countless experimental moments, we gradually learn all of the things that make us uniquely human. In essence, we are guided to do things gradually, ever more successfully, based upon how dopamine systematically rewards and reinforces our calculations (the guesses we make about the most efficient path to a reward) with a release of this neurotransmitter. When we were babies, closing our eyes and putting our head back was pretty successful if we were looking to take a snooze, but that won't get you anywhere if you're looking for a meal. Very quickly, our random trial-and-error guesses led to learning how to get along and manipulate our environment. Our crawling soon led to standing and walking and our squeals and squawking morphed into words that eventually got strung into sentences. All of this and more is a by-product of the differential bursts of dopamine keyed to our seamless predictive experiments.

And there is more. Not only do we learn from the pleasurable jolts of dopamine to approach, do, and engage things (positive reinforcement); we also learn from this same brain chemical to avoid things. Here's an example: You know the answer to a question in class and start to put your hand up. But before it's raised, you put it back in your lap, too nervous and worried that your voice might shake and you will embarrass yourself. Lowering that hand quickly is accompanied by an immediate feeling of relief. Your heartbeat stabilizes, as does your breathing. This avoidance of an experience you anticipate as potentially uncomfortable is as rewarding (negative reinforcement) to the brain as had you been more successful than you imagined. So then, basic learning is accomplished by the layered combination of positive and negative reinforcements.

Sounds simple enough, but wait. The way reality works on our planet, not all rewards are equal, nor is the time it takes to attain them. When we are given a choice, we tend to prefer more rewards rather than fewer and to receive them sooner rather than later. Doesn't that sound exactly like human nature? But if the amount of reward and the time it takes to get it are in conflict (less now or more at a later time), our choices get more complicated. You remember the marshmallow experiments. For some kids, it was simply too tempting not to eat the marshmallow, even when they knew they would get more of that sweet treat if they could wait a few minutes. All of us tend to discount the value of a reward based upon the combination of its perceived importance and the time involved in getting it. The larger, later reward is known as the self-controlled choice and the smaller, sooner one as the impulsive choice. Most people would say having a svelte, attractive body is preferable to the momentary delight of gobbling down a pile of hot, salty french fries. But one reward takes time and energy, while the other requires only a thumb and index finger. Who among us wouldn't prefer waiting ten minutes to get ten dollars over getting one dollar right now? But would that change if we had to wait ten months to get it?

The ventral striatum is the part of the brain that mediates reward experiences, motivation, and movement. To survive, we willingly expend effort throughout our days, and this effort is a product of the decisions we make. Neuroimaging studies show that the ventral striatum activates while we make decisions and this activation encodes the value we attach to rewards relative to their costs, like wait time, effort, and probability. This part of the brain also does something else. It creates *activation signals* that prepare us to expend energy as well as *discounting signals* that help us to choose the action that requires the least amount of effort, making sure we don't put in any more work than we have to. As you will recall, the brain is designed to be very calorie conscious.

Where all of this gets really interesting is when we look at these dynamics in terms of Shields and Swords. These undercurrents are ultimately directed by the indelible slant our brain chemical imbalances exert on the errors we choose to let dominate our decision-making process. Arousal-hungry Swords tend to make riskier, more impulsive choices. Guided more by positive reinforcement, they are also more likely to discount important rewards that are costly in terms of time and effort. Conversely, Shields, driven by their aversion to arousal, are better able to delay gratification. Where they get into trouble in terms of their decision-making is when their affinity for avoidance and the negative reinforcement it provides lead them astray. That student we mentioned (likely a Shield and likely to have known the answer or they wouldn't have wanted to raise a hand) was deprived of the success experience that would have bolstered confidence. Instead of rewarding the taking of reasonable chances (the student might have been wrong), what was reinforced was the strategy to dampen the arousal felt by the anticipation of throwing a hand in the air (avoidance).

Shields tend to overvalue negative consequences and undervalue positive rewards, while Swords do the opposite. Remember those students in chapter 2 who were facing an upcoming test? Let's use them again for an example. Both must juggle short-term wishes for what they would like to do with their time versus the long-term outcome of the test results. Do they study or do something more immediately pleasing? The problem is that the delay (time) dedicated to study is expensive. Both focus on what they are missing as well as what the delay is costing them. For Swords, that cost might be a couple of hours playing Fortnite, watching the latest new movie, or lounging around on social media for a few hours. And coming along with whatever the delay costs happen to be is the absence of some sort of rewarding experience.

As you will recall, Shields tend to be more cautious and less willing to take chances as they go about their business. It's not that they don't like rewarding situations as much as do Swords, for they do; it's just that they place more importance on what they might lose or have to give up by going for the reward. Focusing less on what they might lose by *having to give up a reward*, they tend to place more emphasis on the consequences attached to *not giving it up*. The anticipation of reward is always related to some variation of, "If I do this, then that is likely to happen." In that anticipatory gap of time before a decision is made, Shields and Swords think about reward (what feels important) in differing ways. Shields gain something by leaving the television off (avoiding the higher probability of doing poorly on the test) while Swords can be seduced by thoughts of loss in having to delay a reward, breaking the willpower chain.

Dopamine neurons don't discriminate between a prediction of rewards and the real thing. These events are of equal value and treated by the brain in a similar way. What this means is that we use our prediction of rewards to make our plans and as the basis of our decision-making. And remember, the dopamine response washes out if the prediction is accurate; we only get the bump in dopamine when the prediction exceeds our expectations. Our brain constantly updates our predictions and the surprisingly larger reward we received soon is downgraded and becomes the norm, no longer releasing a dopamine prediction error surge. The dopamine swirling around in each of our brains acts to drive us not only toward rewards but toward constantly increasing rewards as well.

As humans, we appear to be hardwired to strive for more and more rewards. This wiring is probably responsible for our competitive nature as well as what drives our intellectual curiosity, providing survival and evolutionary value. This is also, no doubt, the engine of the material world, the embedded human decision-making connection to every successful marketing ploy. It's likely that our predictive errors are behind every new car or home purchase, every new purse when the old one is perfectly serviceable, even trading in the old boyfriend for a new one. And the same dynamics apply on the other side—fear motivation. Every doom and gloom prognosticator, every longevity-enhancing promise, every miracle face cream in a jar is responding to a prediction.

Other things being equal, the invisible influence our brain chemical imbalances throw into the system has important implications. Because Shields are more sensitive to negative reinforcement, they tend to put a little more weight on decisions that predict greater safety, while reward-focused Swords overweigh predictions promising a positive reinforcement. A Sword's lack of caution is a great boon in their development of social skills and confidence but may be a hindrance when they are tempted to max out their credit card on another piece of expensive jewelry that they can ill afford. And a Shield might be better served ignoring the prediction of a rejection and asking the woman he's attracted to for a date but hang on to his innate caution when caution serves the more intelligent and prudent cause. Clearly, Swords and Shields each could learn a few lessons from the other's playbook.

How? We've found it really helpful for those who identify as Shields to take a critical look at how much of their behavior is influenced by negative reinforcement. Remember, negative reinforcement feels good because it's a by-product of a temporary reprieve from some situation that is perceived to be anxiety creating or dangerous even. All too often these dynamics create decisions that are comfort driven instead of being healthy, constructive, or personally generative. Or, and more important, even accurate. Many of Shields' worst fears are simply that—inaccurate assumptions based upon too few real-world experiences. Instead of learning from the *experience,* all that is learned is the repetitive *avoidance.* Indulging in the avoidance of a potentially constructive experience does two things. It has the effect of strengthening the fear of that experience rather than weakening it and it causes you to miss out on some important and beneficial learning experiences.

Where Shields need to say go and yes more often, Swords' issues are a little different. They need to say stop and no and ponder more frequently. Swords don't have the innate noisy nervous system filters that Shields do and need to find ways of constructing one. What this requires first is an awareness of those moments when you're most inclined to say yes instead of waiting a moment to think about what "yes" means. Saying something as simple as the command "wait" to yourself when you recognize those go signals from inside can create just enough time and thoughtfulness necessary to consider the consequences of the action. Doing this is never going to turn you into a Shield. You won't become a worrywart and you're always going to have more fun. We've never known a Sword yet who didn't profit from learning a little more appropriate caution. But to do that requires work. What comes naturally to Shields is distinctly unnatural for you. But here's the truth: what feels unnatural to you is really a very constructive trick to put in your arsenal.

Tolerance for Ambiguity and Dichotomous Thinking

No one likes ambiguity. It's disturbing and messy and requires much too much energy and thoughtful weighing to parse through the nuance. To make our decisions, formulate our thoughts, and clarify our opinions, we all go for the straightest line between two points. We want a solid yes or no, black or white even though we all know reality is made up of many shades of gray. Ambiguity is emotionally disruptive; its mixed messages are inherently discomforting. Most of us filter these oftentimes confusing and contradictory events through some kind of lens to clarify our thoughts and feelings.

For example, let's explore how we dealt with the political ambiguity immediately following the Trump/Biden contest. Among the by-products of the pandemic of 2020 were feelings of great threat and uncertainty, and an acute awareness of the limits of our control. And then came the election, Biden's win, and Trump's negation of it, heaping uncertainty upon uncertainty. While both state and federal courts rejected the Trump campaign's claim of election fraud as baseless, millions of Americans, and from 70 to 80 percent of Republicans, believed the election was rigged and stolen. How did we sort through the relentless news feed assaulting us? Sword and Shield alike, we are natural-born categorizers and labelers. As storytellers, most of us form some narrative, lean and parsimonious, that lays out the world in ways that make sense to us and fits our attitudes and values.

A significant number of us get our news through social media. One of the reasons for Facebook's enormous success is that it allows users to curate their own news feed. In the quest to gain and keep eyeballs that feed their business models, news sites are less about informing and more about affirming their audience. Social media users are fed the slant on the news that they would like to hear, that confirms and reinforces their worldview. Because they are comforting (not necessarily because they are true), these slants become our truths, leaving us swimming in a pool of "alternative" facts. Our brains are designed to process fact and possibility in very different ways. And words count. The brain represents factual information with a much higher level of activation than it does information in the "possible" category. Words like "may" or "might" produce much weaker cortical activation signals than do words like "is" or "does." This is why the brain is so easily seduced by lies, particularly when they're repeated often enough.

How do we deal with this kind of blurred vision of reality? In our search for explanations, we tend to filter the information glut through an ideological lens, with interpretations cobbled together favoring our particular biases. This is called confirmation bias: the tendency to interpret new evidence as a confirmation of a person's existing beliefs or theories.

We are drawn to simplicity over complexity because it makes our world seem more predictable and certain. We saw this at work after the 2020 election. Elections are won and lost for a host of reasons, even when people may find the results not to their liking or even shocking. Those who were pleased with the results in 2020 simply concluded that Biden had won, while those who were displeased or found the result unbelievable had to make sense of what had happened, construct some sort of story. The story was a claim of blatant fraud. For many, reaching the conclusion that the unthinkable result was caused by systematic vote manipulation satisfied their need to see the world as unambiguous and orderly.

Our need to make sense of things, to understand their causal roots, comes from our need to live in a predictable world. But this need for order and certainty has a dark side—the power to distort reality. In fact, a recent study found that the higher a person's need is to see order in the world, the greater is that person's tendency to see objectional stories as being intentionally fabricated. Our need to feel as though there is order in the chaos is more powerful than our willingness to look at information contrary to our liking as being factual.

Part of what we do to reduce the discomfort of ambiguity is label elements to fit our story line. And any good story must have a protagonist and an antagonist—a hero and a villain. Studies in social psychology suggest that one of the ways people cope with the lack of control they experience in their lives is to blame their misfortune on something nebulous. We've seen this historically and again more recently in the rise of populism and nationalism around the globe. In the story line of our experience, nothing weaves together the disparate events quite so effectively as having an identified enemy, preferably one working sub rosa and devilishly powerful.

So how does this relate to brain chemistry? While Shields and Swords have an equal distaste for ambiguity, they relate to it in slightly different ways. Swords tend to see ambiguity as an obstacle, something to be pushed aside in their race to the bottom line or conclusion. They are busy connecting dots long before all the dots have been presented. Instead of speeding up, Shields slow down when they encounter patches of ambiguity because the lack of clarity represents the potential for danger. They, too, want to reduce the confusion, but not at the expense of missing something that might put them in jeopardy.

The human brain loves clarity. Ambiguity makes it difficult to sort things into the neat piles we like to construct. Once we've thrown something onto a pile, we don't have to give it much more thought. We've picked it up, identified it, and cataloged it. We like convenient piles like moral/immoral, right/wrong, good/bad.

Because Swords tend to be more reward/goal driven, they tend to value decisiveness over deliberation. So what that it might not be perfect? It's finished! This tendency favoring speed over accuracy is linked to their intolerance for ambiguity. Ambiguities, graininess, and complex nuances are cognitive choke points that require a reduction in speed. Many a Sword prefers to plow right through these stop signs and views them not as relevant information to be processed and incorporated into decision-making calculus, but as hindrances.

Want a real-world example? Two people equally interested in consummating some deal are reading through the pedantic legalese of the contract. Both want this part of the process to be over with and both view the bulk of the text as boilerplate. But only one takes the time to read through each passage and picks up the wording in one section that made it unwise to sign. You might venture a guess as to whether this was a Sword or a Shield.

We all like clear-cut answers. Ambiguous detail muddles things. But our Swords scream, "What are they saying!? Get to the point. It's all so complicated." This need to get to the point drives out the middle ground and pushes us toward its either-or. But sometimes it's not either-or; it's this and that. Sometimes there are no clear-cut choices, just messy layers of potential outcomes.

An antipathy for ambiguity leads to dichotomous thinking. English philosopher Alan Watts said more about this rigid type of thinking in one sentence than tomes written on the subject. Watts said, "It's like going to the store to buy a loaf of bread and coming home with only the crusts." Sometimes that old trope about the devil residing in the details actually is true. And if we rush too swiftly to an either-or conclusion, we may miss the pleasure, subtlety, and deeper meaning contained in the loaf. Unfortunately, unlike bread, it can be much more challenging to fully digest.

If you identify with Sword tendencies, you might want to pause for a moment and ask yourself if you are inclined to want to categorize something quickly and then move on. Do you tend to be a "Let's cut to the chase" person? Do you often jump to conclusions? If you answered yes to any of these questions, recognize this Sword tendency and condition yourself to slow down. Rushing forward can lead one to miss crucial bits of information that are vital to the decision-making process. When your natural tendency to be done and just move on surfaces, take a deep breath and remind yourself that a little patience and prudence will yield protection.

The dilemma here for Shields is a little different. They tend to get caught up in the granular details of the loaf and not see or lose sight of the obvious larger picture. If you identify with having these inclinations, you might try recognizing those moments and pushing yourself to answering some version of, "Yes, but what does it all mean?" or "How does all of this relate to the larger point?" You don't want to be so mired down in the minutiae that you fail to take necessary action.

Concentration and Attention to Detail

Some of us are more focused than others. Big-thinking, risk-tolerant, fast-moving Swords tend to be distracted easily. Ever-protective Shields are more focused and have better concentration and attention to detail. They come by way of this naturally, as a by-product of their vigilance. When you have your radar scanning the world for potential dangers, your ability to concentrate and pay attention to grainy detail is enhanced.

Being able to hold your focus and pay attention is integral to efficient cognitive processing, and an important aspect of this essential ability is related to having the right amount of arousal in the system. As you know, levels of arousal are inherited and the differences form our brain types, or stress-coping styles. What's important to understand about focus is that it requires just the right amount of arousal to hold it effectively. A patient once described it this way: "When I hear someone beginning to explain something that's complicated, I find myself tuning out." Focus, of course, is the prerequisite for attending to details, for if we can't concentrate, the details are scattered or not even seen or processed. When your mind is elsewhere, you can find yourself turning the page and suddenly realizing that you have no idea what you just read. This phenomenon can happen if we have a bit too little arousal or too much. A safe and comfortable feeling of stimulation is when we are able to maintain central nervous system arousal within a fairly narrow band.

The fundamentals of this aspect of cognitive processing come to us naturally. It's not like learning to ride a bike or to play the piano; it's innate. We're either pretty good natural concentrators or not. And we've known this since we were kids. If you had a hard time sitting quietly and doing your homework, a hard time remembering what you read, or a hard time getting yourself to sit somewhere long enough to even crack open the book, you are probably a Sword. And while you might have gotten yelled at and admonished for not being more organized, none of this was your fault. The fault was only in the paltry amount of arousal floating around in your system. When you're looking for enough stimulation in the system to stay awake and engaged, you are also likely to be distracted when one activity doesn't offer enough stimulus to hold your attention as long as you might like it to.

Shields, because they are generally a bit on the overaroused side, tend to be pretty good at concentrating and paying attention to what is relevant at the moment. They are focused and attentive, but not necessarily because they want or intend to be. No, their attentiveness is unintended; they explore the weeds as an innate strategy designed to dampen arousal, since they feel that the more informed they are, the fewer unknowns will follow, which is reassuring.

So, when we have just the right amount of arousal available, we tend to concentrate better. But like many things, a small spike in vigilance (think of that as arousal) is good, while too great a spike is not. Studies show that test scores actually increase with some anxiety thrown into the mix, but these same scores drop when anxiety levels get higher and become disruptive. It follows the common inverted U curve in nature where a little is good and too much is not.

Focus and attentiveness are valuable Shield assets, unless the arousal level rises too high and the process gets disorganized. Anxiety causes a disruption in focus similar to distractibility. In this case, an external focus is difficult to maintain because there is so much internal arousal bouncing around that the person is trying to process, make sense of, and avoid. We only have so much bandwidth, and during anxious moments there can be little left over to dedicate to details in the external world.

As mentioned earlier, many children get identified in school as having problems with attention and restlessness. The common diagnosis is attention deficit disorder (ADD) or attention deficit hyperactivity disorder (ADHD). Logic would suggest that a child who is bouncing around the classroom must have an excess of arousal. But no. Instead of having a surfeit of arousal, they have a deficiency. Coping with this deficit, they look around for ways to increase arousal in order to feel normal and to function in the way they would like to.

Commonly used to treat ADHD, amphetamine-type medications, like Adderall, Dexedrine, and Ritalin raise dopamine levels in the frontal cortex of the brain and allow for significant improvement in focus. There is also now evidence that a deficiency in the transporters that carry dopamine to these areas of the brain might contribute to the lack of attention seen in these syndromes by reducing dopamine delivery to the frontal cortex. This neurotransmitter imbalance, left untreated, has a clear role in handicapping our Sword's cognitive potential. And, as you know, impulsivity is linked with dopamine imbalances, a dynamic that compounds a Sword's difficulties around maintaining focus. This area of medicine remains controversial, as some parents are reluctant to "medicate" their children with ADD or ADHD. But consider this argument: A diabetic cannot produce enough insulin because of production problems in the pancreas, and someone with ADHD cannot produce enough dopamine because of production problems in the brain. Here we have two different organs unable to manufacture enough of one of their main chemicals. Same problem, same solution. The brain is a far more emotionally connotative organ than the pancreas, an unfortunate consequence for children struggling with their imbalanced brain chemistry to concentrate and improve their cognitive potential. Behavioral therapies are also critical in helping those with this diagnosis, but maximizing their success starts with a similar rebalancing act, but now focused in their brain chemistry.

There is an overlap between focusing difficulties and reading problems. Somewhere around a third of individuals with significant reading difficulties also have been diagnosed with ADHD. But interestingly, children with dyslexia also exhibit something else. This all-too-common syndrome appears not to be simply a weakness in reading skills, but one that is also associated with hidden interpersonal strengths. Anecdotally, there are lots of reports suggesting that some kids with dyslexia also have more finely tuned social skills. And, in a recent study comparing children with and without reading problems, those with dyslexia (based on MRI data) were also more emotionally expressive and showed stronger connectivity in the key brain structures that support emotion generation and self-awareness. It would appear that many children with dyslexia may possess important social strengths and higher levels of emotional intelligence.

As you know, Swords tend to be more keyed into the external world, are highly sensitive to social cues, and tend to favor speed and words like "yes" over accuracy and words like "no." It may very well be that their less noisy nervous systems allow Swords to concentrate and focus on different aspects of the world around them than the ones that garner Shields' attentiveness. Perhaps a Shield's more internally driven focus pays attention to granular details in the event that they may pose some degree of danger, while Swords may place their laser focus not on avoiding some potential harm but on the possibility of some rewarding experience. Swords and Shields tend to view the value of experiences in different ways. Swords place greater emphasis upon novelty/adventure, interpersonal events, and cut-to-the-chase conclusions that may lead to positive outcomes. On the other hand, Shields emphasize experiences that are familiar and predictable, which contain lots of contemplative time, and examinations of elements they are dealing with that may pose some danger. Let's be very clear here—one set of priorities is not necessarily better than the other; they're simply different, leading to oftentimes-dissimilar decisions, choices, and outcomes.

Let us remind you for a moment of the purpose of understanding the workings of your personal relationship to arousal. The bottom line is that we either sort of like its presence or dislike it and those preferences are expressed in both strengths and weaknesses. Understanding these vulnerabilities allows you to interact with the weaknesses you'd like to work on and turn into strengths.

The most important vulnerability for Swords is their tendency to be blind to or minimize and gloss over important details they later regret not having considered. The decisions we make have consequences and regrets are odious and largely capable of being prevented. A couple of exercises may be helpful here; one is retrospective and the other prospective. Think about some of the decisions you've made that you've later had regrets around. These can be anything from not marrying Bob to having married him or perhaps putting your hard-earned savings into a bad investment. See if you can come up with four or five that fit that category. For each one, write down what details you missed or minimized in making the decision you did. This should be done with as much honesty and detail as possible. Now for the prospective part of the exercise. Read over the details on this list and push yourself to come up with common elements, threads that have been repeated. Where did you put your focus and what details did you miss? Keep this list where you can refer back to it, and the next time you have an important decision to make pull out that list and make sure you don't repeat the same mistakes. Where was your focus misplaced? What kind of details did you fail to check out and appreciate? For an upcoming decision, see if you can use this information to make sure you put your focus where it is most helpful and don't disregard the important kind of details you may tend to gloss over.

While Swords' focus is too often seduced by their hunt for positive rewards and their attention can turn a blind eye to negative details, Shields face a different dilemma. Their focus is directed by their desire to avoid potential dangers, and the details they tend to miss are the positive elements in their decision-making process. Instead of being blindsided by the bad, they tend to lack sensitivity to the good. They are so hypervigilant about the possible negative outcomes that they often miss out on the positive. Even though Shields tend to be quite good at concentrating and paying attention to detail, it's important for them to challenge themselves to examine all aspects of a given situation.

One helpful exercise for Shields is to construct a list of wishes not realized or opportunities you wish you had been free enough to have explored. This wish list can be anything from "I sure would like to have purchased that house when the market was depressed" to "I wish I'd been a little more participatory in that dinner party the other night." See if you can come up with four or five of these wishes. For each wish, write down what you were avoiding (the target of the focus). Usually, these avoidances are in the realm of possible mistakes or anticipating feelings of emotional discomfort.

Be as specific as you can. In making the decision for each of these items, you protected something on the downside, but you also caused yourself to miss something important on the upside. Now write down all the positive things you might have gotten had you said yes instead of no. Keep this little exercise in mind the next time a decision needs making. Remember, you lean a little too heavily on the side of caution. Try, for a change, giving at least equal weight to the possible benefits and upsides of saying yes to the decision. Push yourself to write down as many details as you can about what you would gain from being affirmative here. We're not trying to re-mold you into someone who is reckless; what we're hoping for is that you give yourself a little more balance.

Sensitivity to Feedback and Feed Forward

How we make decisions is the result of a complex matrix of calcu-lated predictions (feed forward) and the results or reactions we get to our actions (feedback). All of us are most comfortable doing what we do best, and Swords are in the middle of their comfort zone when their expectations are clearly delineated and where they can predict the future most accurately using feed forward: con-necting anticipated outcomes from past experiences. Conversely, Shields' heightened natural arousal levels sensitize them more to feedback. It's not that they don't use prediction and feed-forward expectations (they do), but they tend to be a little more sensitive to how those predictions are doing in real time (feedback) than are Swords. Because they have gotten used to dealing with a barrage of continuous sensory input, Shields tend to rely more on the mo-ment (and the feedback they get from it) to shape their actions. It is the moment-by-moment interplay between what they say and do and how they read their impact on the environment that makes them so capable in situations with shifting demands (and maybe having sufficient levels of stimulating neurotransmitters like nor-adrenaline helps, too).

Why is all of this important? The object here is to build on what comes naturally and to learn to acquire those things that might be helpful but don't come so easily. Being more reward-oriented, Swords are very good at predicting positive outcomes. They do this by cataloging past actions and function most effectively in situations where expectations are clearly defined. Where they can get into trouble, of course, is when the past isn't a good predictor of a positive outcome in the present. Such circumstances are when there are unpredictable changes that must be accommodated. Part of the problem here is Swords' tendency toward doing the same things repeatedly even though the circumstances have changed, a manifestation of their rigidity. And the other part is their resistance to using feedback as it comes in as a loop to refine and alter their actions.

The greatest gift Swords can give themselves in this regard is a commitment to paying closer attention to small changes (feedback) they become aware of while in process and trusting the value of employing this information to refine their actions. The best way of doing this is applying a kind of internal Socratic dialogue. Ask yourself: Is what I'm doing working? If not, what do I see that I can use to modify what I'm doing to create the outcome I'm looking for? And here's the most important question to ask yourself: What details are there that I may be ignoring because they don't fit with my plan or the goal I'm looking to achieve? Seeing and processing or taking into account are very different things. There are no visual differences between Swords and Shields, only how they value or find relevant the details their eyes take in.

Derek came back from a weekend fishing trip in La Paz, Mexico. He had a great time with his buddies and brought home over one hundred pounds of fish. Within days, he talked himself into the idea that buying a commercial fishing boat would be a very profitable business venture. When he passed the idea by his fishing pals, each came up with at least one reason that this was a really complicated and fraught plan. We won't bother you with the details his fishing friends came up with for why they thought this venture could fail, but they were many and specific. Undaunted, Derek moved ahead, bought a very expensive boat, and had it sailed to La Paz. A month later the pandemic hit and tourism crashed. I'm sure you can guess how Derek's plan turned out.

In terms of this business venture, Derek demonstrated a very high level of focus, planning, and organization. What he lacked was the willingness to evaluate the myriad feedback details that ran counter to his dream. It wasn't that he didn't see or hear them; he simply chose to ignore or discount them.

A Shield has different potential shortcomings when making a decision. Because of their protective nature, Shields tend to focus on what might go wrong. Where they get tripped up is in over-weighing negative feedback and discounting the positive. Feedback, of course, is simply information. As it comes in, it's our job to interpret and evaluate it. Shields tend to put a minus sign next to otherwise neutral or even sometimes positive information or feedback. As good as they are at paying attention to details, they all too often don't see the positive and affirming information in the mix.

Annie told us a story recently about an experience she had at a party. There was this attractive man standing alone who caught her eye. She was in the midst of a conversation with one of her girlfriends when she saw him shyly look over again at her. Clearly, he found her of interest. This time she held his eyes and smiled at him, hoping he might come over. Not wanting to be rude, she let her friend continue with her story. Annie glanced over at the man again, hoping to catch his attention. This man was getting plenty of feedback. He simply didn't quite know what to do with it even though it was unabashedly positive. And sadly, maybe that's the reason they didn't connect that night. Processing her response to him as positive, he would've had to risk trusting his senses. This guy had to be a Shield.

For you Shields, the constructive growth is not in becoming more sensitive to feedback in general, but in becoming more sensitive to *positive* feedback. You've got negativity and covering your backside down pat. What you don't have is a good radar for information that is affirmative. We're not suggesting that you give up your pessimistic tilt but rather that you assign an equal value to relevant positive information.

Thinking Speed

Daniel Kahneman, in his Nobel Prize–winning book, *Thinking, Fast and Slow*, describes a two-system process for how we think and make decisions. System 1 thinking is fast, impressionistic, intuitive, and employs a kind of gut reaction for knowing what to do. This system is always on, producing intuitions and judgments. Our brain feasts upon seamless, coherent, and simple stories that inform our decision-making. We humans rarely choose the more difficult road when there is an easier one to take, no doubt simply because ease burns fewer calories. But in that it's fast, System 1 thinking often leads to snap judgments, jumping to conclusions, and erroneous decisions caused by unconscious biases. Our brain's proclivity for System 1 thinking is what gives conspiracy theories their seductive power. This is because of our wish to construct clear, easy-to-understand stories that bring a comforting order into often chaotic and messy events and situations. There is little more disturbing to the human mind than disorder. The presence of disorder suggests chaotic randomness, leaving one feeling out of control. The beating heart of every conspiracy theory is a simple explanation for a set of facts that is anything but simple, but if believed leads to a greater sense of control.

We typically revert to System 2 thinking only when we hit a problem or something unexpected arises. At that moment, we consciously slow our thinking to take a more measured, critical look. Slower System 2 thinking is more analytical and directed toward the kind of problem-solving that requires taking more data points into consideration.

As you might imagine, understanding Shields' itchy relationship with arousal, they tend to spend a bit more time in the slower

System 2 thinking and decision-making mode than do their Sword cousins. Why? Tending to be more harm-avoidant and protective, Shields are suspicious of the simple, goal-oriented story that their fast System 1 thinking provides. They are more likely to value the importance of downside risk and tend to look more carefully for missing pieces of relevant information. Swords, conversely, tend to be less concerned about negative outcomes and more focused on raising their level of arousal. In fact, it is their built-in need for arousal that is the source of their blind spot, encouraging them unconsciously to value speed and an all-too-easy coherence building over accuracy.

Shields aren't necessarily more interested in analytic thinking than Swords; they are compelled to do it by their nature. In fact, they don't feel comfortable *not* doing it. This works both for them and against them. They can be granular in their incorporation of detail but tend to make false negative errors. However, they are much less concerned with making a false negative error then a false positive one. The reason for this is, of course, that they tend to overvalue negative consequences and undervalue positive rewards.

Not being able to calm yourself easily and naturally because good old serotonin isn't available to tamp down the arousal in the system leads to feelings of anxiety and the perception of danger. Shields have busier amygdalae than do Swords. And having a busy amygdala leads to more false negative signals and a more frequent state of hypervigilance and high arousal. Shields, very early on, learn that they can exert a bit more control over these unpleasant levels of arousal by turning their focus inward whenever they can. This is why they like to have contemplative moments in their lives when they can simply be quiet and keep the external world at bay for a while.

Routine Building

Swords have a natural affinity for building routines because performing them increases arousal. The drop of dopamine they give themselves in anticipating the completion of a routine provides the very motivation that gets it started.

Having a surfeit of arousal, Shields tend to focus on the immediacy of their feelings. Unfortunately, that focus on the present doesn't carry with it the motivational carrot to build healthy routines that Swords have at their disposal. Let's take developing an exercise routine, for example. Instead of their attention being attached to how good they will feel after completing it, Shields are more likely to focus on the fleeting feelings of the moment like "I don't feel up to doing this right now" or "It sounds like an awful lot of work and it's too damn hot!" For Shields, sticks are often the motivational spur that gets their attention. Hearing your doctor say, "You've got to lose twenty pounds and start exercising or you're going to have a heart attack or stroke" is the kind of thing that is motivating to a Shield.

To be clear, routines are not the same as habits. We all develop habits naturally by unconsciously repeating certain behaviors whether or not they benefit us. Routines, on the other hand, are something we have *to build*. We notice habits after they are formed, but routines usually require some planning and intentionality. Routines, like habits, are neither good nor bad, but they certainly can be either healthy and constructive or not so. Think of routines as consciously formed habits. Swords are eager to find ways to link together chains of behavior that lead to the reward of a dollop of arousal. Remember, dopamine is released in the anticipation of a reward. Give Swords a way to anticipate a dopamine hit and they will do it.

Building routines is one of those ways. Setting some goal and achieving it, or even having some accidental, one-off experience that turns out to be rewarding, can set in motion the building blocks for routines. The brain casts its approval by encouraging repetition and what's repeated (for Swords) tends to be behavior that amps up arousal. The brain doesn't distinguish between good and bad routines; they are all equal opportunity inhabitants. The way the brain processes a repeated chain of events leading to a massive online buying spree is as rewarding to the brain as is climbing onto a treadmill at 6:00 PM, although one may prove to be ruinous and the other essential for health. The central challenge for Swords is to call upon the judgment provided by the prefrontal cortex to comment on the direction in which a nascent routine is heading.

Too often, our routines are hammered together in a haphazard fashion, leaving us with some mishmash of healthy and not-so-healthy routines. And, also too often, the prefrontal cortex stands paralyzed at the thought of giving up some arousing routine even though we know it is self-defeating.

Here is a way Swords might go about evaluating the constructiveness of their routines. We ask our patients to take a typical week and make a log of all the things they do during their waking hours and then to look back through it to see what the repeating patterns are. Creating this awareness is the first step toward sorting out which patterns are constructive and which are not. Later in the book, we lay out some specific guidelines for constructing healthy routines in the areas of eating, exercise, sleep, and emotional regulation (self-soothing) designed specifically to leverage Swords' strengths and innate tendencies.

Shields are not natural routine builders. Because they are not in need of bumping up arousal, they don't possess the same motivational cues to build the reward-driven routines that Swords use. Unlike Swords, who tend to be more reliant on the past to inform their present, Shields tend to exist in the moment. They live there not because of some Zen-like skill, but because it feels safer not letting their guard down. Ever. Because of their vigilance, they tend toward an "I'll wait and see how I feel about doing it" mindset instead of one characterized more by a routine-building friendly "I'll do it whether I feel like doing it or not because I know it makes me feel good afterward."

It's not that Shields don't build routines; it's that their routines are not always healthy. Asa turned off his familiar route home from work and pulled into the parking lot of a liquor store. Before he even made it five feet past the door, the clerk retrieved a half pint of Smirnoff vodka and a packet of Tic Tacs and put them on the counter. Asa grinned at the clerk and, as he took out his wallet, said, "I'm not sure being this predictable is a good sign, Ben." Back in his car, Asa unscrewed the cap and took a swig from the bottle. He turned on the radio, listening to music and taking sips until the bottle was empty. After ditching the bottle in a nearby trash can, he got back into his car, threw some Tic Tacs in his mouth, and started the engine. Driving again, he thought about how he could now have a couple of glasses of wine with his dinner without receiving eye rolls from his children or admonitions from his wife about drinking too much. Yes, this was a daily routine for Asa, but in reality, this repetitive chain of behavior is simply a self-soothing ritual and a decidedly unhealthy one.

Shields, too, can profit from charting the idiosyncratic patterns that characterize their daily behavior. We recommend looking at how you spend your waking hours for at least a week. That amount of time is usually sufficient to tease out any kind of patterned routines. How many of your routines do you think are healthy and how many not? How many patterns/routines do you recognize as being designed to avoid feelings of discomfort? How often do you find yourself saying something like, "I should do...," while finding some excuse not to? Are the excuses related to anticipating how you'll feel doing those routines? Constructive routines usually involve some amount of discomfort. Discomfort-avoiding Shields tend to defer and put off anything smacking of pain. But remember, pain can only be postponed, not avoided. Deferring pain (not exercising, for example) only results in the pain of the predictable (and painful) health-related consequences associated with a sedentary lifestyle.

Routines—both constructive and sabotaging—tend to coexist unless challenged directly. It's not that we can't separate the healthy from the harmful. Identifying what works for us is not the problem. Giving up what doesn't work is. In the chapters ahead, we're going to encourage you to take on the work to break routines that don't serve your best interests. For Swords, this means being willing to relinquish routines that exist solely for the sake of creating arousal and don't serve your greater good. What's at stake here is learning to tolerate lower levels of arousal and the feelings of discomfort that giving up unhealthy routines creates. The ask for Shields is different. You must be willing to take the leap of faith that the healthy routine will pay off in a way that compensates for the discomfort required to build it. We're going to show you exactly how to do these things by leveraging the natural inclinations of your brain chemistry.

CHAPTER FOUR

Work—
Examining Obstacles
to Ambition, Success,
and Decision-Making

*How Our Personal Brain Chemistry
Plays a Powerful but Largely Hidden Role
in the Most Fundamental Approaches
We Bring to Our Work and Careers*

WE WANT TO CONTINUE OUR story by exploring the ways in which our brain types interact with how we go about our everyday work, for between the lines of our job titles, roles, and responsibilities lies an unseen tangle of dynamics fired by our neurochemistry that influences how successful we will be. The built-in traits of our brain types spring into action as a response to stress, and little else is as stressful as our work lives where survival of the fittest can sometimes be a daily bare-knuckle fight.

We all know the extrinsic factors that lead to more successful careers, such as education and technical skill development, but what follows is an examination of work's important intrinsic factors, those influenced by our brain chemicals. One construct that is a distinguishing human characteristic is fire in the belly, focused and applied desire, or belief in action—better known as ambition.

Obstacles to Ambition and Success

Ambition and success are yoked dynamics. While being ambitious doesn't guarantee success, becoming successful rarely happens without ambition. For some, ambition is animated by a long-held passion or desire, while for others it is driven by fears and insecurities. Want and need are a powerful combination, and although the proportions of each may vary widely, most of us are motivated by some blend of the two. Measured by conventional standards, it's hard to be successful without ambition: our persistent motivation toward a goal. But this drive for accomplishment has not always been viewed in a positive light. Indeed, in some Eastern traditions being ambitious can be seen as a negative and a trait that ties us down to worldly pursuits and prevents us from experiencing the more virtuous states of serenity, wisdom, and a spiritual life. Even today, we speak of ambition as "healthy" or "unhealthy." Healthy ambition is usually understood as the development of one's gifts without creating too many sacrifices or casualties along the way. And unhealthy ambition can be seen as a naked competitiveness that is greedy and blind to its destructive consequences to self and to others.

Unfortunately, science doesn't shed a lot of light on ambition, for it has not generated much in the way of scholarly study, in large part due to its ill-defined nature. Here are a few things that we do know. On the trait pairings from the Myers-Briggs Type Indicator, the biggest gap is observed between Extroverts and Introverts (you might read that pairing as between Swords and Shields). Among Extroverts 85 percent identified with and defined themselves as being ambitious, while only 67 percent of Introverts did. One study, examining differences in workers' promotion rates over a three-year period between Introverts and Extroverts, found that those rated as more ambitious were promoted more frequently than those rated as less ambitious. Other studies link optimism and a proactive personality style to objective measures of success and satisfaction. Score one for the Swords here.

So, how are we shaped to relate to the challenging worlds we all inhabit? We have our parents and extended families as role models, and we are bent this way or that by what they say and do, as well as by their expectations of us. Certainly, our levels of cognitive efficiency, fears, and educational and socioeconomic backgrounds influence the expression of ambition, as do our anger, envy, competitiveness, energy levels, sexual drives, and deepest feelings about ourselves. But beyond all these complex dynamics lie the influences of our brain chemistry. Swords and Shields tend to have patterned and predictable assets as well as obstacles to ambition and success.

In a retrospective moment recently, Larry lamented that although he had an interest in student government, he never took the chance to run for office. He said, with a bit of sadness in his voice, "I remember there were a couple of offices I wanted to run for. I even wrote out the speeches I wanted to make, but I was always too anxious in the end to follow through on any of it." Was Larry lacking in ambition? We think not. He certainly had the wish to take on those risks of putting himself to the test but wasn't able to act upon it. His low level of serotonin flattened his dream and robbed him of experiences that might have bolstered his image of himself. Instead, his discomfort paved the way for a pattern of avoiding challenges, and a trail of regrets and other avoidances of challenges he wishes now he had taken on.

Let's take a closer look at some of the ways Shields can get in their own way in achieving their dreams.

How Shields Can Underreach and Create Obstacles to Success

How do we learn to tackle something as nebulous as ambition when we have a nervous system characterized by uncomfortably high activation that predisposes us to avoidance, risk aversion, and pessimism? Not easily, but it is possible with understanding and effort. As a protective mechanism, Shields tend to rein in aspirations, particularly those that require increased stress, exposure to criticism, emotional conflict, and risk-taking. It's not that they don't have the dream of accomplishment and moving beyond the ordinary; it's just that they can sometimes sabotage and undercut themselves.

The higher or more complex the ambition, the greater is the degree of uncertainty. Swords are usually pretty sanguine when faced with the prospect of a muddy critical path and uncertain outcomes. They are much more likely to say, "Sure, why not give it a try?" Shields hate uncertainty and can stand in awe watching their Sword cousins dance with it, even seeming to enjoy it at times. Where Shields anticipate jeopardy in uncertain circumstances, Swords' natural optimism allows them to be more tolerant of the unknown. We all live in a probabilistic world, but Shields are more likely to overemphasize the costs of the worst-case scenario, influencing their decision-making.

So how do Shields examine their connection to ambition? First, let's define a work ambition as setting a specific goal and mustering the energy that pushes you toward its accomplishment (or maybe we can just call it plain old going after what you want). Any kind of examination of ambition for Shields requires picking through the influence of their big three obstacles to ambition and success: avoidance, risk aversion, and pessimism.

Avoidance: Reframing Arousal. We've discussed how Shields tend to regulate itchy and noisy nervous systems by finding ways to keep their reading of arousal in check. This same process sets the boundaries that define and constrain ambition.

Here is a good exercise to get a personal barometer on whether or not your relationship with arousal interferes with your ambitions and may limit your success. Think for a moment about what you would like to accomplish, what you would like to try to do if you could be assured that throughout the process you would feel relaxed and comfortable. What might you do if you weren't anxious and hesitant to go after it? Don't just keep a running list in your head; write it down. And take your time. It can take several days to build a proper list. A reminder: the items on your list shouldn't be things like "I'd do such and such if I could be guaranteed not to fail." Failures are a necessary part of any complex process and to be embraced and learned from. Their absence can never be guaranteed. In fact, their presence is often a sign that you are stretching and challenging yourself in expanding ways. Instead, frame it as: "I'd like to do such and such if I could do it without feeling nervous and uncomfortable doing it."

Feeling nervous and uncomfortable is a simple by-product of arousal. These feelings are just the activation and subjective experience of the chemicals that fire our bodies. For Shields, having a little too much arousal sends signals through the limbic system, dampening the reward circuitry and firing the alarm circuits. A Shield's interpretation of these signals interacts in predictable ways in terms of how they go about achieving their goals. These chemical signals can be seen as either simply intense feelings or signs of danger. Labeling these feelings as dangerous leads to some unfortunate choices. The moment a Shield says no to the experience, they feel relieved and that very feeling is the reward for the avoidant behavior and stamps it in.

Avoidance is a strategy designed to reduce arousal, or even its anticipation. In cognitive behavioral therapy, we teach avoidant people to become more comfortable with arousal. One way of doing that is to simulate the feeling of being overly aroused. You can do this by taking short, forceful, rapid deep breaths for at least a minute. Doing this brings on the symptoms of an anxiety attack, albeit one that is very short acting. The point of doing this exercise is a simple one. By being able to bring on the scary buzz of anxious feelings, you learn that anxiety is simply a chemical storm that ends on its own if we don't stoke the flames. And we also learn that we have control over these feelings. By inducing the experience, we come to understand that we bring on these heightened states of arousal and that they are not dangerous.

The trick here is in learning to reframe the feelings from a sense of danger into an opportunity to create control. Shields often feel in the borderlands of anxiety. At those moments when you step over and you get, or anticipate getting, anxious, try to reframe the experience. Some people use, "Oh, it's just a chemical storm," to label the feelings, while others use words like "intense and interesting" or "I'm feeling excited," for that is exactly what is happening in the nervous system. The value of reframing is that over time and with practice, changing how we label our feelings (particularly a surge in arousal) positively alters our relationship to those uncomfortable feelings. And this alteration has the effect of increasing the number of things we feel comfortable enough to do, reducing avoidant behavior.

Go back to the list you created of the things you might do if you felt comfortable and relaxed doing them. Pick something from that list and think for the moment about saying yes and embracing the specifics of the experience (the more detailed and specific the thoughts, the better). Make note of how you feel. If the thought of saying yes makes you a little anxious, that's normal. You are thinking of doing something you wouldn't normally do, something new. Contemplating doing something new is supposed to increase arousal. It does that with everyone. Say to yourself, "These are normal, excited feelings I'm having." This exercise isn't something you do once. It's a drill you go back to over days and each time take some more challenging item from the list. The litmus test here is, of course, to eventually pick one of those items and breathe life into it. Do it!

Something else you might find helpful is creating an Avoidance Log. It should include all those activities you tend to avoid but that may actually be beneficial to your success.

First, write down the work-related actions that you tend to avoid. These might include something like avoiding taking on some voluntary role or special project that would be viewed favorably by the powers that be and is doable but challenging. Next, list the *physical, emotional, and situational triggers* that set avoidance in motion. These might include everything from getting queasy when you're faced with a task and feeling panicked at the thought of your work coming under scrutiny to getting a last-minute invitation to an after-work social gathering. And now make a note of the rewards (feelings of comfort or relief, however fleeting) you get from indulging in the avoided action. It's important to be brutally honest with yourself here. An avoided action is always rewarded by a reduction of arousal, however momentary.

By this time, you are getting a lot more familiar with some of the sneaky ways you trick yourself into sabotaging goal accomplishment. It's time to take that list of avoided actions you've been keeping track of and rank-order them from "least emotionally uncomfortable if I had to do it" to "most emotionally uncomfortable." As a challenge, take on the behavior at the top of the list ("least emotionally uncomfortable").

The stretch here is expanding your comfort zone and learning how to tolerate the emotionality that accompanies unfamiliar, non-avoidant behavior. Having mastered this "least emotionally uncomfortable" avoidance, move on to the next one on your list of avoided behaviors.

Changing Your Risk Profile. Shields naturally focus on hurdles instead of satisfactions, on the anticipation of emotional discomfort instead of pleasure. Nowhere is this manifested more insidiously than in their relationship with ambition. Ambition, of course, isn't just accomplishing tasks and projects; it isn't even the skill set, however well filled out and impressive it may be. Ambition is an attitude. It's about belief in yourself, an awareness of your worth thrust into action. And yes, it's about your risk profile.

The truth is that most of us don't give much thought to our personal risk profile; we simply act it out unconsciously. For most Shields, risk aversion comes naturally. From infancy on, their noisy nervous system broadcasts danger signals to most anything that raises, or even threatens to raise, their level of arousal. Long before explanatory language is formed, they tend to develop a list of largely unconscious and, in many instances, false assumptions about what is and what isn't a threat. Unfortunately, we carry those inaccurate assumptions with us as we get older and they all too often follow us into adulthood. Most frequently, these inaccurate threat assumptions go untested but make up our risk profile nevertheless.

The downside of an untested risk profile is that it limits our experience in the world and influences things as fundamental as levels of confidence and self-esteem. Shields know they can have a hard time taking reasonable chances, but, over the years, many have developed multilayered excuses and ways to explain away their behavior.

John developed his skills from the ground up in a large auto body shop. Over time he could repair a fender and wield a paint gun as well as anyone, and soon he was promoted to making estimates for insurance companies. John was a diligent saver and put a significant part of his paycheck into a mutual fund investment account. And although he had no formal education beyond high school, he was ambitious, intelligent, and, from early on, had his sights set on having an auto body shop of his own. John had saved enough to finance his dream of creating his own company just as the Great Recession hit. In Los Angeles, commercial real estate took a big hit and John's wife encouraged him to take advantage of the moment and buy one of the properties he'd been looking at. A perfect venue came onto the market with a distressed price tag. John sat down with his wife and, after they ran the numbers, everything came up with a go signal. He could finally make his dream come true. John entered an escrow and then backed out, fearing property values would continue to plummet. Over a couple of years, John did this a number of times, each time with different commercial real estate brokers, all who eventually soured on working with him. Sadly, he watched property prices dip and then rebound before his eyes while he dithered and couldn't get himself to say yes and mean it. The risk felt too great and now he feels a welling of anger and regret.

Ambition can easily be curtailed by a risk profile set in motion not by logic or good business acumen, but by our brain chemistry. It doesn't always manifest as a lost business opportunity; it can be as subtle as failing to communicate to the someone you report to that you understand what you bring to your job and that your value should be acknowledged. In a conversation with a director in a pharmaceutical company, Clare related a call from HR asking her to identify which of her senior managers she considered to be flight risks and which she was confident were not. Only those seen as likely to leave if not given raises went on to receive one. What's the lesson here? Certainly, it's not that corporations value being passive and deferential. Or that they don't have sensitive risk profiles of their own. On the contrary, they value those who raise their hand when it's earned and appropriate and honor the value they bring to the team.

Not all alterations to one's risk profile are quite so abstract. Colin wants to be seen and acknowledged, but his risk aversion and fear of exposing himself to criticism has held him back. With an MBA from UCLA on his résumé, he works at a national bank and is the youngest portfolio manager in this bank's history. In staff meetings with the chief investment officer, Colin often thinks he has some cogent and valuable things to say, but it's difficult for him to raise his hand and share his thoughts. The fact may be that he *does* have better answers. He's done his homework; he always has. The hidden truth is that he's actually a little cocky about how much he knows and his skill set. But even his cockiness can't overcome the social anxiety that mounts during these staff meetings, leaking in from the time the door closes and paralyzing him. Avoidance, Colin's default strategy for managing discomfort, stands in the way of him reaching all the goals he's set for himself.

For someone like Colin, a series of personalized strategies grounded in cognitive behavioral therapy provides a road map for becoming less avoidant and risk averse. The following is an exercise we devised for Colin to do:

STEP 1: DEFINING THE GOAL. Colin first needed to articulate his goal clearly. He wrote: "I want to express and defend my opinion in a staff meeting." Please note that this kind of statement is very different from, "I want to feel comfortable and confident enough to express my opinions in a staff meeting." Confidence is the reward for a brave act, not the prerequisite.

STEP 2: DETERMINING THE LEVEL OF MOTIVATION. Colin was then asked to assess his level of motivation on a scale from 1 to 10. It's very important to have priorities clearly stated. Lukewarm motivation is just that. After all, what's at stake here is learning to tolerate some uncomfortable feelings, previously avoided.

STEP 3: RISK ASSESSMENT. Colin constructed two lists: one for Threats (possible negative outcomes) and the other for Values (possible positive outcomes). Colin had seven entries on the positive side but only one on the negative: "My voice might quaver and make me go blank."

STEP 4: REFRAMING. Colin was asked to reinterpret or reframe the emotions he anticipated feeling as *excitement* rather than *anxiety*.

STEP 5: REHEARSAL. Colin practiced what he wanted to say in his head five times. Next, he had to rehearse out loud five times. He started in front of the mirror, his barber heard one version, and the last time he was on the train to work, pretending to be on his cell phone.

STEP 6: THE AVOIDED ACTION/THE BRAVE ACT. Right before the staff meeting, Colin took some deep breaths and instructed himself to get excited. As a Shield, he was naturally already aroused. If he were to be told to calm down, it would not match how he was feeling and would be disconcerting. Having him get pumped up and excited was congruent with his natural emotional state.

STEP 7: REINFORCEMENT. After a successful staff meeting, Colin completed the very important step of intentional reinforcement. Positive outcomes need to be burned in in some way so that we remember them and have an active access to them in the future. This is how we slowly rewire our brain. Some find writing a note to themselves helpful and others just tell the story aloud, to themselves or someone else. In this case, Colin held his dog in rapt attention as he told her what he had accomplished.

Having a low tolerance for risk can be a very unpleasant and embarrassing state of mind sometimes. But being risk averse is not all painful. By having their threat detection set to high, Shields feel oddly protected and anxious simultaneously. And this protective feeling is rewarding. That is precisely why this dynamic is so durable and not easily changed.

What is important for you Shields to consider in terms of ambition is to make sure risk aversion works for rather than against you. Risk is about assessing and managing outcomes. Psychologically, risk is about uncertainty and our tolerance for ambiguity. In choosing career paths, as in other arenas of their lives, Shields unconsciously tend to choose careers that value a healthy amount of risk aversion as well as those that require the ability to tolerate uncertainty. Put another way, they are more likely to avoid choosing careers where a healthy amount of risk tolerance is an asset. For instance, in a study of surgeons versus internists, surgeons were shown to have a much higher need for certainty than internists did. Internists can second-guess themselves as they parse through a blizzard of sometimes-confusing data, to a patient's advantage. Surgeons, in contrast (who are more likely to be Swords), can't afford much in the way of second-guessing or they wouldn't be able to make the first cut. You can imagine the kind of certainty an Indy driver has to have to mash that gas pedal: "I will survive this race." There are careers or even niches within careers in which risk aversion is an asset. Choose wisely.

Beyond career selection, how Shields process outcomes plays into their expression of ambition. Our ambitions are expressed throughout our lives. An integral motivational element of ambition is our need to be seen and acknowledged for the value we bring. Some of this can and should be done internally, but with rare exceptions ambition eventually needs some sort of payoff in the external world. To receive the fruits of our ambitions, we need to expose our uniqueness and gifts. We need to trust our talents, and that requires taking some chances, saying yes to reasonable risks. Colin, as you will recall, began doing just that. He risked speaking up and presenting his ideas and those risks paid off for him. Shields need to take a leap of faith and shoot higher, choose to become more aspirational. They need to learn to put their belief in themselves into action. This takes understanding that their tendency to reflexively say no to themselves is self-defeating and, just as important, often inaccurate. Shields' central task, when it comes to risk-taking, is in finding a way to get to saying yes. Yeses that affirm their value and put actions out there into the real world increase the probability of being seen and judged accordingly. As we noted when we gave Colin his exercise, courage is not something we sit around and wait for before making a move. It's not something we wish for and it's not something we can get by fantasizing about it. *Courage is the reward of a brave act.*

It's up to you to take some actions for yourself that might just propel you ahead. Those often scary and brave actions backfill with the feeling of having been brave. That is such a good feeling and one that leads to other brave actions, creating a positively accelerating cycle.

Pessimism and the Burden of Doubt. When Amelia Earhart was twenty-four, a pilot overhead spotted her and a friend standing in a field and dove at them, presumably to frighten them and watch them run. As the plane pulled out of the dive near them, Amelia, who stood in rapt attention, said, "I believe that little red airplane said something to me as it swished by." You can believe it most certainly wasn't, "I could never do that!" That vividly remembered moment changed her life and aviation history. As it would turn out, Earhart wasn't the greatest female pilot of her time and neither was she the greatest navigator, but she was missing something that often haunts Shields when it comes to ambition and that element is doubt. She knew what she wanted and went after it with clarity of purpose and gusto.

Interestingly, doubt is not always a negative when it comes to thinking about things we want to accomplish and getting them done. In an experiment with students, one group was given the phrase "I will" to say and the other group the words "Will I?" They were asked to say the words before they knew the task they were about to perform, an amalgam where they were given a word and asked to come up with as many other words as they could using any combination of the letters from that word. Which group do you think outperformed the other? No, it wasn't the "I will" group. Those of you who thought the "Will I?" group outperformed the other, you are correct. There is something about posing the question that backfills with a feeling of resolve, an affirmative kind of inner voice, an answer that says yes. More about constructive ways doubt can be used a little later.

As we've indicated, Shields tend to be pessimistic. Because of their protective nature, they think ahead and wonder and make predictions about the possibility of hidden dangers. The upside is these proclivities work; their predictions often save them from making a variety of mistakes. The downside is that their threat detection on steroids also works; it can stifle and stunt the important aspirational thoughts and feelings that comprise ambition.

Schopenhauer, Nietzsche, and Camus are among history's most pessimistic philosophers. They also all found ways to make their negative thought patterns work for them. Not all of us are so fortunate. We suspect that they may have come by their pessimism naturally, that their negative thoughts and conclusions may have been unknowingly influenced by their imbalanced serotonin. "Unknowingly" is the operative word here, because that portion of the variance unaccounted for by their brain chemical influences can shift critical thinking from neutral to negative. Logic and looking at the empirical record can result in an accurate negative take on an event or process. But imbalanced serotonin can take one to a negative position even when the empirical record doesn't support that direction. Recognizing our hidden influencers (personal brain chemistry) has the potential of freeing up our thought processes, allowing for fewer decisions that create false negative errors. And examining unconsciously driven pessimistic thoughts and feelings and how they relate to what we set out to do in our lives can be illuminating and helpful.

That said, the truth is that when we are feeling anxious and worried about this outcome or that, the admonition to be more positive doesn't help much. In fact, trying to force positive thoughts inevitably fails and tends to leave the person just as anxious, but now embarrassed for feeling the way they are feeling, a double whammy.

But you Shields take heart. Sometimes there is a payoff for certain kinds of negative thoughts. There is an interesting body of evidence derived from studying the effects of a particular kind of negative thinking called defensive pessimism. In essence, defensive pessimism is a strategy in which the person anticipates that a future event will go poorly (even if similar events in the past have gone well), spinning out low expectations for the outcome and a detailed list of all the things that might go wrong so they can be planned for and avoided. Remember, the feeling of anxiety is the awareness of cortical activation or arousal and employing this strategy has the effect of harnessing that itchy energy and deploying it to constructive uses. Feeling anxious, we have two choices: to allow it to spin around in our heads or to grab that energy and use it to systematically troubleshoot and compensate for all the little obstacles that may derail the event and lead to a disaster.

During the pandemic, we suspect that there were a whole lot of Shields who quite naturally practiced defensive pessimism. And dotting all those i's and crossing the t's no doubt saved some lives. In fact, being prepared to prevent negative outcomes has some real health benefits. Surely, Shields worried more than did the Swords during the dreary months of lockdown and they were also those most likely to wash their hands, swab down surfaces, and wear masks.

A study following anxious students through their university years found that those who practiced defensive pessimism had greater levels of confidence and self-esteem, probably because they were able to imagine, predict, and avoid more negative outcomes than the group that didn't employ that strategy.

For those of you who would like to practice this exercise, you might try the following. Before your next event—let's say it's a presentation you have to make—write a list of all the small details that would go into making that a successful experience, and then describe how those details could go wrong. Even the most obvious items should go on this list, things like "misplace my car keys" or "a stain on the blouse I want to wear." Write down everything from "forgot to check the time it would take to get to my destination" to "don't have enough gas in the car" to "didn't charge my laptop and phone" to "my PowerPoint deck is sequenced improperly" to "we lost power and I don't have technology to rely upon." Pushing yourself to run through this written list of contingencies is an anxiety-reducing rehearsal, and by imagining your way through the worst-case scenarios you will feel more reassured and ready to take on whatever lies ahead.

A reminder: For Shields, the most common hidden stumbling blocks they encounter in those areas of their lives where they would like to be successful are tendencies toward avoidance, being a bit too risk averse, and being held back by negative thoughts. What is important to remember here is that these tendencies aren't derived from logic, your innate gifts, capacity, potential, or even reality; they are an artifact of your brain chemistry, your simple luck of the draw. You needn't let these tendencies define you. Simply recognizing their source can be enormously freeing. But the other liberating component is entirely up to you. Learn to recognize the challenging situations you tend to avoid. Lean in and feel the activation in your system. It's just arousal, just your unique brain chemistry talking to you. It's not dangerous. No one dies from arousal. What is dangerous is the experience of successes that are missed when a distaste for arousal and avoidance make the decision instead of logic, desire, and belief in yourself.

The same goes for being too cautious, too passive, too risk averse. The awareness of risk doesn't equal a bad outcome. Clichés are made from this truth: nothing ventured, nothing gained. Shields tend to venture too little and, unfortunately, their gain is often in some proportion to the constraints of their timidity. The risk-averse mindset isn't fired or maintained by deductive logic and rational thought, but by having a bit too little serotonin floating around the system. Having a risk profile is important and has great survival value. It's just that having the danger threshold set by a slight brain chemical imbalance isn't the most intelligent strategy. Carve out a couple of areas at work where taking some measured chances might result in some sort of positive payoff.

Another exercise that can be useful is to select a person in your life who you think always "plays it safe"—obviously a Shield—and list those avoidance behaviors that you have thought might be holding them back. Can you recognize yourself in this person? Does it feel like you're looking into a mirror? This exercise is not meant for you to be judgmental of someone else, but to see your own behaviors more clearly and objectively. It can be humbling and you may even laugh at yourself, but the goal is to have a better understanding of yourself and your behaviors.

And now to negative thoughts. The truth is, if you're a Shield, you won't have to look around for them; they will find you in bucketfuls. But it's not the presence of negative thoughts that's diminishing; it's when we let ourselves be defined by their presence and allow them to shape and narrow our experiences. Those of you who come to your pessimism naturally might try harnessing those threatening thoughts using the exercise we've described earlier. You're never going to be a wide-eyed optimist, and that's perfectly all right. But neither do you have to let your penchant for a bit too much doom and gloom etch in the architecture of your life and become the self-fulfilling prophecy it might. Use that threat-assessing energy to your advantage and you just might find that your confidence increases along with your experiences and that you even find a couple of unexpected sunny patches along the way.

We all like to feel in control. There is probably nothing more primitive than that need, which has animated life from the beginning. Learning to understand and better tolerate (yes, override) our own brain chemistry is the prerequisite for bringing real—and sustainable—control to our lives.

Obstacles to Swords' Approach to Ambition and Success

As we mentioned, Amelia Earhart wasn't the most highly skilled pilot or navigator. Earhart wasn't even the best communicator. She had some serious challenges when it came to making sure she had all the right radio parts and knew how to use them properly. But whatever she lacked in technical acumen she made up for in sheer desire, belief, and boldness. Having a PR man for a husband didn't hurt in spreading her story, and between the two of them, they were quite a duo in creating a very splashy career. Did we say splashy? Yes, we did. Earhart wasn't pushed from behind the curtains onto the stage of life; she leaped to it from the balcony. Flying hit all the right notes. In those early days of flight, thrill, uncertainty, and danger were her companions every time her wheels left the ground. Impulse control and careful planning were mid-level priorities at best. Tedious checklists, dry runs, and attention to detail were not what held her focus for long. Of course, none of these things held her back from slipping into legend, mystery, and an all too early end.

Amelia Earhart was clearly a Sword. She had that compelling "it" factor, something many Swords have. What she likely didn't have was a vigilant and noisy amygdala. What she possessed, as do the other Swords among us, was a very sensitive reward center.

The brain's reward center is stimulated by our old friend the neurotransmitter dopamine. We couldn't survive without dopamine. If we couldn't find ways to get an occasional hit of it, personal existence would be about as interesting and pleasurable as living as a hunk of lichen on a rock. The problem is that our brains don't discriminate very well between good rewards and those that don't serve us so well.

As a part of the reward circuitry, there is a group of specialized neurons that comprise what is called the incentive salience circuits (networks of dopamine neurons that signal desire/wanting). And it's because of this network of neurons that Swords can get into trouble. Lacking sufficient dopamine, they are slightly more prone than their Shield cousins to indulge in their impulses, have difficulty delaying gratification, and be distracted by their craving for novelty. These Sword-related tendencies comprise the challenges to meeting their aspirations, career success, and accurate decision-making.

When it's acted out, this reflexive quest for dopamine to feel alert and normal can lead to the brain getting hijacked, resulting in compulsive behavior such as drug, food, sex, and gambling addictions. But even when these dopamine-related dynamics are not nearly so dramatic, Swords can have issues that wreak havoc with how they approach their work and make everyday decisions.

Novelty Seeking. Shields often take refuge in the comfort of the familiar and can actually have an aversion to novelty. On the other hand, Swords can be driven by their need for it. Anyone—let's imagine William Shatner for a visual—trying to qualify for the astronaut program probably wasn't deterred by falling out of a tree when he was a kid and found progressively more exciting ways to create challenges. An aversion to novelty leaves Shields plenty of contemplative time to noodle around in their heads, while Swords need the external world to keep them stimulated.

Dopamine is released in response to the anticipation of a reward. The operative word here is "anticipation," for as you will recall, dopamine is the motivator, not the appreciator. Dopamine gets us to do the things we do but is silent and doesn't help us appreciate those things once we have them. The pleasure of an experience is all front-loaded. As you can see, all experiences aren't rewarded with a dopamine hit (sitting down and doing your taxes); only thinking about a new and interesting experience is. And as you can imagine, being a bit dopamine deprived naturally makes novelty a bag full of M&M's. Novelty and cortical activation are intimately entwined. Doing the same old thing doesn't do it. If you want to bump up arousal, find something new to do. But it's the "find something new to do" that can cause trouble for Swords.

As children, many a Sword was identified as being distractible. The kiddy version is having your eye caught by the fly buzzing on the windowsill when you're supposed to be reading. The adult version is a little more sophisticated and can take the form of getting off track on a work project, spending too much time returning to an online shopping screen, or romanticizing your guitar-playing days and googling all your old buds with the idea of restarting your band again.

Willa, thirty-eight, has all the ingredients to be the successful writer she's long had the aspiration to become. But success has eluded her, much to her surprise and disappointment. Largely self-taught, she stutter-stepped her way through a patchy formal education. Never having completed the BA in English she worked on for more years than she would like to remember, Willa taught herself the essentials and devoured any material that caught her attention at the moment. Her twenties were spent telling herself she was going to finish her degree, and her thirties, to this point, have blown by her in a whirlwind series of uninteresting jobs chosen because they were less than challenging so she could devote her energy to the passion in her life: writing. And she's written. And she's gotten real encouragement from credible and critical sources as to the quality of her writing. None of this is anything new, of course. Her writing has paralleled her life, with moments of brilliance here and there interspersed with longer periods characterized by agonizing writer's block and too many cigarettes. Willa describes herself as an intuitive writer, one who loves to be overtaken by the Muse. But her waiting for the Muse to strike is really an indulgence and a dodge for not doing the hard work of staying with something she's started and then finds herself unable to finish.

Funny, smart, and cynical, she has a hundred beginnings and no endings. Her character sketches are sharp and colorful, but they exist only on the pages of one of the notebooks scattered around her apartment. In her dreams, she brings these wonderful characters to life and sees them struggle and grow their way through a layered, well-plotted story. Her days are spent opening her notebook to a blank page soon to be filled with the beginning of yet another new idea or situation she wants to explore.

Willa only recently has been dealing with how her brain chemicals have derailed her career by causing her to indulge in the distraction of novelty and allowing it to trump the slog of follow-through. For the first time she is resisting the temptation of moving on and forcing herself to work her way through a detailed outline. This is something her third agent asked her to do after gushing over one of the character sketches and setups she had shown her. That was over a year ago. Willa hopes the agent will still remember her! Regardless of the outcome, she's excited at the progress she's made in beginning to regulate her focus.

Novelty comes to its attention-grabbing status quite naturally. Our brains are designed to ignore the old and familiar and focus on what's new. Our attentiveness to novelty has important evolutionary value, for this powerful signal carries essential information that alerts us to possible dangers and rewards. When something new comes along and we pay attention to it, our brain releases dopamine, indicating there's potentially something of value to be learned here. As we've said, dopamine makes desire feel more important and pressing, creating an action. But wanting a dopamine hit isn't necessarily linked to "liking" the result of that desire. In other words, we can "want" something we know we don't even "like" when we get it—a form of decoupled desire. Willa didn't like her distractibility even though she was compelled to allow her focus to go there.

Truthfully, in today's world distractibility is a challenge for everyone. The problem is most humans today have shorter attention spans. Marketers definitely recognize this. The way television commercials are edited is as technical as it is manipulative. In essence, using a machine that measures eye fixation, they make the edit to the next segment of the commercial as soon as the eye gets tired of being where it is and moves on. The human brain is surprisingly plastic. This means that the brain has the ability to adapt and reorganize neurons based on inputs and stimuli. Unfortunately, over the past decades we've trained our brains to be less attentive instead of more.

Researchers at Microsoft studied subjects using electroencephalograms (EEGs) to analyze brain activity. They found that since the year 2000 the average person's attention span dropped from twelve seconds of concentrated focus before drift to just eight seconds in 2013. Even goldfish manage to focus their attention for nine seconds at a time! We can only speculate what's happened to our attention span in the years since the Microsoft study was conducted. Sadly, modern technology appears to have rewired our brains so that we have even shorter attention spans. Studies show that we tend to spend more of our time flipping through random topics but probably with less depth and patient thoughtfulness.

This presents issues for us all but particularly so for Swords. Imagine that you're sitting at your desk struggling through some complex decision-making chain, the conclusion of which has important consequences. The task is complicated and you feel uncomfortable and take a big, deep breath. Suddenly, a text pings on your screen. You've been saved. It's a lunch invitation from an old friend. You respond. You check your email. Before you know it, you're on your favorite news feed. Just for a moment, you tell yourself. A headline grabs your eyes. You've got to read on. The dopamine is flowing. Your real work now sits out of sight, covered by multiple screens.

Swords' brains are vulnerable to getting kidnapped by novelty. Novelty stimulates a dopamine release, saying a version of, "Hey, take a look; there could be something in this for you here." If we lived in a static environment, it might be useful to give that emergent event serious consideration. But in our world, novelty is as near to us as a keystroke. Might it stimulate a new idea for Willa? Yes. Might it also lead her down an ever-branching chain of endless other new ideas, thoughts, and content to be explored? Yes again.

Is this energizing and exciting for Willa? Yes. Does it work for her? No. Part of the problem is that the brain doesn't necessarily like what it wants. What was exciting yesterday for Willa now feels more familiar and she is aware of the holes in the idea and the tedious work that would be required to deepen and flesh it out. Sadly, Willa's brain today doesn't like what it wanted yesterday.

Science has shown that mindfulness meditation is good for the brain, for it helps maintain the health of our neurons and brain mass. And it's helpful for people like Willa. After meditating for twenty minutes each day for six weeks, she found that she was less distractible and able to put her attention where she wanted it to be and keep it there for longer periods of time.

Delay of Gratification and Impulse Control. These two constructs are intertwined dynamics in many Swords, and present as hidden hurdles to their goal attainment and work product. Being successful in the work of our choice is tricky enough when we approach it with clarity and a full understanding of where all our internal levers are and how they operate for and against us. But imbalances in dopamine don't present in an immediately obvious way, for they just seem to be the "way we are and always have been." And that's exactly right; getting shorted on the activation side of the nervous system is a part of our natural state of being and becomes an embedded part of our personal identity. The task here is to be able to tell the difference between decisions that are made with logic and rationality and those that are influenced by our brain chemistry.

Because they are reward sensitive, Swords can have a difficult time delaying gratification. Despite the little that Willa has to show in concrete accomplishments, she is very ambitious. Since the time she was in high school, she's had the goal of someday writing something beyond the funny, poignant, and always very human sketches she writes. Because of her relationship with arousal, putting in those necessary hours to reach her goal has proved difficult.

"I'm a sprinter, not a marathon runner," she told us. "I always wanted to write long form, you know, the big, breakout novel that everybody wants to read. Oh sure, I get it that I'm a dreamer, right? Every writer wants that, but I get winded after page five and have to get up and wash a window or find a room to vacuum. To write the way I would like to means that I have to plot the whole sweep of the story out, force myself to sit down and not only think it through to the end, but actually write it. And then when I'm through, I'd have to rewrite it. It's all so daunting that just thinking about it makes me want to pull the covers over my head."

Being able to forgo short-term gains for long-term, more substantial rewards is a very valuable capability. We described the children's version of delaying gratification in the marshmallow studies. What happens in the adult brain when we are given a choice between getting something small now that we want (a gift certificate) and something more valuable (a larger gift certificate) that requires a two- to four-week wait to receive it? Using brain imaging, those people who went for the immediate reward showed heightened activity in the reward center of the brain, while those who chose to wait for a larger reward showed more activity in the prefrontal cortex—the brain circuits that exercise more thoughtful judgments and decisions. While the subjects in the study weren't identified as being Shields and Swords, you can be pretty sure that those who took the reward immediately and whose reward center lit up were, in fact, the Swords.

The information we receive from our senses—sights, sounds, smells, as well as the anticipation of a reward—boost dopamine levels in the brain. And having lower levels of dopamine in the brain makes us act more impulsively. It's difficult for Willa not to go for the immediate dopamine hit attached to something she can accomplish quickly, for that is the strategy she's gotten used to using to regulate the boredom and restless itch of emotional discomfort she feels in her brain. Sadly, Willa has always felt that there was something wrong with her as she watched her friends stake out long-term goals and find ways to reach them. She attributed her struggles to simply being lazy, but in fact, these issues have nothing to do with laziness. Nonetheless, not only was Willa stuck in her career, but her belief that a "character flaw" was responsible for her lack of success robbed her of confidence and eroded a trust in her gifts.

The relief she felt when we explained the roots of what she saw as her failings was palpable. Willa wanted to take on the challenge of dealing with her brain chemistry in a different way and proved to be an eager and effective student. We gave her an exercise that some of you Swords might also find helpful. Willa committed to doing three things for a week. First, she agreed to turn her phone off at 11:00 pm and not turn it on again until after breakfast. The second thing she agreed to was not indulging in social media or clicking on a news feed until 6:00 pm. Not surprisingly, this freed up considerable free time. In addition to her daily meditation, the third part of the exercise (and the one proving to be the most diffi-cult) was to commit to two separate ten-minute periods each day when she did absolutely nothing. Nothing meant exactly that: just sitting comfortably in a chair, her feet on the floor, hands in her lap, and her eyes closed. While this may not sound like much, for a Sword an exercise of this kind is not easy. The goal of this exercise for Willa was to form a different relationship with contemplative time—time spent in the intentional absence of outer distraction and stimulation.

You'll be interested to learn that she's now 150 pages into a novel (that's about 140 pages more than she's ever written on a single story line) and going stronger every day. It isn't that the temptations don't still come along and beckon with the promise of a dopamine release in her brain. It's that she's learned to be just a little bit more comfortable with and accepting of that old feeling. She's learned to simply make note of it and continue on with whatever she's doing.

Speed, Persistence, and Errors. As you know, being reward sensi-tive makes Swords' risk profiles different from those of Shields. The sweet lure of a possible reward builds in a tolerance for risk. You've seen how important it is to be able to take measured risks, but tipped too far in the opposite direction, problems can arise. The translation of ambition into success requires staying on some critical path. Unfortunately, risk tolerance favors the mirage of shortcuts with lower-probability outcomes. "Slow and steady" would not be the motto for any Sword we know. Trading accuracy for speed, Swords are vulnerable to taking a quick approach to problem-solving. Success, at any juncture along the critical path, requires accuracy and some attention to detail. Focusing on minutiae, patience, and accuracy tends to be sacrificed for getting through tasks quickly. But it is not simply accuracy that can be an issue for Swords; perseverance presents one as well. Swords and Shields are equally intelligent, but Shields tend to be more persistent in completing tasks as they increase in difficulty. It's not clear whether it's getting distracted or bored or just plain tired, but Swords tend to give up in the face of increasing difficulty, while Shields push doggedly through.

Irrespective of the specific goals we might have, unforced mistakes are the enemy of success. Where Shields tend to make false negative errors, Swords fall on the other side, making more errors that are false positives. Being stimulation driven and reward sensitive, Swords are built to respond. They tend to act before they think. Shields, being the more cautious creatures that they are, tend to think first and only then act. That critical difference creates a vulnerability in Swords. They focus more on what they anticipate getting rather than upon those elements in the calculus that might hurt them. These are the dynamics for making false positive errors. What we've found helpful for Swords is, when facing any decision with important or far-reaching consequences, to take a forced break in the process to examine not what could go right, but what could go wrong. Swords, because of their infatuation with stimulation, naturally want to speed the process, because with a goal in mind movement forward is exciting. It is in the midst of this fizz of excitement that Swords can miss the red flags that Shields see. Red flag blindness can lead to the kind of critical mistakes that blunt success.

LET'S TAKE A big step back for a moment. What exactly is success? Obviously, in the broad sense, success is subjective and can mean many different things. In the narrower angle of its relationship to work, we would define success as a satisfying engagement of our curiosities, talents, and acquired skill sets that line up with the acknowledgments we receive for the fruits of our labors. And, of course, even this definition is idiosyncratic and subjective. Most simply, success in your work is probably just having no spirit-killing complaints or regrets and liking what you're doing.

During these times of such rapid cultural, geopolitical, and economic change, it can be difficult to measure success, for it can seem like a moving target. Have we realized our aspirations? Are we accomplishing our goals? Is there a good fit between our perceived value and the compensation reflecting it? Is our work engaging? Is there intrinsic satisfaction in what we do? How will our value be assessed a year or two from now? Of course, there are many more questions we could pose, but it's clear that our relationship with work is complicated.

Our wish is for you to be as successful as you would like to be and in any way you would frame success. Where we think we can be helpful here is in passing along some invaluable soft skills— skills that require working with and often against your brain chemistry trends. No well-prepared warrior would leave home with but a shield or only a sword. To be successful, we need a good offense as well as the protection of a defense. There are a couple of things we have found to be very helpful. Shields can learn something of value from the Swords' natural inclinations and vice versa for you Swords. Differences in brain chemistry are powerful influences, but they should never be thought of as limiting. These influences we are born with rule things in; they don't ever rule them out.

Shields are more persistent. They don't give up so easily and move on as you Swords tend to do. Swords should remind themselves that they don't have to have everything right now. Swords need to question their exit strategies and make sure they are based upon logic and reason and not boredom and fatigue. Sometimes it's smarter to wait. And for you Shields, is it just your brain chemistry that's causing the gloom and pessimism? Learn to take a few more chances and bet on your being able to handle more of those higher-arousal situations you tend to avoid. Trust in your skills; expose them more directly; bet on yourself. Being a little more hedonistic won't kill you; it will feel good. Swords seemingly have it all, charm, optimism, and an ease with others. You Swords are effective in getting your way, but sometimes by being overly aggressive. You can get others to follow you by being coercive. But studies show that if consensus building is part of your leadership strategy, your assertive tendencies can get in the way. And for you Shields, it's time for you to flash a little more boldness. You are good at building consensus, but you would be more effective leaders risking the exposure of more of your thoughts and ideas.

Swords should ask themselves how their reward sensitivity plays out in the accuracy of their decision-making. And Shields should examine the ways in which their avoidant proclivities may hold them back. Imagine how leaning in the opposite direction of your innate reflexes might have positive payoffs. Take on and embrace that lean. It's only a few chemicals floating around your body that hold you back.

We know what we are suggesting isn't easy. And the reason it isn't easy is because your brain chemicals have been building habits and pushing you around for a long time. That doesn't mean it's not worth trying. What trait from the other team do you envy or find difficult, that you would be willing to challenge and gain greater self-control over? Take on the challenge and see what you can do with it. See what it brings you over time. Remember small steps are good, for they often lead to larger ones.

CHAPTER FIVE

Brain Types: Adaptation to Shifting Workplace Demands

How Our Brain Chemical Imbalances
Influence a Core Set of "Success Factors" Critical
to Survival in Today's Flux of Change

THE CHALLENGES CREATED BY THE pandemic have still not been knit together. The virus swept over us like a tsunami, leaving behind a decade's worth of changes in only a matter of months. Technology has always been the driver of change and the virus sprayed it with an accelerant. Most of us had to build some new skills when we were suddenly having to adapt to working remotely. Business trips became Zooms, meetings became emails, and emails have transitioned into instant messages. There has also been a shift in how workers are employed. Fully a third of organizations across the country have replaced full-time employees with contingent workers. And with all of this, we are scrutinized more closely than ever before. We've witnessed the increased use of monitoring technology to check on emails, chats, and computer usage. Yes, our big brothers and sisters are watching. And these changes are not going away anytime soon. In a survey of hundreds of business leaders, four in ten said their organizations have made changes they intend to keep in place after the lockdown, particularly increased time working from home and a greater focus on digital services.

So, how can we keep up, stay relevant in this avalanche of organized chaos? We believe one of the ways is to ensure our competitiveness, and that requires adapting to and blending in with the flow of change. And to do this, we need access to every ounce of consciousness and intentionality we are capable of. Querying scores of business owners and leaders, we have identified a list of personal qualities prized by today's corporate culture. These "success factors" are accountability, flexibility, confidence, discipline, and self-direction. We all understand these qualities and know why they are so valuable, so we aren't going to spend a lot of time defining and describing them. Rather, we are going to explore the obstacles to being able to embody them with consistency. Our brain chemical imbalances bring predictable challenges to each of these modifiable qualities. Mastering them is independent of specialization, expertise, and technical acumen. These soft skills are not wishes, intentions, or hopes—they are actions, what we actually *do*, how we *are* at work day to day.

Accountability

On the face of it, accountability seems so logical and obvious a quality to possess. Accountability is our capacity to understand and assume responsibility for how we influence and shape our circumstances. You are probably one of those people who feel accountable at work. Most conscientious people do. But where we can get in trouble is in exactly *what* we are accountable to. This requires a personal honesty and clarity of mind that can be diminished by the machinations of our imbalanced brain chemistry. Sounds pretty straightforward, right? Well, not quite when you scrape through the surface.

Jim, a Shield, would be the first guy to raise his hand when asked, "Who sees themselves as accountable?" He's one of those hardworking types, a family man, someone you know you could count on in a time of need. His company, as well as the whole sector, underwent a severe contraction during the lockdown. His group still lags behind and hasn't hit their targets for four quarters. Jim has approached his career very seriously and is invested in not only his continued viability but the well-being of his reports as well. You would like him. He's one of those people who look you in the eye, and when he asks how you are you feel as though he cares about your answer. During the lockdown, he worked from home and his worries about the dangers of the virus set the high level of vigilance maintained by his family.

Now Jim is back in the office working with half his group (the other half still working remotely) and feels as though he has tried everything. But what he's really done is hollow out the effectiveness of his group by becoming a one-man show. He would tell you that his micromanaging is a result of the loss of control he felt when his group all began working remotely, that it was harder to stay in touch, that his numbers were understandable given the downturn. But that's not the whole story. Jim has a blind spot. As group leader, he has been careful to set reasonable goals and incentives for his reports. Yet, despite his efforts, his group continues to underperform. Instead of taking a step back and looking at the big picture, Jim throws himself ever further into the mix with his micromanaging. The true failure lies in his not delegating responsibilities properly. His staff has become demoralized by his second-guessing and his tendency to step in and take over projects better left to the competency of others. This has caused them to become less motivated and increasingly inclined to step back and let him take over. Jim's anxious meddling makes his fear of failure a self-fulfilling prophecy.

Avoidance is the engine of Jim's micromanaging. Even though he was in on the hiring of more than half his group and has been an active and adept teacher, it has been difficult for him to trust their competencies and allow them the natural learning curve of failures and mistakes. Assigning reasonable responsibilities and encouraging autonomy are things he pays lip service to but rarely come to pass. The truth is that Jim has been more accountable to his anxiety and fear of failure than he has to the growth and productivity of his group. When work and the control levers it provides get connected to anxiety-reducing strategies, the result is never a positive one.

Jim is an anxious human being. He has always been one. It's natural to ask ourselves why when we're feeling anxious. Looking for ways to deal with that painful discomfort in a personal way is healthy, being accountable. Trying to reduce your anxiety by controlling those around you is not. Jim was pretty upset when we pointed this out to him. But after only a little probing, the truth came tumbling out. He talked about how hard it was for him to relinquish control. And soon, he spelled out stories of how this played out in his helicopter tendencies with his children at home, much to his wife's dismay.

We had Jim construct a spreadsheet ranking each of his reports from weakest to strongest. For each, he came up with a reasonable task to be completed by them with autonomy. This was a very stressful task for Jim because assigning responsibility required his opening an anxious gap of trust. For each of the assignments, he wrote down "worst fear" and left room for a score of 1 to 5 in terms of successful completion.

It took a bit of nudging and encouragement for Jim to actually pull that first trigger. But what he found over the course of this three-month project was that his "worst fear" was the lowest probability outcome and, to his amazement, scores of 4 and 5 were the highest probabilities.

It's impossible to be accountable to the growth and effectiveness of our teammates when, in truth, we are being accountable to modulating our anxiety and fears of failure. How often do you look

beneath the surface to gain a clearer picture of your emotional motivations? If you are a Shield, can you identify any ways in which
your anxiety levels or avoidant tendencies affect your accountability to the group? How often do you regulate your personal stress
level while calling it something else? How often do you put your
anxieties and fears to the test? These were the questions Jim struggled with. Gaining some understanding that his behavior toward
his reports was, in part, related to his particular brain chemicals
was greatly relieving. We're not sure whether that deeper snapshot
into himself was what gave him the confidence to put his doubts to
the test, but we do know that once he had done that, his anxiety
level slowly faded and was replaced with a growing trust in the
competencies he hadn't believed possible in his group.

Emily, a Sword and general counsel for a large insurance company, has a very different issue with accountability. She has anger
issues. When things don't go right for her, it's always someone
else's fault. Among the hidden dangers to her career was that she'd
lost the trust and loyalty of those around her, damaging invaluable
alliances. Beyond her position, she was an intimidating force.
People steered clear of her when they could and deferred to her
when they had to. Emily's go-to defense for a real or imaginary deficiency was to look around for who to blame. Curiously, she never
looked to herself.

When Emily is stressed (and she is stressed most of the time),
she discharges her tension with angry, overblown, and sometimes-
cruel comments. Where Shields are vulnerable to self-blame and
internalizing their mistakes, Swords tend to look to the external
world for explanations. Although Swords feast on cortical arousal,
even they dislike it when levels get uncomfortably high and they
look for ways to reduce and discharge it. Emily spends much of her
day with arousal in the red zone, making her unaccountable. She
has been swamped by her neurobiology.

We asked her to take the self-control/emotional regulation sub-
test of an Accountability Quiz, below:

I notice that I feel irritated and angry at work.
Never ☐ Rarely☐ Sometimes ☐ Frequently ☐ Most of the time☐

I must admit I do tend to blame people for problematic issues at work.
Never ☐ Rarely☐ Sometimes ☐ Frequently ☐ Most of the time☐

I believe I'm right even though others may disagree with me.
Never ☐ Rarely☐ Sometimes ☐ Frequently ☐ Most of the time☐

Other people's inadequacies seem to hold me back.
Never ☐ Rarely☐ Sometimes ☐ Frequently ☐ Most of the time☐

I'm quicker to criticize than to compliment.
Never ☐ Rarely☐ Sometimes ☐ Frequently ☐ Most of the time☐

I look to other people's faults more often than my own.
Never ☐ Rarely☐ Sometimes ☐ Frequently ☐ Most of the time☐

Emily was saddened, but not surprised, by her results. The very day she took the quiz, Emily had yelled again at her assistant for not reminding her of an important conference call that she missed. She had shrieked, "You have to be more proactive and responsible. Don't think you're getting away with this!" When Emily stomped back into her office, she saw her assistant's IM and email reminder to check her calendar for the conference call. It was Emily—not her falsely accused assistant— who needed to be more responsible.

Seeing how often she answered "Most of the time" was a wake-up call for Emily, and she was only slightly consoled when we explained that it was her brain type that influenced her behavior. But this recognition was enough to get her on board with our suggestions to help her take back control of her behavior. Although Emily can't change her brain chemistry, she did learn to override it and gain greater control over her anger. In addition to committing to a simple mindfulness meditation technique for a month, Emily signed on to an emotional regulation strategy designed for Swords who look for external ways to discharge stress. The goal of the strategy is to move the locus of control from the outside to the inside through the exercise of intentional self-control and inhibition.

Here are the elements of the strategy we gave Emily to work on. The embedded goal here is designed to awaken her freedom of choice. The expression of anger needn't be reflexive. We asked Emily to do the following when she felt that old familiar need to discharge:

1. Simply be aware of the impulse to express negativity (silently taking note of how she felt and her wish to hurl that feeling outward).

2. Remind herself that this awareness, this pause, is an opportunity and strategic moment.

3. Make an intentional shift from reflex to choice (just knowing that we *can* express our angry feelings brings an awareness that we don't necessarily *have to*).

4. Exercise inhibition (assuming the challenge of resolving the moment without having to resort to anger, blame, or sarcasm).

Emily also mapped out a series of goals and rewards (the best way to motivate a Sword is to hold a reward out there). She kept a log of every instance where she consciously inhibited an angry impulse. The first goal was to reach ten consecutive inhibitions of her trademark angry buck-passing and complaining. There were some start-over-from-scratches along the way, but after the third week of trying she had earned her first reward—the gift of a massage. And to expand her capacity to delay gratification (very helpful for most Swords), the bar was raised to twenty consecutive withheld outbursts to earn her next reward—a delectable weekend at a spa.

This process has been very interesting for Emily. To her amazement, she realized that as she inhibited her criticism of others, she felt increasingly in control (she had feared just the opposite).

What's more, Emily realized that her efforts at work had paid off in ways she hadn't expected. When one of her children asked, "Why are you being so nice to us?" she knew something very important had shifted for the better.

So, what, you might be wondering, did Emily do with the buildup of arousal she had to deal with? Curiously, blame had been conflated with the illusion of control. But it was only when Emily began to use the tool of conscious inhibition that she gained a real sense of self-control. She learned that curbing the expression of her angry outbursts had a calming effect on her. "I felt like if I didn't blurt out my angry feelings that I would burst. Paradoxically, taking a moment and giving myself a choice to do something different brought that terrible tension down." She's actually feeling more accountable now not only to those around her but also to herself.

Anxiety and anger distort accountability. Both are related to high levels of arousal. Shields interpret it as anxiety and internalize it, while Swords interpret it as anger and seek to discharge it. Both of these high-arousal states are obstacles to clarity and accountability. In service of an "accountability check," Shields should look to make sure that logic and rationality are the real basis for decisions, not attempts to modulate discomfort. And Swords might examine any role that anger and the assignment of blame play in their dealings at work, holding themselves as both the source and the solution.

Flexibility

As we've described, Shields grow up being more emotionally reactive than do most Swords. Their typically uncomfortable level of heightened arousal can leave them with a baseline of low-level anxiety. The noisy amygdalae they have in their brains leave them responding in real time to the sensory, cognitive, and emotional demands they encounter throughout their days. To make these shifts effectively requires that they learn from early on how to move fluidly from one event to the next. This response to moment-by-moment change (that they get good at) allows them to learn to be flexible (well, more like forces them to be). It's their essentially reactive nature that makes Shields so flexible and adaptive to change. If anything, Shields are flexible except when they're not.

Letitia is the owner of a successful hair salon. She has her own private area where she gives haircuts to those (primarily women) who enjoy the perfect cappuccino or espresso she has prepared for them and are willing to pay the premium for her special touch. A single mom, she has two small children she loves dearly who are in daycare and she considers herself to be at the top of her game.

After Covid temporarily closed the salon, she hunkered down into survival mode, waiting the virus out, expecting everything to be the same when it was over. It wasn't. She assumed all the old rules and procedures would be the same. But as much as the old paradigm had worked and as much as she assumed it would work again, it didn't. Normally laid-back and accommodating, she suddenly found herself irritable, much more anxious, and feeling out of control.

Clients had gotten used to staying at home and many still felt vulnerable. She got requests that she come to them and cut their hair outside in their yards. And clients of her staff were also calling in, trying to arrange home visits for haircuts. Letitia had always had friendly and sensitive relationships with her employees, but even they began to make demands that only increased her anxiety. They had gotten used to being sequestered and the expectation of coming back into the salon full-time caused them to ask for flexible hours and to be able to do some of the home calls their clients had requested. She had always been proud of herself for being accommodating to all the various changes. But now everything seemed to have turned free-form and chaotic.

Shields lose their flexibility when they feel on the verge of losing control and having to change their risk profile. Letitia normally has a very long leash, but when she got to the end of it, it snapped. Payroll would have to be adjusted, how she managed appointments would have to be more flexible, the hours where she could expect staff to be at the salon were now being challenged, and half her staff were revolting, refusing to wear the masks that some clients expected them all to be wearing. Shields tend to be people pleasers and, as we've described, are risk averse. But Letitia knew there was no way she was going to be able to please everyone, and every solution seemed fraught with danger. One of her most valuable skill sets had vanished in the presence of changes that demanded leaps of faith and measured risks.

What Letitia needed to do was take a deep breath and remind herself that a part of the danger she felt wasn't real and was simply a by-product of her brain chemistry chattering in her head. Letitia sat down with her accountant and rewrote the protocol for how the salon was to now function. She knew all of the new procedures wouldn't please everyone, but she also knew that trying to adhere to the old ways was no longer viable. Overriding her anxiety, she pushed herself to adjust to the changing conditions and, so far, under very different conditions, her salon seems to be thriving.

Shields run up against their limits to flexibility when they have to confront their aversion to risk-taking. Remember, flexibility for Shields is a by-product of how they modulate anxiety through hypervigilance—it feels safer to change because the circumstances have been altered. Where they get into trouble is when these new, altered circumstances force them to change their risk profile. If you are a Shield, make sure that your discomfort around risk isn't tending to make you cling to the old rather than embracing the new.

Now, Swords have built-in obstacles to flexibility. Dealing comfortably with change is not a Sword strong suit. Swords are most comfortable in situations where applying rule A to problem A predicts a successful outcome. But in conditions where business models are being shredded and the chaos of change is the climate of the day, applying rule A to problem A becomes ineffective when problem A is a hybrid of what it once was. Flexibility can be difficult for Swords because it challenges the comfort they have developed by heavily relying upon past experience.

Eric feels as though his career has hit a lull. What he doesn't realize is his responsibility in the seemingly rudderless situation he finds himself in. Eric, a fifty-two-year-old bank executive, is experiencing an all-too-common dilemma: the resistance to change. As he explains, "Look, I know the banking industry has gone through convulsions these last few years, but that doesn't mean you have to start doing things a whole different way and trashing everything that worked before. I want my twenty-five years of experience to count for something. We did a lot of things right and I can't see the need to go around revamping all our procedures." But this is a bad attitude if you want to stay relevant and still be in the running for upward mobility.

Flexibility and responsiveness to change requires as much unlearning as it does learning. Shields' emotional reactivity causes them to continue to learn anew and the dynamic of learning anew is essentially unlearning the old. Swords, unfortunately, can have a hard time with this. Eric was very fond of the frequent business trips to meet with each of his regional managers. He enjoyed the face-to-face contact, the camaraderie, and the drinking dinners after their meetings. He certainly understood why the lockdown prohibited those business trips and grudgingly adapted to doing those meetings online. But the use of certain technologies has a learning curve. Eric found himself reluctant to push past the glitches and commit to learning the technology and making the best use of it. The bank had a software-based phone system that allowed calls to their business number to come through to their computers, where he could answer with a headset or on the computer microphone. Instead, he chose to continue to use his cell phone for internal calls and calls to clients. This slowed things down internally because not all cell phone numbers were in the company directory and it wasn't possible to use the speed dial features of the software. And even though Eric got Zoom meeting requests, he continued to make voice-only calls because it was easier than making a video-enabled call.

Something important was missing for him. He looked forward to the day when his teammates would be able to resume patterns more comfortable and familiar to him. The cost savings of substituting video meetings for cross-country flights weren't lost on him, nor was the fact that communication and efficiency didn't appear to suffer in this switch from in-the-room to on-the-screen meetups. Eric wasn't even impervious to the eye rolls he got in response to his repetitive grumblings about how he couldn't wait for the old days to return. The truth is those good old days are gone forever. Had he spent a tenth of the energy on grappling with the new technology that he did complaining, Eric wouldn't have earned the "Luddite" moniker whispered behind his back.

Things took a turn for the worse when new banking regulations came down from the Federal Reserve. As you may surmise, compliance is an important requirement in the banking industry. The report from the Fed was lengthy and complex. There was only a small sliver that Eric was required to master, but the new regulations intimidated him and he found ways to circumvent them. His assistant, worried that the department was skirting federal requirements, broke rank and went to HR.

It was during this time that Eric reached out to us. What became quickly apparent was that his rigidity and resistance to change wasn't simply relegated to work but had echoes in every area of his life. Eric clung to deeply entrenched habits. He did the same exercise routine he had done in college. He expected to have steak every Monday, salmon every Wednesday, and pizza every Friday and felt deprived whenever his wife deviated from this menu. He used the same brand of razor blades, shaving cream, and bar soap he'd used since he could remember. When we pointed out that he seemed a little rigid and routine bound, he laughed and said his wife kidded him about it all the time. He went on to tell us how he liked driving the same route to work every day and how there was something comforting about that. Shaking his head with a grin, he said, "I still buy the same Jockey underwear I've always worn."

Sure, routine building is good, but even better is the ability to change those routines when circumstances demand such a change.

The skill set here is flexibility, and its obstacle is the kind of rigidity and resistance to change that is a vulnerability for Swords.

Eric wasn't simply resistant to change; he romanticized having one foot stuck in the past. But along with all this stubbornness, he was acutely aware that his rigidity posed a problem for his career advancement.

When we made a few guesses about other aspects of his behavior, he looked at us as if we were psychics. We assured him we were anything but, and that the guesses we made were based upon what we thought his brain chemistry imbalance might be. "You mean some of the things I do," he said, "are based on my chemistry? I always thought it was that I learned a lot of this from watching my father do things." We told him it may very well have been related to his father, but that the similarities were likely a combination of modeling himself after the man as well as having inherited his brain chemistry.

Eric had developed a kind of "if it's not broken, don't fix it" philosophy and then institutionalized it. His story line, his narrative identity, had cast change as a hidden enemy. We set out to help him make a critical edit in that story line. Recognizing his rigidity was related to his brain chemistry and the comfort of habit was the first step. This understanding of habit simply as repetition and familiarity and not choice set in motion a newfound freedom. We had Eric start small, making minor changes to some of the things he was used to doing. Early on, he had a big insight. "Do you know what I learned?" he asked. "I learned that I always thought the things I did were the best way of doing them and I just realize that they weren't; they were just mine. They weren't better or worse; they were just things I was used to doing."

Eric also learned that change takes effort and the willingness to experience some discomfort along the way. What seemed to intrigue him was that his story line wasn't some fated version of his destiny, but something he could choose to edit, interact with actively, and alter. Change became a challenge, and his willingness to engage that challenge resulted in many fewer complaints and grumblings and a

lot more adaptiveness. He even bought himself a new shaving system and helped his daughter set up a Zoom call with friends.

Confidence

Not everyone can run like Usain Bolt, play basketball and dominate
the court the way LeBron James does, or return a backhand the way
Serena Williams is able to. Outstanding athleticism is genetic. We
might try to improve our skills in any of these arenas, but we would
inevitably bounce up against our physical limits. Certain aspects of
who we are as human beings have ceilings, and while we can push
toward those upper boundaries, we eventually hit them. The success factors we are exploring here are a little different. Instead of
being relatively fixed and stable, they are mindsets you can interact
with and change in constructive ways.

Confidence in work is one of those dynamic internal states that,
while seemingly a constant, is in fact quite fluid. There are no metrics for confidence. It is not charm or charisma or assertiveness,
and it has nothing to do with being outgoing or some sort of social
butterfly. Confidence is content and context specific.

Even though this story may seem a little off point, it shows just
how fluid our sense of confidence is and how context specific.
Many years ago, a university psychology professor rounded up a
group of paired students (young women and men) who were
bonded emotionally. Each of the couples had to have been in a mo-
nogamous, intimate romantic relationship for at least six months.
The point of the study was to observe how those couples handled
being in unfamiliar and possibly challenging circumstances. The
professor, along with the students, flew to Tibet. They, along with a
group of accompanying Sherpas, began to climb to the base camp
of Mount Everest. The weather turned bad as they neared their destination, and by the time they got to the camp they found
themselves in the midst of a terrible storm. None of them had
signed on for the terror they felt as freezing blasts of wind carried

some of their tents away. While this experiment was meant to be somewhat challenging, no one had been able to foresee the storm that befell this group. What became apparent was the competence of the Sherpas. Now, remember, each of these couples had been selected because they were in long-term, bonded relationships. By day two of this raging storm, a surprising number of the women had left their partners and found Sherpas to bond with. Their mates may very well have been alpha males on campus, but up on these oxygen-deprived mountain sweeps the alpha males were the Sherpas. Clearly, context matters.

As humans, we are all born storytellers. By the time we reach adulthood, whether we think about it or not, we have constructed a narrative identity or personal story combining the highlights that have shaped our lives and give meaning to the ways we see ourselves. It is that accumulated narrative database added to over the years that acts as a ready barometer for how we feel and assess ourselves. You can ask anyone, "On a scale of one to ten, how happy are you?" and they would have an answer based upon how they interpret their unique story. Confidence follows the same guidelines.

One form of psychotherapy actually looks at the personal stories people have constructed about their lives, and the goal is to edit and modify those story lines in positive and constructive ways. Interestingly, this type of therapeutic intervention has been shown to be as effective as medication and cognitive behavioral therapy.

As in other areas of our lives, confidence is an important success factor at work. Let's see if we can define confidence in this context: confidence is a set of inner beliefs about our comfort and trust in the core skills we have that fall under our job responsibilities.

During a national sales conference, two regional managers were brainstorming a new strategy over a working lunch. Later, one of them threw her hand in the air and pitched the strategy to the group. And yes, she mentioned at the outset her partner's participation, but she was the one bold enough to flesh out the idea and field the barrage of questions it stimulated. Which of the two members of this idea-generating duo do you think the group remembered?

If you are a Sword, you have a built-in advantage. Your relationship with arousal does some positive things that interact with confidence. Because of your brain chemistry, you tend to be more optimistic and, just as important, you tend to be more risk tolerant and less vulnerable to social anxiety. Put another way, welcoming a little bump in arousal allows you to throw your hand up first. But wait. For Swords, arousal cuts both ways and can be both a blessing and a curse. You know where the devil lies, and rather than worrying about details, Swords can get carried away looking for a dopamine hit. Attention to detail—the quiet, sometimes-tedious work required to document and substantiate "big-picture" ideas—can be neglected.

Craig had good ideas, seriously good ideas. He was known for them. He was also known for abandoning them when it came to the more careful fine points of follow-through. But that wasn't the primary obstacle he faced around the issue of confidence. No, Craig's challenge was a mixture of confidence run amok and not being able to say no. He is an architect and came to us with symptoms of stress and exhaustion. And despite the fact that he runs on the treadmill for an hour each morning before dawn, his blood pressure was poorly controlled.

His description of an average day made both of us want to curl up somewhere and go to sleep. After nine or ten hours at the office, he would head home for a quick dinner before helping with bath time for his twins. After tucking in the kids and reading them a bedtime story, he would go to his computer and work on one or another of the personal projects he has going on. Rest was only after the second or third call from his wife, and sleep on a good night was a scant five hours before fumbling with the alarm and making his way to the treadmill. With him always the first one in the office and the last to leave, his only break was his usual delivered pastrami on rye sandwich wolfed down over a working lunch.

Craig is an intelligent and talented man and, without a doubt, he could probably master everything he set out to do—if only he would focus on one thing at a time. But that's not the way he chooses to go about things. His style is attempting to do them simultaneously. In addition to overseeing his demanding architectural practice, he is developing a productivity app he hopes to sell to large corporations. This requires him to work with a number of programmers and, of course, he insists upon wanting to design the "look" of the app himself. Recently, his professional association asked Craig if he was interested in doing a weekly podcast. He has been writing and doing the recordings in a room at home set up as a mini recording studio. He has been juggling all of this along with working on a book dealing with the influence of new materials on architectural design. Did we mention that he serves on two boards and has just been asked to join another one? Probably not. Too exhausting to even think about. And now Craig just brought up that he is thinking that he might volunteer to coach his kids' soccer team.

We weren't sure if Craig was looking for admiration or sympathy for all he was doing. Maybe it was a little of both. But we steered him back to why he had chosen to come in to see us. What Craig didn't like to talk about were the persistent rumors he'd become aware of that he was overleveraged and distracted. In fact, he had recently lost two important projects that he's not yet been able to replace.

Wanting to do too much and being right on the verge of actually being able to pull it off can be a very tricky thing to deal with. We certainly didn't want to dent Craig's optimism and belief in himself, but we did want to show him the role that his brain chemistry played in his ever-expanding swath of activities. We explained that mistaking low levels of dopamine for boredom and a feeling of deadness can cause people with his brain chemistry to live in dread of contemplative moments. And how because of this, they will do almost anything to make sure that there isn't any time for these moments to occur. Craig didn't seem to quite buy what we were saying, but it was a dead giveaway when he said, "I'm game to try anything you suggest, just so long as it doesn't mean sitting around having nothing to do." Now we had something to work with. Sometimes what you don't want is exactly what you need and an obvious starting point for a journey to do things a little differently.

To describe Craig as capable would be an understatement, and he certainly didn't suffer any doubts about his many talents. But what appeared to be an abundance of confidence and surety about himself was, in part, a by-product of how he modulated low levels of arousal. His restless shifting from activity to activity ensured a steady stream of stimulus input. The tedious but necessary attention to detail most projects require didn't engage him, for its stimulus value was too low, causing Craig to set the task aside and search for something "more interesting." It was that relentless hunt for the more interesting that posed a threat to his business.

We started Craig with two assignments. First, we got him to agree to try a ten-day trial of a mindfulness meditation app he downloaded on his phone. Then we instructed him to work on a list of what we labeled "Details I'd Rather Ignore." We explained to him that the first strategy would allow him to expand his tolerance for periods of low stimulation, which would pay off by making him less distractible. The meditation trial turned out to be less than successful. He claimed that trying to focus on his breath made him want to do anything but feel himself breathe. We switched it to a more tolerable fifteen-minute "purposeless moment" where he agreed to sit in a quiet space with his eyes closed. No other instructions. That Craig could handle.

How he dealt with the "Details I'd Rather Ignore" list surprised us. He came in with three pages saying, "I had no idea that I had all these things floating around in my head that I wasn't taking care of. It's no wonder I'm losing business. I wouldn't put up with anyone who let this many things fall through the cracks." He patted the list with a palm as he went on, "When I look through this, my eyes cross and all I want to do is go online and troll through the portable pizza ovens I've been looking into."

There it was! There isn't a Sword who doesn't love a new purchase. We knew exactly how we were going to motivate Craig to plow through his list of necessary details. His ordering that new pizza oven was going to be a reward for accomplishing some much-needed and tedious tasks. Real confidence requires proof. While

Craig had an abundance of attitude, exuberance, and optimism, his follow-through and attention to detail had been sorely lacking and had sabotaged his accomplishments. His willingness to tackle the "stuff that doesn't hold my interest," as he put it, made a huge difference in his work product. "I knew I was neglecting the small stuff and when I stopped, I realized how important it actually is and how I distracted myself by not doing it. Not jumping around and doing so much has actually let me finish more rather than less. Feels pretty good."

Issues that influence confidence take on a more circuitous route for the Shields among us. With them being more familiar with the dark underside of things, their posture in the world is typically a more defensive one. While Swords can ignore important details, Shields get lost in them. For them, details feel like friends, and the more they immerse themselves in them, the safer they feel. And because of their itchy relationship with arousal, Shields tend to be risk averse and avoidant. The combination of these dynamics can make the development of confidence a difficult process. Confidence is expressed with a certain boldness that often feels uncomfortable and unsafe to Shields who can find themselves standing on the sidelines waiting for just a little more information to come in, in order to act.

Beth found herself in a position where her reluctance to draw conclusions based upon what she felt was still incomplete data drew the ire and impatience of her boss. Let us tell you a little bit about Beth. She was the youngest daughter in a large Catholic family. After a Jesuit education at Fordham University, Beth decided to become a nun. Having grown up with two sisters and four brothers, she yearned for the structured and serene life she imagined would be hers by dedicating herself to a life of study and service.

Due to a few unforeseen turns in the road, Beth began questioning her "calling" and, in the days before her final vows, decided against a religious life. Using her education and following her interest, she got an administrator's job at a large Catholic hospital in Los Angeles.

Beth was dedicated to her job and thrilled with being given the task of collecting and analyzing data on updating procedures for infection control and patient safety. Six months into her projects, she was being prodded for results. And even though she worked long hours, speed was never her friend; accuracy was. After all, she is a Shield.

When we met Beth, she was afraid she was going to lose the job she loved. In her midyear review, her boss told her that unless she had something to present soon, she would find someone who could deliver results. Beth was devastated. She didn't know which was worse: losing her job or sacrificing accuracy for speed and rushing conclusions she didn't yet feel confident making. Beth was anxious, had no appetite, and below the surface was angry at herself for having this crisis of confidence. This was not the first time and it sent shivers of doubt through all of her decisions of late.

In working with Shields on confidence, the first thing we do is help them separate fact from brain chemistry artifact. The purpose of this is twofold. First, being able to discriminate between "this is in fact dangerous" and "this feels dangerous even though I know it probably is not" brings the anxiety level down a peg. And second, it provides the content around which we can build strategies designed for them to safely begin to take reasonable risks. It is through taking these reasonable risks that Shields build their confidence.

Beth could have gone on for another six months and collected another mountain of data, but truth be told, she had more than enough to make firm conclusions on 95 percent of the issues and provisional conclusions on the other 5 percent. The more she talked about the projects, the clearer it became that her perfectionistic tendencies were the real culprits getting in the way of writing up these reports. And then she revealed the real kicker. She had been told that when the reports were finished she would be asked to present them orally to the board. It was her dread of public speaking that was at play here. As long as she could continue to collect more information, she could avoid having to get up and talk in front of a group. She had sabotaged her talent and capability because she didn't know how to deal with her relationship with arousal.

To override her fear of arousal, we put together a performance anxiety reducing strategy similar to the one we used with Colin, from chapter 4. For Beth, we did a little twist on the strategy. Near the end of the process, she would make her presentation to us. In the ramp-up to that day, she tried out every excuse to avoid actually having to present to us. We just kept reminding her that if her goal was to keep her job, she'd have to break through her discomfort. When the day finally arrived, Beth came in dressed in a way we had never seen before. She wore a tailored charcoal suit and introduced herself as if we'd never met. She went through the presentation like a real champ. Her presentation at work followed two weeks later, and she was highly praised by her boss. All that rehearsal had paid dividends.

Discipline and Self-Direction

What are the propellants that fuel self-direction? Certainly, among the primary ones are ambition, being able to visualize and understand the path forward, and the combination of focused curiosity and imagination. Being self-disciplined and directed not only feels good when experienced but also is a major attribute when we bring that energy to work. In fact, self-motivation has been identified as one of the most important factors in a person's overall performance. The reasons this is such a valued quality in a work situation are pretty obvious, particularly when you are looking around for those most capable of handling more responsibilities or those you are interested in wanting to retain. So, what could get in the way of something that is valued by management and feels so satisfying and enlivening in the experience?

Sadly, a lot can get in the way of maintaining self-direction and it all spins around our relationship with arousal. Swords and Shields tend to have similar *obstacles* to their internal motivation, but the *underlying causes* of these pitfalls are as dissimilar as their differing brain chemistry. Both Shields and Swords can be overly reliant upon external sources of feedback or guidance, and both can misidentify core tasks. Let's look at why this is so for each of these brain types.

> Chris has great, unrealized potential. Brimming with optimism and an infectious smile, he warms the room with his appearance, making those around him feel seen and appreciated. Willing to take on extra projects, his enthusiasm sadly isn't accompanied by follow-through. Chris overpromises and underdelivers.

The preceding description was copied from Chris' annual review. When he shared this snippet with us, he prefaced it with, "I'm the go-getter at work. No one has to tell me what to do or how to juggle all the things I am responsible for. And here's the kicker: my manager told me that he was hoping in the future that I might, and I am not paraphrasing, 'exercise a little more autonomy in the future.' How insulting! I feel like I got totally slammed."

Well, certainly not totally. But how do we listen and take in criticism? No one likes to hear something negative about themselves, but getting angry and going into denial is pretty self-defeating. As Chris continued to go over his review with us, a through line began to emerge. He would be the first person to describe himself as disciplined and self-directed, even though the truth is he is not. What he revealed in the first session were some classical blind spots that Swords have with maintaining consistent internal motivation.

As we've described, those of us with too little natural central nervous system activation are left reward sensitive. What this means in Chris' situation is that his decisions, large and small, are shaped by what will produce small dopamine hits, increasing arousal and leading to his sense of greater comfort. All of this, of course, was operating beyond his conscious awareness.

So, what impact does being reward sensitive have on Chris' capacity for internal motivation? We asked him to describe his responsibilities and to write them down in two columns. The first column was labeled "More Interesting" and the second column was labeled "Less Interesting." Chris is a smart man. Finishing his lists, he looked up and, with a grin, said, "I know where you guys are going with this. That second column is harder to stay with. Look, I start out strong, but having to deal with a lot of tedious details is just plain boring. I'll get an idea and put this down and jump into something else that's just more interesting."

The "jump" has to do with impulse control and dealing with the "tedious details" has to do with being able to delay gratification. These are both aspects of a Sword's brain chemistry and reward sensitivity and they lead to a common obstacle—distractibility. And distractibility is a powerful enemy to discipline and self-direction.

Building on this, the by-product of distractibility is often procrastination. Chris, after discussing the results of attentional lapses, told us failure to complete was a part of his MO. "This is embarrassing to admit, but I lose interest a lot," he said, looking away. "And sometimes, when I hit a roadblock or things just seem too difficult at the moment, I just give up. When I was a kid, they gave me Ritalin. I used to hate having to take it, but it did help me to stay on track better."

Boredom, losing interest or focus, and lack of sustained endurance (giving up) are all possible Sword vulnerabilities, as is a history of ADHD. One of the first things we did with Chris was to suggest a mindfulness meditation. We got a dismissive eye roll. What finally convinced Chris to commit to twelve weeks of meditation was a study we told him about. Researcher Lidia Zylowska and associates found that 78 percent of their participants (these all happened to be people diagnosed with adult ADHD by the way) who practiced mindfulness meditation reported a reduction in their ADHD symptoms. And as a bonus, the researchers also found the participants performed significantly better on measures of attention and concentration.

Procrastination and failure to complete are often related to another Sword proclivity—a largely unconscious dependency upon external guidance. Swords function at their best in a feed-forward environment. Unlike feedback, feed forward is not an after-the-fact critique of performance. Rather, feed forward has to do with laying out clear directives and expectations before a task is started. "Jumping all over me for my deficiencies has never been a very effective motivator for me. It always feels like pointing to the barn door being open and only makes me feel bad about myself."

When we explained the feed-forward concept to Chris, he lit up, saying, "Yeah, I'd love to have my manager set up the priorities, step out the specific expectations, and set timelines. I'll never get that. My manager isn't going to take the time to figure all that out." And we agreed. Most managers don't have the time, inclination, or energy to do that for their reports. Chris needed to learn to do that for himself and we gave him that task.

Seemingly pleased with himself, he came in with a chart that de-tailed a list of the six projects he was working on. For each he had fleshed out the detailed scope and expectations, and each was as-signed a specific time it would be completed. Chris would provide his own feed forward. He was disappointed when we put on the brakes and said we wanted to add in one other hurdle to sustained motivation—incorrectly identifying core tasks. Swords can have a kind of Swiss cheese approach when it comes to identifying which of the tasks they are assigned are the most important and timely. They can have a kind of inattentional blindness (focusing on one thing that causes others to not be seen). We showed Chris a video on this phenomenon where a group of people passed a ball from person to person. The task is to count how many times the ball is passed. "Thirteen times," he said. "Did you see anything else that struck you?" we asked. When he said no, we replayed the video, tell-ing him that he'd missed the big bear before we hit play. He couldn't believe his eyes. There amidst the ball passers, a man in a bear suit walked out into the center, faced the camera, and then moonwalked off. Google this (Inattentional Blindness—How Many Passes) and watch it for yourself.

We use the video to talk about Swords' frequent proclivity to choose the task that is most interesting and most likely to be stimulating (providing a little dopamine hit) first. After all, Swords, being reward sensitive and on the prowl for excitement and something to activate them, are naturally drawn to doing the things that have the most potential for pleasure and enjoyment. Asking the viewer to concentrate on how many times the ball gets passed is what causes the inattentional blindness in the video. For Swords, their blindness is caused by their relationship with arousal, their unconscious need to seek it out. We had Chris take another hard look at the chart he'd brought in, taking the bear into account. His assignment was to go through his list with the very conscious intention of prioritizing by importance and timeliness while stripping out interest and stimulation. With a hybrid look of "I can't believe this" and chagrin, he changed the priority positions of four of his six positions.

Before we let Chris go, we had him read aloud his less than celebratory review. What struck us was how his anger had melted away and been replaced with a real sense of personal responsibility and control. We'd given him some tools to override his natural brain chemistry and hope he will use them in his journey. Chris now has an understanding of the pull his particular brain chemistry has on his decisions and has a good chance of reducing their self-defeating power.

As we mentioned, Shields' issues around self-discipline and direction are much the same as for Swords, even though the underlying causal connections are starkly different. Certainly, not all Shields experience obstacles in this area, but when they do, these impediments can profoundly affect their performance.

Rather than looking for ways to increase cortical activation, Shields are on the lookout for ways to avoid getting hurt. Instead of being reward sensitive like Swords, they are sensitized to the possibilities of being harmed in some way and motivated to avoid it.

Shields, being harm avoidant, exist in a relatively steady state of hypervigilance. And it is this emotional state of being chronically on guard that can interfere with staying disciplined and motivated. That kind of vigilance comes with the price tag of the energy drain that is required to sustain it. Shields' hypervigilance can lead them to overthink, doubt themselves, and be paralyzed by the time sink of perfectionistic tendencies, all additional energy sponges.

The successful completion of tasks is another variable that is linked to self-discipline and motivation. Shields often fail to complete important tasks, not because they're lazy or don't have the technical skill set, but because of their reluctance to make critical decisions. As you know, Shields are risk averse and often would rather dawdle than take necessary chances that might be in error. As we've indicated, Shields tend to make false negative errors. One of the things we've found helpful to Shields in this regard is to ask them to construct a list comprised of "Things I Worry about That Haven't Come to Pass." Unfounded fears tend to swim back into our unconscious, but if we put our needless worry into words and write them down, they are stored in a more retrievable and impactful way. The memory and impact can be used as real and factual reminders of false fears during times of doubt.

Risk intolerance is a major component of Shields' failure to sustain motivation to complete a task successfully. They don't tend to give up as quickly or easily as some Swords do, but when they do, risk is a likely culprit. We all like to think that we make our decisions using logic, but the truth is that our emotions, particularly fears (for Shields) and desires (for Swords), play a huge roll in decision-making. David Ropeik, author of *How Risky Is It, Really?: Why Our Fears Don't Always Match the Facts,* puts it this way: "Risk decision-making isn't conscious, and it's not what we would define as rational in the sense of evidence-based. It's emotional, it's in the context of how the information we have feels, and that depends on our life circumstances, our education, our health, our age." And we would add to that list and underline "brain chemical imbalances."

As you know, the amygdala is one of the key regions involved in evaluating risks and making decisions. That part of the brain is responsible for triggering feelings of fear by signaling the presence of a potential threat to other brain regions. Responding to the alarm, the body starts to release stress hormones and prepares to react in one of three ways: flight, fight, or freeze. Of course, the amygdala is designed to protect us from physical harm, but the kind of itchy amygdalae Shields have amplifies the possible consequences of the microdecisions required to bring projects to completion. Some Shields' work is guided by an unspoken and unconscious mantra: *When in doubt, don't.*

But human decisions aren't driven solely by fear. Our brains have a counterbalancing system, a region called the ventromedial prefrontal cortex, which assesses whether the amygdala has overreacted, allowing the brain to evaluate decisions with a little more rationality. These two brain regions are intimately connected and exert influence on each other. The amygdala signals the ventromedial prefrontal cortex that something is potentially threatening. The prefrontal cortex takes a moment to review the alert in context and comes to a conclusion as to whether the threat is serious and how to respond.

Processing risk can be tricky for Shields. The amygdala and the prefrontal cortex enter into a kind of competition for who will call the shots. Remember Shields tend to have noisy, overactive amygdalae that aren't always sanguine with the calming logic bouncing back from the prefrontal cortex. Because they have too little serotonin, Shields' amygdalae often prevail, causing them to make decisions large and small from fear instead of rationality. This decision-making brain circuit exists obviously in the brains of Swords as well. Like Shields, they weigh in when competing courses of action are called for. But where Shields zero in on the costs, Swords focus more upon the possible benefits.

While Shields' distaste for risk is probably the primary cause of their issues around decisive task completion, they can have another closely related obstacle to completion. That possible pitfall is their tendency to become infatuated with and rely upon feedback. Shields love feedback and the information, sense of progress, and encouragement it contains. Because of their brain chemistry, Shields often suffer from self-doubt. Moving ahead and making difficult decisions is hard for them. Feedback along the way, of course, makes those tough decisions a bit easier. But this affection for feedback has a downside. Managers don't look favorably on having to provide too much and too frequent feedback on a project. And waiting for it or asking for it prematurely can read as needy and insecure.

What we've found helpful in this regard is to take on the challenge of creating your own feedback. Any task or project can be approached in that way. Take the time to go through your project (either on paper or in your mind) step-by-step. At each step, give yourself a thumbs-up for completed or thumbs-down if it hasn't yet been completed. Most of you will find the thumbs-up steps outnumber those you are more critical of. For the ones you have questions about, ask yourself a few of these questions: "Why don't I think this is working?" "Do I need more information to move ahead?" "Am I procrastinating?" "Am I being perfectionistic?" "If I made some decisions right now, could I move the process ahead?"

Now here's the fun part: This process is a reflection of your relationship with yourself. For many Shields, this personal relationship is a rocky one. What helps is to become an ally instead of a nit-picking critic. Having a positive relationship with yourself takes courage—courage to trust in yourself and courage to push yourself to make hard decisions. What hard decisions are associated with your projects and which decisions, if made today, would move those thumbs-down steps to a neutral position or maybe even a thumbs-up position? No one needs more constructive self-soothing than do Shields. Encourage yourself. Sure, push yourself to do better. Trust yourself to make the decisions you need to make. A successful relationship with yourself is one part self-discipline and one part encouragement.

The third obstacle to successful completion is the misidentification of core tasks. We've discussed why Swords misidentify core tasks. Shields can have their own trouble in this regard, but for different reasons. Shields sometimes talk themselves into working on certain aspects of a project while letting others go, without being aware of the deeper reasons why. When your basic posture is a defensive one, the world can seem a dangerous place. Wishing to avoid the anxiety attached to difficult, stressful tasks can lead Shields to distort their ability to prioritize their importance. Because of this, we've found that it's helpful, particularly for Shields, to regularly challenge how they are prioritizing their work process. We've also found it helpful to prioritize the tasks both in terms of importance as well as in terms of how much anxiety is attached to tackling them. Are you more likely to put off those tasks that cause more anxiety? If so, do those tasks first. Challenge the anxiety head-on.

BEING HONEST WITH ourselves, we probably all have our own little glitches in how we approach our work. We all have certain things that come more easily, that we are clearly better at, and even those aspects we'd rather not see in ourselves but have been pointed out to us and we secretly know are true. While the personal styles we bring to our work are not all attributable to brain chemistry, those we've explored certainly are. It might be helpful to take a few minutes and think about how some of the traits linked to your brain type might be expressed in how you are in your work. Are there any themes you recognize? Do you see ways in which you behave in any of the stories and issues we've described? If so, is there something you've learned about yourself? What? What small shifts would you commit to taking on? For each of those shifts, the only real obstacle is your willingness to face and challenge the ways you allow the discomfort of arousal to push you around, the ways old brain type habits can materially stand in the way of achieving greater effectiveness and success in your work. Be good to yourself—get a little uncomfortable.

CHAPTER SIX

Managing Down, Up, and Across

*Leveraging your Shield/Sword
Knowledge to Manage Up, Down,
and Across More Effectively*

UNLESS ONE OF YOUR COWORKERS is a neuroscientist, you probably know more about brain chemistry by now than anyone you deal with at work. A question you might still be asking is whether our theory of Swords and Shields is an oversimplification. The answer, of course, is yes. Most things we take for granted as true are oversimplifications. Assuming it's safe to sail through an intersection when we see a green signal light ahead is an oversimplification. We do it because it moves traffic along and, most of the time, is safe. But not always. The way reality spools out is always jagged, layered, and contradictory. But that doesn't mean that simplifications don't pack value, for they allow us to generalize, observe themes and trends, and make much better than chance predictions about a variety of actions and decisions. We think the more important question isn't whether our brain type theory is an oversimplification, but if it is a *useful* one. We've found it to be exactly that. We're going to show you how to put your growing knowledge of brain chemicals to work in all of your employment-related interactions in very practical ways.

Before getting into the formal content of this chapter we'd like you to try a little experiment. First, make a list of the names of those people at work who are critical to your success. The list should include everyone from your boss, or maybe bosses, to anyone who reports directly to you, and also the peers you interact with who are essential to your job security and the expression of your talents and skill set. You might even include here, if appropriate, your partner in life. These are all people you know. We want you to use your knowledge of each of them to make these important relationships more effective. By now, you've learned a lot about how Shields and Swords think and act, their strengths and weaknesses. We want you to put that understanding to work. Go through your list of names. Think about each one of these people and what you've observed over your experiences with them. And now the fun part—write down "Shield" or "Sword" after each name. Sure, it may feel like a bit of a stretch, but if you really think about these people, you'll have a pretty accurate guess about which they are. After doing this, you'll never see them in quite the same way again. What will become increasingly apparent is something that's been hiding in plain sight—their brain chemistry. The benefit here is that it may make some of their behavior less aggravating and less related to you personally. And more important, your understanding of their brain type will allow you to relate to them in ways that will optimize your effectiveness.

You know if you're Sword- or Shield-leaning and now you've identified the likely brain chemistry of the significant people around you. By "significant," we mean those who may help you as well as those who might hold you back, for one may be as important as the other. This information will provide a valuable backdrop for you as you read on.

Whether your work culture is top-down, democratic, chaos/ laissez-faire, or downright cutthroat, an understanding of brain types and their assets and vulnerabilities is a valuable management tool. We are all managers. Even if you have no one who reports directly to you, you manage up and you manage your relationships with your peers. This tool can be used irrespective of the direction; it can be used to manage up, down, or across. Making educated guesses as to the brain chemistry of those to whom you report will inform the most valuable ways of dealing with them. Employing this same tool will make you a better leader, teasing out both greater teamwork, productivity, and morale from those who report to you. And in managing across, you will learn how to gain the kind of cooperation that is essential for your well-being and success.

Managing Down

If you are in a managerial position, you are clearly already doing a lot of things right. Our goal here is to refine your leadership skills. The way we can be helpful is in leveraging your understanding of your reports by suggesting some small but significant changes in your interactions with them. In one respect, these relationships are comprised of two human beings relating to each other in the context of a power differential. But at another level, there are two sets of brain chemistries in the mix that can exert a powerful influence on the outcome of these everyday interactions.

As managers (and we mean anyone who supervises someone else's work product), you have your own duties and responsibilities far beyond making sure your reports stay on track. Because of this, management can become haphazard and shoot from the hip, particularly when other issues are more emergent and of a higher priority.

We believe effective managers are good teachers and good teaching takes an investment of time, energy, and attentiveness. Unfortunately, these commodities are in short supply in today's work world. We'd like to offer some tips that will make you a better teacher while saving you time. These bumps in effectiveness require a little front-loaded observation and listening. But the payoff of this investment will be increased efficiency and productivity in the future, with less energy and stress expended. We also believe that effective managers are open, authentic, and empowering to their reports. It is the product of these qualities that bears the fruit of collaboration, and it is understanding the importance of your role and how it relates to the team's goals that drives success.

What follows are examples of management strategies that are effective and productive, collaborative and empowering.

We want to start by telling you a little bit about Janis. Viewed superficially, Janis is a woman who is simply underperforming, in terms of not only the expectations of those around her but her own expectations as well. But digging deeper, she's much more interesting and her underperformance is much less a fait accompli than it may seem. Janis, twenty-five, was tested in grade school and found to have an IQ of 143 (for perspective, only approximately 5 percent of the population score above an IQ of 125). Despite her intellect, she clawed her way through high school. Her BA took her six years instead of four. Possessing an astonishing vocabulary and polished verbal skills, she managed to interview her way into an aerospace job with a starting salary of $90k and a bright future.

One year in, she feels her job is in jeopardy. As a classic Shield, Janis sparkles at proposing and initiating but is never satisfied with what she's done. Instead of anticipating praise, she expects to be pink-slipped—on a daily basis! It's always the devil or the deep blue sea with her; to get something done, she has to be more anxious about the consequences of not turning something in than the feared assessment of her work product. She has no idea how often and unnecessarily she gets in her own way. Too often, she takes work home with her or stays late at the office. Although she doesn't tell anyone, Janis takes an Inderal (a beta-blocker that can be helpful to those who experience performance anxiety) before her weekly meetings with her manager to make sure she can control her voice.

Janis brings "the perfect is the enemy of the good" to new heights. Her obsessive reworking of material doesn't make it better; it simply makes it different. She very rarely makes a mistake but even more rarely gets assignments finished on time. In looking back through her records, we found her old WISC (the widely used Wechsler Intelligence Scale for Children) results. Besides her high IQ were some small but telling dips (relative to her overall IQ) on the subtests that measure concentration and attention to detail. In that pattern, we saw the early fingerprints of anxiety, for it is that anxious state that interferes with our ability to concentrate and attend closely to detail. As you know, Shields tend to excel in terms of attention to detail but not when anxiety levels get too high. Of course, as a manager you wouldn't have access to such detail, but understanding that anxiety is in the loop here is a small inferential leap, even if you only look at Janis' underperformance.

So how do you manage someone like this woman, who possesses so many gifts and great potential but isn't delivering it to the group? You might imagine the trouble a Sword could have in managing Janis effectively. To a Sword manager, Janis' horsepower alone should make her self-confident. It doesn't, but a Sword would be likely to admire her idea-crunching power and make the assumptive leap that her intellect would necessarily lead to confidence. And Swords are speedy; they get on task and push quickly to the end. A Sword manager would likely be very impatient with Janis; her work is excellent, but it's always late. She would likely be seen as unreliable and be the recipient of exasperated verbal admonishments.

And what if her boss is a Shield, like Janis? A Shield manager (possessing coping strategies similar to Janis) might err on the side of being overly empathetic and compassionate with Janis to the detriment of her productivity or even her belief in herself. Relating to anxious people as if they are wounded is counterproductive. Doing so underscores their worrisome, self-critical natures, leaving them weakened and feeling even more deficient. They need to be understood, not babied. And alternatively, a Shield manager very well might find herself angry with Janis (we often react negatively to qualities we see in others that we do not like in ourselves).

Whether her manager is a Shield or Sword, there are a few things a manager who has identified Janis as a Shield might do to personalize and sharpen their communication with her and make the interactions more effective.

Using respect and transparency, the goal of a managerial communication should be to enhance positive motivation toward a jointly held goal. You want to be pleased with your report's work product and they, too, want to be pleased with it themself. Toward that end, a conversation between Janis and her manager might look something like this:

"I just read through this and I find your work to be excellent. Clearly, you're very gifted. The only note I have is that, once again, you turned it in nearly a week late, holding up other members of the team. I don't know if anyone told you, but we all noticed. Janis, I was disappointed. This has become a pattern—thoughtful work but invariably late. You're obviously too capable to be pleased with these time frames. It makes me wonder if you're too critical of yourself and that maybe because of that, these projects take longer than they should."

Armed with her Inderal, Janis responds in an unwavering voice, "Beginning any project makes me really nervous. I do what I used to do in school, which is wait until the last minute and then work like crazy to get it done. And then once I finally get it started, I keep changing it over and over again. I'm never satisfied, even when I finally turn projects in."

"I thought it might be something like that," her manager might say. "This next assignment I'm giving you shouldn't take more than a week. Let's try a little experiment here. I want you to start on this tomorrow, send me a rough draft of where you are by Wednesday, and then have the finished draft on my desk by Friday. Remember, nothing is perfect. Nothing. Don't let trying to make it perfect get in the way of your finishing. And Janis, you might try giving yourself a little encouragement along the way and a little less of the

judgment. We all need that from time to time. You're a very valuable member of our team and I want you to remember that."

Let's take a closer look at this simple snippet of dialogue between Janis and her manager. It is far richer than it may appear, for
this sort of conversation hits Shields like Janis at five sweet spots
(the more the better).

SWEET SPOT 1: Rich, authentic feedback. As you will recall,
Shields are used to responding to real changes in real time and are
highly responsive to those changes. As this relates to Janis' work product, those changes are the information provided by the richness of
the feedback loop. This constructive, "mixed" review provides her
with some very specific reactions and critique, which all Shields
thrive upon.

SWEET SPOT 2: Stimulating a harm avoidance alert. The tardiness comment and using a word like "disappointed" bumps up the
anxiety around completion and acts as a powerful motivator by activating any Shield's harm avoidance system. Emotionally laden
words like "disappointed" should never be used as a manipulation,
but they are helpful as an authentic and appropriate comment.
Chronic tardiness *is* a danger to Janis' career and issuing this alert
is constructive.

SWEET SPOT 3: Pointing out the causal connection between perfectionism and procrastination. As described, the combination of
perfectionism and procrastination is a common vulnerability for
some Shields. When these issues are present, Shields are aware of
every perceived flaw or imperfection and can feel shame around
their presence. Often, they are unaware of how their fear of imperfection leads to procrastination. Simply talking about it
without judgment can be helpful. This kind of dialogue sets the
stage for a deeper understanding of the "tardiness" and, even
more important, it communicates an understanding of its causal
roots—perfectionism.

SWEET SPOT 4: Collaboration. Having identified the cause of her
lateness, the manager becomes a collaborator and ally in Janis'
struggle with an overzealous critic. But beyond that, her manager

has provided Janis a strategy to counter the impact of her perfectionism. Encouragement is powerful on its own, but the manager has also activated an underdeveloped aspect of Janis' relationship with herself. Janis was asked to try being less judgmental and more affirming. She was also given a strategy that short-circuits her perfectionism by not allowing her the indulgence of time. Janis needs to learn that she doesn't need more time, but to use time more effectively.

SWEET SPOT 5: Awakening reward sensitivity. "Thoughtful work," "gifted," and "valuable member of the team" were comments that provided Janis a positive assessment of her work product and team value. Shields tend to have muted reward sensitivity. By communicating these earned words of praise, you awaken the possibility of her being motivated by reward instead of the avoidance of punishment. The acknowledgment of her strengths and her value to the team may make her a little more reward sensitive over time.

Let's shift our focus. Now we would like to talk about another underperforming employee—someone who is a Sword. But first, let's review some of the things we know about Swords and what motivates them. Because Swords are drawn to stimulation to compensate for too little natural arousal, they are easily distracted. Why? Because the stimulus value of moving to something new is greater than the value of staying focused on something more familiar, particularly a task that requires attention to detail and concentration. What else do we know? Swords can have a hard time delaying gratification for the same reasons. Swords also tend to be more optimistic, a dynamic that cuts both ways. Optimism is a plus interpersonally or when you are in sales mode. But it can be a negative when in a fulfillment mode where results trump heightened expectations (the proof is in the pudding kind of thing, not the rosy promise). You also know Swords are reward sensitive. Because of that, they tend to be more tolerant of risk and less sensitive to possible punishment and negative outcomes. This dynamic and their optimism is what makes them vulnerable to making false positive errors (overweighing the possibility of positive results).

Reward sensitivity and optimism can lead us to seeing things as potentially more beneficial and as less dangerous than they in fact are. Decisions made with this mindset can lead us to saying yes when saying no would have been more prudent.

You may remember Chris from chapter 5 and how he received a less than positive note in his annual review. Like Janis, Chris, too, has considerable potential but continues to underperform, according to not only his expectations but also those of his manager.

His manager gave him this mixed review:

> Chris has great, unrealized potential. Brimming with optimism and an infectious smile, he warms the room with his appearance, making those around him feel seen and appreciated. Willing to take on extra projects, his enthusiasm sadly isn't accompanied by follow-through. Chris overpromises and underdelivers.

As you may recall, Chris was upset. What he didn't tell us until much later was that his manager let him know that his delays had caused "serious downstream delays" and something to the effect of, "You're on thin ice here. This is a warning."

While we don't doubt that the review was accurate or that the manager intended to be helpful, we do think that she could have given much more beneficial feedback if she knew that Chris was a Sword and had taken his particular brain type tendencies into consideration. She could have had a conversation with him that would have been more helpful and that better served both their goals.

Let us give you a little deeper backstory on Chris. He was one of those kids who would have scarfed down that marshmallow as soon as the experimenter left the room. While Chris learned to read early, his comprehension of the material lagged far behind. In grade school he was prescribed Concerta (a non-amphetamine stimulant), and by junior high school he was taking Adderall (an amphetamine and stronger stimulant). He continued using the Adderall while he was in college for all-nighters before tests. Like many Swords, his life is replete with unfinished projects, the latest of which are an exercise bike still in its unopened crate in the garage and a fence he tore down and promised his wife he'd replace. He lives in a world of believed intentions and interests, passionately engaged and easily discarded.

So how might Chris' manager have reviewed him in a more constructive way? We are suggesting something like the following that takes into consideration his brain type: "Chris, everybody loves your ebullient personality. Face-to-face, you're charming, always on point, and we all come away confident in the timelines you promise. But looking at you on paper is a very different picture. You leave important projects uncompleted or orphaned, and blown timelines have led to some costly delays. I think you make a real contribution here, but based simply on the empirical results, you're not irreplaceable. That said, we really want you to succeed. You're working on six different projects now, a lot of balls to keep in the air. As far as I'm concerned, all of these projects have the same relative weight and priority. Off the top of your head, which is the most interesting and which is the most tedious? OK, I want you to put your time and energy into that boring one. We're going to talk next week and you can tell me the progress you've made. You excel in the idea department, but follow-through and struggling with the details are what give the ideas their real value. I want you to assign short-, medium-, and long-term goals and time frames to each of your projects. Be realistic, not optimistic, because when we meet each week I'll expect you to meet them. I'm looking for you to stay focused here, Chris. I'm not sure how you work, although I'm sure you know that all the research on multitasking suggests it's not effective."

How is this feedback both helpful to Chris as well as serving the company goals?

1. Addressing focus/distractibility issues. Identifying and commenting on a real problem can be of value, especially when the message is delivered in an understanding way.

Chris certainly knows he's not a detail guy and is distract-ible. Having his manager partner with him and offer possible solutions can be empowering. Swords love work-ing on projects where they get the most bang for their buck. Those tasks that they see as tedious and boring are the ones they typically place last in the queue. This man-ager might also have reminded Chris that working on the more boring projects first might be helpful because the more interesting projects could be used as rewards for get-ting through the ones that are less personally engaging.

2. Tempering optimism with realism. Reminding Chris to be realistic as opposed to optimistic in terms of his timelines alerts him to the downside of his wishful expectations.

3. Pointing out the possible negative consequences of his shortcomings. It's dangerous to overestimate your secu-rity and deny potential threats to it. This manager doesn't need to mince words. Chris should know he has some se-rious deficiencies. Most often, Shields have one eye open to what might come along and be harmful to them. But as a Sword, Chris tends to be relatively insensitive to possible damaging repercussions and might very well need that re-minder of the negative consequences to keep him on task. On the upside, his manager also tells him that she wants him to succeed. Moreover, she has some concrete steps he can take and a timeline for completing them.

4. Providing feed-forward guidance. The most important communication this manager could give Chris would be to provide him with specific feed-forward guidance. Swords frequently underestimate the length of time projects take to complete, say yes to taking on too many, and then feel guilty for letting their promises go unmet. And, of course, when we feel guilty, we often feel angry at the person at-tached to those unpleasant feelings. This manager's explicit

directive and a set time for completion gives Chris something to focus on with very clear boundaries.

While none of these things will necessarily ensure Chris' success,
they can go a long way toward providing him the understanding
and structure in which Swords flourish, increasing the probabilities.
An important win-win for both parties.

Managing Up

So, how do you manage up? How much thoughtful intentionality
do you bring to your relationship with your boss? How can understanding your boss' brain chemistry help you? Think about it. Are
they a Sword or a Shield? By giving this some careful thought, you
may pick up some dynamics that would be helpful in bettering this
relationship.

When Your Boss Is a Sword. Susan is a product development executive at a large technology company. She reports directly to Blaine,
who heads the department. Recently, Susan came into our office
steaming. She'd left plenty of time to finish her meeting with Blaine
and drive over, but he'd made her late. She'd been early as usual for
their weekly face-to-face and yet one more time had heard: "He's
just gone for a coffee and will be right back." "Twenty minutes later
is not right back," she complained. "One of these days I'm going to
show up twenty minutes late and he'll be right on time."

Over the next hour, we heard enough from Susan to know that
her boss was difficult in ways he would have trouble understanding
or acknowledging himself. She wasn't the only one grumbling behind his back. According to Susan, most of those who reported to
him had their own "Blaine stories" they shared among themselves,
each less complimentary than the other.

"I get him," she said. "You know I get him." And she did. Susan,
as a Sword herself, recognized many of her own tendencies in
Blaine—but she was quick to point out that he was worse because

he was so "entitled and self-centered." Our job was to encourage her to use the tools she already had—her understanding of Blaine's brain chemistry. But first, we had to help her get out of her own way.

If Susan was going to manage her relationship with Blaine in a more effective way, she would have to get beyond the anger that bordered on contempt for the man. Being a Sword, Susan was prone to directing her anger outward. The truth is, she had plenty to be angry about. They had gone through two series of layoffs in the past three years. It wasn't just the two critical teammates she lost in this last round of cuts; it was his lack of understanding that the workload had increased, with all her reports having to take on additional responsibilities. To make matters worse, Blaine required her team to attend his biweekly book club meetings, which, by team consensus, were useless and took time away from tasks critical to their production schedules. And the kicker was his using the team as an in-house focus group to help him fine-tune a seminar he was developing on "team motivation." The irony of it all exasperated them. Their plates were already full, and these meetings (largely unnecessary in her mind) just added to their burden. Then there was Blaine's showboating. He would boast about his negotiating prowess, insisting upon getting involved in the company's dealings with prominent influencers he found of interest and celebrity endorsements. Susan and other members of her team thought he was giving away the store. Susan came to think of him as self-involved and as a schmoozer. While he was in the commissary chatting, everybody else was working, with Susan doing her own work and much of his. Yes, she was in a rage.

Anger, however justified, gets in the way of being smart. Blaine was one of those political savants who had evidently been agreeable to all of the right people. He believed himself to be bulletproof and had a lot of influence at the company. The pandemic and ensuing production shutdown foreshadowed yet another round of cuts. Susan found herself being less discreet about her feelings toward Blaine and knew her brewing anger was a threat to her personally. She could be the next one on the chopping block.

Instead of waiting to see how things shook out with the next round of layoffs, as she had done in the past, Susan decided that this time she wasn't going to sit around. She was going to try to shape the results. As a fellow Sword, she recognized Blaine's penchant for using feed forward. Susan went to him with a detailed strategy to save the designer in her group she felt was on the bubble. "I think there is a way where we can save Alan," she told Blaine. "With the new catalog, we need more people, not fewer, and I have a plan." By the end of their discussion, Blaine had co-opted her plan as his own, only making minor tweaks to the bullet points Susan laid out.

Blaine stopped her in the hall one day and told her he was thinking about asking everyone to read *Emotional Intelligence*, to be discussed in an upcoming staff meeting. When she said, "You mean reread," she could see by the look on his face this was not a good direction to go in. It was all Susan could do not to say something like, "Do you know how old that book is?" Instead, Susan said, "Interesting choice, Blaine. Makes me think of another one. You're a big-picture, generalist kind of thinker. There's a newish book called *Range* by David Epstein. It's about the ability to see convergence, how the pieces fit together, versus being a specialist." When she got the email asking her team to read *Range*, she smiled quietly to herself. By empowering Blaine, she'd empowered herself. She knew he liked ways to shine as much as she did.

Susan's one-on-one meetings with Blaine have long become constrained by the righteousness of judgment. Judgment narrows information flow, resulting in our learning less and less over time that's new and valuable. This inverse relationship between information and judgment is stunting. We suggested a little experiment to Susan. We asked that instead of bringing assumptions and judgments to her meetings with Blaine, she bring a mindset of curiosity and amusement.

"He's not amusing," she retorted.

"But isn't that itself amusing? That someone who sees himself as charming is lacking the very quality he prides himself as having?"

"I think it's pathetic."

"And so it may be. But isn't there something amusing about bearing witness to the blindness of his actions?"

"I see an insecure little boy showing off for the girls and crashing into a table of glasses."

"Exactly."

The most important thing Susan did to better manage her relationship with Blaine was transform her anger and disrespect for him into much less toxic emotions. And all from the perspective of understanding Blaine's likely brain type.

Over the next couple of weeks, we did a few empathy exercises with Susan, with the goal of lowering the temperature of her anger and perhaps helping her gain a little window into her own tendency to externalize blame. The first exercise we had her do was designed to elicit curiosity. Her task was to find out three personal things from Blaine she didn't know. Even though she told us that she didn't care and wasn't interested in learning anything personal about him, she agreed to try just to humor us. Susan found out that Blaine was born in Nebraska, played football in high school, and loved Mexican food.

The second thing we had Susan do was share a personal story of her own with Blaine. She asked what had drawn him to the tech sector and then told him that her father had wanted to work at IBM in the early days but got drafted and spent time in the Navy. Blaine came back with details of his own. She learned that Blaine had a superstar older brother who died when he was nine years old and that his father had been a failed actor before managing a paint store. This man was no longer simply her boss, a blowhard, and an implacable foe; he was complex and all too human.

Next, we had Susan practice becoming a little more dialed into how she was feeling and understanding why she felt what she did. She described how she would simply think about Blaine and become stressed and annoyed. We had her jot down her feelings when things came up and reflect on them. And as she continued to talk to Blaine on a more personal level, she reported that her feelings had started to change. She talked about a conversation she'd had with Blaine after a meeting when the others had left the room. She watched him push a box of donuts farther out of reach and found herself telling him that she had struggled with weight when she was a girl. He listened attentively and related a story of his own when as a teenager he had severe acne and how devastating it had been for him.

It's not clear that Susan thinks any more highly of Blaine, and she will probably continue to find things he says and does irritating, but she is no longer quite so angry. She sees his palpable insecurity and neediness. By humanizing him, she's managed to humanize herself, becoming a bit more accepting. By not seeing him simply as the "other" and holding him at a distance, Susan found herself having gained some growing trust. Increasingly, Blaine has sought her out for her thoughts on how best to pitch keeping the group intact. With a shrug, she told us they'd run all the numbers the other night over margaritas and Mexican food, saying, "He's really not a bad guy."

When Your Boss Is a Shield. Shield bosses present a whole host of very different obstacles to having an effective relationship with them. While they are likely to admire optimism, they are often less likely to reward it, suspecting some important data is missing that might present some danger. Less swayed by enthusiasm and more by close attention to detail, they are moved by proofs instead of promises. In that they tend to think more slowly (and accurately) than their Sword cousins, their decisions can be frustratingly slow. Having a "reactive" coping style, they are less interested in what worked yesterday and more in what will work in today's changing conditions. Whether they let you see it or not, it's important to remember that Shields tend to be anxious. And while it's certainly not your job to calm them, it's to your advantage to have your actions prove to be reassuring. We all tend to put a little of ourselves into how we see others, and given that Shields can delay gratification pretty easily, those expectations will likely be applied to you as well. Motivated more by the avoidance of potential harm, Shield bosses won't take kindly to any actions on your part that rip away the cover from their backsides. And last, it's important to understand Shield bosses' risk profile. Being risk averse, they will always take the smaller gain to avoid the larger loss.

These were some of the things we discussed with April when she came in, concerned about the future of her job. April really wanted her job. No, she needed it. As a single mom, she had no room for error. She'd worked for Karen for the last four years developing the children's division of a once successful party-planning company. The pandemic and economic downturn crushed their business. Karen had always been parsimonious, and when the lockdown came she hunkered down. She put all the equipment into storage, got a small-business loan from the government in order to keep paying her employees a reduced salary, and planned on waiting things out. The weeks passed, the money slowly ran out, and April was on unemployment.

Karen had just reopened her business when April first came to see us. April was provisionally rehired, dependent upon her being able to reinvigorate the children's division. Unfortunately, the rebound was nowhere near what they had hoped it would be, and even many of their most loyal customers had drifted away. April didn't need anyone to tell her that her job was on the line and that staying with the status quo would lead to only one thing—being unemployed once again.

To keep her job, April knew she would have to get creative and that would cost real time and energy. And Karen would have to buy into her ideas. It hadn't taken much thinking to identify Karen as a Shield and that could be a problem. If April knew anything at all about Karen it was that she didn't like to take chances. And her risk aversion wasn't any secret, for she pointed to it as one of the biggest reasons her company had survived over the years. Rather than throwing up her hands, April got busy. She devised two strategies: one a business development blueprint and the second a plan to get Karen to go along with it.

What did April know about Shields and Karen that would be of help here? April knew Karen was really good with numbers and paid very close attention to details. She knew Karen was anxious. In better days, they would share a little gallows humor about feeling overwhelmed with the buzz of life. She also knew that Karen tended to hold on to negative impressions and that meant she would have but a single shot at this.

April got to work. As much as she wanted to let Karen in on her ideas, she held herself back. To make this work, everything had to be already in place, for if there were any cracks Karen would find them and it would be all over. There were never any redos with Karen.

April got her cousin Eric to help her construct a digital platform that combined a Zoom event with guest-sent party swag boxes and TikTok videos. For the face-to-face parties, she found an interesting unused space she could rent by the hour for laser tag and paintball parties. Both of her strategies were accompanied by a marketing plan, a budget, and projections. April knew Karen would overthink every detail and try to take it apart. To counter this, she would do the overthinking. She would be overprepared. Over several nights, she went through her verbal pitch, stopping to jot down each question she anticipated Karen asking. Then she did the same for her marketing plan, budget, and projections. On the night before the big meeting, it was well past midnight when she turned the light out.

She awoke early having dreamed of three more possible questions Karen might ask. After writing down the answers, she knew she was ready.

"I kept putting myself in Karen's place, and when I did, I knew just how she was feeling and what to say that would be reassuring," she told us a couple of days later. "I was really excited, but I kept reminding myself to keep 'risk averse' in my mind and it really helped. I don't think there was any detail she didn't ask about and I was glad I did my homework and then some."

"And so?" we asked.

April continued, "I can tell you this: she said that when I showed her that if we didn't grab this space, someone else would, she started to take it much more seriously. Can you believe it? I was shocked. I was prepared to get shot down, and I didn't. She didn't say yes, but just getting beyond no with her is huge. What she told me was that she was going to run all the numbers by the accountant and would let me know."

Even when we use all the right tools in all the rights ways, it's not a lock that things will go our way. When Karen got back to April, her answer was no. She didn't feel comfortable investing in the fleshing out of the digital platform or the at-risk marketing costs incurred in giving the products a try. A week or two later, April and Karen parted ways amicably. April was once again jobless. But there is a postscript to this story. Learning of April's availability, Karen's chief competitor asked her to come in to talk. She went in armed not only with her natural talent but also with a detailed plan for what a children's division might look like. Maybe this time all of April's hard work will come to fruition.

Managing Across

For teams to function effectively, members require clarity, collaboration, and cooperation. Managing across can be tricky. Humans, be they Swords or Shields, can have important control issues. For Shields, these dynamic issues are born in anxiety and the need to regulate uncomfortable feelings that can have little to do with the work product. Swords come to their control tendencies by way of their impatience. They tend to use fast, reflexive thinking in their decision-making and can have little tolerance for those choosing to make decisions in a slower, more deliberative fashion. The fact that Swords' decisions tend to be less accurate than those of Shields can be a source of annoyance. As you will recall, Swords flourish in situations where past is present and dynamics are predictable. Because of their reactive nature and cranky amygdalae, Shields perform best in changing, unpredictable circumstances, leading them to put voice to "but what if" questions. Such questions are likely to garner an eye roll from a Sword who values alacrity over what can seem likely useless musings.

Clashes can occur over issues of just how much information is necessary to make a thoughtful decision. Pulling the trigger is often the last thing a Shield wants to do. As they are naturally cautious and avoidant, it's much more difficult for them to say yes than no. Saying no means that they retain the option to collect more information, leaving them feeling less exposed to risking a mistake. Swords, in contrast, feel enlivened by making bold decisions.

While Shields often envy Swords' cheery, optimistic natures, it is hard for them not to express their built-in pessimism. It's certainly not that they want to be downers; it's simply that it can be hard for them to contain their negative thoughts.

Bottom line? Shields get itchy with decisions and actions that Swords find comfortable, and vice versa. And remember, this all spins around our relationship with arousal—Shields trying to tamp it down and Swords to ramp it up. In the midst of all those quotidian interactions, comments, and decisions is the unseen burble of our brain chemistry at work. All those microconversations that may appear rational and reasonable on the surface are a little more complicated than that underneath. In between the lines of what we say and do are the invisible brain chemical fingerprints of each of us as we try to regulate our feelings, being subtly bullied by our unique relationship with arousal.

So how do we work in teams when our brain chemicals push us around, where there are no power differentials to suppress or cajole our brain chemistry leanings? The answer is somewhat haphazardly. To bring a little more clarity to the situation, we propose the following: First, make a list of the coworkers you have most contact with and who are important to getting your job done. Maybe you've already done that, even made your guesses as to which are Swords and which Shields. None of the names on this list should be reporting relationships.

For each person on the list, put either a plus or a minus indicating that the relationship has elements of tension, misunderstandings, or conflicts (+) or the relationship is typically easy and issue-free (-). Now throw out all the names with the minus.

Let's take a look at your new, leaner list. Are more of these people similar to your brain type or to its opposite? Sometimes working closely with someone quite similar can be unnerving, particularly if we harbor negative feelings about ourselves. For each person on the list, jot down some quick thoughts as to what the issues are that you have.

Now comes the hard part, requiring great personal honesty and a bit of insight. Going down your list, write "yes" or "no" as to whether or not you can see the issues you've observed as possibly being related to one or another of the brain chemical traits you're now familiar with. For those on the "no" side, look again. Remember: honesty and insight. Could it be your brain chemistry that's at play? If you still come up empty, maybe we just have to concede that there are difficult people out there and some personality types that can be challenging.

We hope now your list is shorter still with only those names with a plus and "yes" after them. So, what do you do? The most important step is to ask yourself this question about the issues you have with this person: "Is there some way that I can not take these issues personally? That I can see them as an unintended consequence of this person's brain chemistry?" We've found that there is great freedom when you can answer yes, for answering yes means it's about them, who they are, and not about you. It means that the behavior is not something that they necessarily intend; it's just the way they've learned to be. They don't do those things to annoy you; they do them unconsciously and without intention.

Understanding the reflexive nature of these glitches goes a long way toward reducing irritation and easing frayed nerves. Reminding yourself that these people act in the ways they do because of their brain chemistry can free you from interpreting their actions as being insensitive to you and your style of working. Of course, putting this to work takes practice, and there is a learning curve. One technique we've found helpful when you feel the tensions rising is to give yourself a secret smile and think, Oh, they are being such a Sword [or Shield]. What comes along with this is a little dab of compassion, the same you would like extended to you at those moments or around the issues when you are deep in the cups of your own itchiness around arousal.

But it is more than just feeling less thwarted, frustrated, or irritated by them; it's that the psychological distance you create by getting them, seeing them, and understanding them at a deeper level allows you to use everything you've learned so far. You are armed with a powerful tool, a lens through which to see what drives behavior, giving you a deeper understanding of yourself and those around you. Putting this understanding into action will make all of your relationships at work more effective.

Perhaps the biggest prize of all here is that the acceptance you give to the foibles in others has the payback of feeling a more generous acceptance of yourself. But before you get complacent, this personal understanding and acceptance has an obligation—you have to pay it forward. Acceptance is not passive. Acceptance is the prerequisite for meaningful action. No one knows the things you need to work on in the detailed and intimate way you do. We didn't call this book *Override* for nothing. Look at those things you do to modulate discomfort that may create problems for you and issues for others. See if you can identify the moment you become aware of the feelings that push you in one direction or the other. Create a visual for yourself. Picture this moment as a V in the road ahead. One side leads to an action that you're used to. For example, if your tendency is to avoid, that's the reflex. If your tendency is to jump without careful thought, then that's the habit. Our habits are comfortable, but they aren't necessarily constructive or good for us. Challenge the habits you notice that don't optimize your gifts; override the reflex; try going down the less comfortable side of the V in the road for a change. Start with small moments where you notice your indulgence in the comfort of the familiar and work your way up to more important ones. Dare yourself to toughen up. Take the smarter action, not the more comfortable one.

We've found that these less reflexive and more intentional actions really pay off in managing across relationships. Clarity of purpose should be the engine that animates your decisions, not your brain chemistry. Thoughtful intentionality can lead to intelligent decisions. Slavishly indulging in your brain chemicals cannot.

You might consider taking a moment here and thinking about the following: What have you learned about how you manage your relationships at work? How can you apply what you know about both yourself and the person to whom you report in a way that will allow you to be more effective in that relationship? We've found writing this down to be helpful to the translation of general thoughts into specifics. If you have people reporting to you, what have you learned that you can use to make yourself a more effective manager? A better leader? Again, be as specific as you can. Your reports don't fit a single mold. They are likely some combination of Shields and Swords. Applying this angle of understanding the likely brain chemistry of your reports, what changes can you make to better manage those relationships? And what have you learned about your peer-to-peer relationships? Even jotting down a sentence or two about each of these important interactions will help create a clearer mindset for dealing with them in the future.

We've asked you to do some serious work here, work that requires inferential thinking and great personal understanding and honesty. You won't get much of value simply speed-reading through this material. The most valuable nuggets, the ones you can make most practical use of, can only be harvested by examining each of these critical relationships carefully. Put in the time required to do this and your investment will pay off handsomely. While this kind of thoughtfulness will allow you to more effectively manage important relationships, the big win is in better managing the relationship you have with yourself. We all like to feel in control. Real control is the freedom to make decisions that are healthy, constructive, and rational.

CHAPTER SEVEN

Romantic Love: Lust, Longing, and All That Jazz

How Lurking below Our Conscious Awareness Lies a Web of Evolutionary Survival and Reproductive Strategies That Shape Our Patterns of Attraction and Laced into That Teeming Mix Are the Indelible Influences of Our Brain Chemistry Imbalances

WHO HASN'T EXPERIENCED THE GIDDY fixation on a potential romantic partner, with its wishes and high hopes? And who hasn't made a few mistakes with new love along the way? Who hasn't been hurt? It has happened to all of us. Attraction spins off the most powerful of human emotions. It can be baffling, wondrous, intense, or heartbreakingly painful. And even to the most sophisticated, it's complicated. Not only is it complicated; the most basic causal roots that stimulate and sustain attraction aren't available to us at a conscious level. These unconscious forces determine not only who we will be attracted to but also whether the attraction will be fleeting or sustained. And interacting with these gut reactions are the dynamics of our personal brain chemistry type. We don't guide our attractions and feelings of love; we are guided by them. Nowhere does nature provide more of an instinctual launch to our feelings and actions than it does with attraction. But rather than making us smarter, it can make us dumber—at least for a while. To gain some control, the trick is to understand our reflexive reactions and make them more conscious. Of course, by doing so we take away some of the mystery of attraction and desire, but by becoming more conscious of our hidden pushes and pulls we are better able to find and retain happier and more enduring relationships.

All living things have a life force, a will to survive. You see it in the scurry of a frightened spider or the frenzied disturbance of an anthill. You also see it in the clash of antlers of rutting deer and in the besotted words scrawled tenderly in every love letter ever written, for built into each and every one of us is an urge beyond personal survival, an urge designed to ensure the survival of the species. Survival is about reproduction and nature leaves little to chance. Mother Nature ensures our compliance by following two fundamental rules: make things easier rather than harder and make them pleasant instead of painful. In fact, the easier and more pleasant, the higher the degree of success. *Ease* is accomplished by making something habitual and unconscious and *pleasant* is cemented in place by tying in the brain's reward and chemical systems. While we think of attraction as a romantic construct, its foundations are anything but. We don't intend attraction; we notice it. What could be easier? Observation requires no effort to get there. And to add a guarantee to success, romantic attraction is rewarded by an immensely pleasurable sexual finish, ensuring that all who get there want to return again and again.

THE EXPERIENCE OF attraction weaves through every great love story, inspiring the emotional wallop of countless books, movies, and love songs. The power of these stories is related to our identification with them, how they make us feel in raw and exhilarating ways, reminding us of our own entanglements with love. Romantic actions seemingly play out in sweaty palms and eager kisses, but beneath the roiling emotions is a system of strategies designed by evolutionary forces animated by hormones and neurotransmitters that dictate the ancient ritual of human connection. Unrelated to anything remotely romantic, these strategies obey the unconscious dynamics of sexual selection, reproduction, and survival of the species.

So, what exactly is attraction? Some chemical X factor that you can't quite describe but certainly know when you feel it? Some sense of having discovered a long-lost soul mate? A potent sexual desire? A promise of safety, status, security? The connection to a sense of inexplicable joy and thoughts of tomorrow? Attraction is an amalgam of bits and pieces of all these feelings and more. It's what makes us want to have babies. Its roots run deep and are embedded in the whisperings of our ancestral past.

Attraction: Gender-Related Sexual Selection

Sexual selection is an aspect of natural selection in which more successful genes are passed on generation by generation. This isn't a new concept. In the nineteenth century, an evolutionary biologist conducted a study in which he examined birth, marriage, and death records of nearly six thousand people born between 1760 and 1849 in small Finnish villages. The study looked at four aspects of life that influence survival and reproduction:

1. How many live beyond the age of fifteen

2. How many get married and how many do not

3. How many marriages a person has

4. How many children are born to each marriage

About half the people died before the age of fifteen (of course, this was before the dawn of modern medicine). So, 50 percent had traits that didn't favor natural selection and didn't pass their genes along to the next generation. Of the remaining half, around six hundred didn't marry and had no children. Scratch them from the pool as well. The number of offspring had by those in the remaining group varied between zero and seventeen. Some had more than one partner. With one partner the average was 5 children, and with four partners the number increased to 7.5 children. Men benefited more than women in terms of having more children because they tended to remarry younger women. Now, there is no way to know exactly which traits were selected, but the genes of the roughly twenty-five hundred people who successfully reproduced and passed theirs along most certainly had some differences from those whose gene pools were discontinued.

Those twenty-five hundred people would likely not have reproduced their DNA had they not been aware of their attraction to their mates and if these attractions didn't enhance and reinforce the sexual experience. Would we have human reproduction without attraction? Maybe not. Surely, attraction is not an accident, any more than are our food preferences. So why exactly do we get together? There have been many theories attempting to explain why humans are drawn to mate. Freud and Jung thought that when choosing partners people were attracted to aspects or (for Jung) archetypes they found in their opposite-sexed parent. Others have suggested we look for similarities (values, attitudes, worldviews) in our mates or that we are drawn to characteristics or attributes in our partners that are complementary to the ways in which we see ourselves. Still other theories posit that attraction is transactional in terms of an exchange of valuable resources.

Of these various theories, seeking similarities garners the greatest empirical support but doesn't explain much other than the comfort of the familiar. What a growing body of science tells us is that we all respond to a sexual/reproductive urge and that we are guided by some gender-specific, hardwired strategies to achieve those goals.

One well-documented theory that has confirming data across dozens of species links sexual attraction/selection to parental investment. Across species, females invest more in their offspring and are choosier, while males invest less, are less choosy, and compete more openly for females. Women, of course, make a disproportion-ate investment in childbearing and child-rearing. And because of this investment, they are drawn to men who seem most likely to make a similar commitment to shared parenthood. Men become as discerning in their mate selection as women when they choose to invest in marriage with an eye toward having a family.

But we've gotten way ahead of our story here. Let's set the stage and tell you about a couple we know—Cate and Charlie. While we've chosen them to explore the dynamics of attraction, we might very well have chosen Charlie and John or Cate and Jane, for the underlying dynamics are similar. The human urgings of sexual de-sire and intimate connections are artifacts of survival and reproduction. The "supporting motivations" that nature devised are what we are conscious of, whether or not they are attached to a wish for reproduction. Same-sex attraction carries the instinctual motivators for reproduction even though those unions don't pro-duce progeny in and of themselves. We chose a heterosexual couple simply because they most typify the forces of attraction and its unconscious goal—reproduction.

Getting back to Cate and Charlie, dark and intimate, the restau-rant sits cantilevered over the Pacific Ocean. Charlie is at a window table set with candles, a white tablecloth, and a bottle of very nice Chablis costing a bit more than his budget affords. Charlie found Cate on Bumble and this was the night of their first face-to-face meeting. He'd arrived early and ordered the wine, and stood when he saw her walk through the door. Upon seeing Charlie, Cate smiled shyly and made her way to the table. He took her hand for a moment and pulled out her chair for her. Beyond the window, silver waves rolled in, stirring the ocean floor under a moonlit sky. You get the picture—pretty romantic.

Both Cate and Charlie have anticipated this moment, each bringing their own set of secret hopes and expectations, fears and insecurities. Will there be chemistry? Will it be reciprocated? Will they want to see each other again? Charlie had gone out of his way to try to ensure the right mood and Cate had dressed just a shade more daringly than usual. How this plays out is as modern as digital technology and as ancient as the primeval forest.

We can't peek in and listen to their conversation, but whatever it is on the surface, this meeting is about one thing they are likely not talking about: reproduction. Cate and Charlie are young, but even if they were meeting far beyond their reproductive years the echoes of unborn children would be still be a powerful shaper in their feelings and actions.

The impulse to find a mate is universal. And while we think of this in the context of long-term commitments, the sexual impulse and the patterns of attraction that fuel it can often be short-term. In the United States, about half of all marriages end in a divorce. And what about infidelity? Estimates of adultery for both men and women vary between around 25 and 75 percent. These numbers don't include the numerous sexual experiences men and women have before entering a committed relationship. Of course, Cate and Charlie aren't thinking about any of this as they move through the beginnings of getting to know each other. But as they are getting to know each other, let's take a look at some of the science that describes the dynamics of the unconscious strategies that may be at play between the lines of their conversation.

Across cultures, studies show that women (more than men) tend to be drawn to potential mates who are ambitious, are educated, and show a potential for earning capacity. Even in the recent past, men controlled more of the resources, but what changes might we notice in these times of shifting social structure? Would parity in socioeconomic status change these preferential dynamics? Studies suggest not. Women *with* resources tend to be attracted to mates who are financially successful even more than do women *with fewer* resources. As a holdover from the past, these gender preferences remain despite changes in economic and educational equality. And what do men find most compelling? Despite the changes in gender equality, a woman's physical attractiveness is a stronger predictor of marriage than her IQ, educational level, or socioeconomic status.

So far, Charlie and Cate are batting a thousand. He likes the way she looks, and surely she made some unconscious note of the bottle of wine he bought and the mention of the school he went to, slipped neatly into the conversation.

Across cultures, men marry women who are younger than they are. With each divorce, men marry progressively younger women. On average, for the first marriage the discrepancy is three years, the second five years, and the third eight years. In case you're wondering, Charlie is thirty-one and Cate is twenty-eight.

Cate couldn't help but notice the expensive watch Charlie wore (the human equivalent of clashing rams' horns or the opulent flash of a peacock's tail). Studies show that a common tactic for men is to show off evidence of their money and status, while women place more emphasis on enhancing their appearance. With Cate's choice of wardrobe, both those boxes are checked. We are all beneficiaries of our mating instincts and wouldn't exist without them. To be successful in our ancestral past, women and men adopted different tactical approaches. And these strategies, while not processed consciously, are alive and operational today.

Attraction is a complex set of cofactors that serve natural selection. We experience these layered inclinations not as intentional interventions, but rather as noticed preferences. Such inclinations are designed to ensure a single goal: reproductive success. As you will remember, even those couples who don't want to have children carry with them the artifacts of childbearing: sexual desire and the desire to form intimate connections. Reproductive success is defined as passing along one's genes to an offspring healthy, fit, and nurtured enough to pass theirs along as well. To serve that goal, studies show that we tend to be drawn to potential partners who have comparable "mating value." Men and women with higher mating values tend to be pickier in their choices than do those possessing lower mating value. This, no doubt, serves a dual purpose: to avoid disappointment and heartache and not waste precious time.

Our bodies provide lots of help in nudging the process of connection along. We can easily see this at play in the animal kingdom.

When primates are in heat (estrus), it is pretty apparent. Apes check out the scent of females' backsides for evidence of ovulation and, in some species, there is a glaring visual cue provided by genital swelling. We know cats are ready to mate when they screech and spray their urine.

Humans do not broadcast their peak fertility and sexual readiness quite so blatantly. In humans, ovulation is concealed. Or is it?

While the evidence is still debatable, there do seem to be clues, however subtle, of changes—physical and behavioral—in a woman during her menstrual cycle that signal ovulation. Some studies show that women mid-cycle (ovulating) are drawn to more overtly masculine and aggressive men for short-term flings. And other studies suggest that mid-ovulation, not only are women more flirtatious and dress more provocatively but also the soft tissue of the face becomes more symmetrical and their skin changes, becoming more textured and rosier. At other points in their cycle, women prefer longer-term relationships with kinder, more conscientious men. Our ancestral past would suggest that masculine features and dominance over other men indicated greater genetic fitness. None of this, of course, is thought to be driven by conscious thought.

And what about men? In a study involving scent, men were asked to smell the T-shirts worn by young women who were either ovulating or at other points in their cycle. Results showed the men smelling the T-shirts that had been worn during ovulation exhibited higher levels of testosterone than those men smelling T-shirts worn by women during other times of their cycle. Testosterone levels in men are sensitive barometers of sexual interest and feelings of prowess and effectiveness. In heterosexual men, levels rise during a conversation with an attractive woman, remain the same or decrease during a conversation with another man, and plummet for a time after losing an athletic contest. Interestingly, testosterone also flags a bit when men move into committed relationships and then drops again after they have children.

Whether a woman's ovulation is entirely hidden or not, its relative opacity does have evolutionary value. Whereas women have no doubt about the men they've slept with, men can wonder about the paternity of the offspring of the women in their lives. In the evolutionary past, a woman might choose to mate with one man but point to another more suitable one as the father to better ensure the future of her child. These men would have to take the women's word at face value, believing they are the biological fathers of the children, and thus be motivated to stick around.

So, back to Cate and Charlie. She did take special care with what she was wearing to meet him. He clearly finds her attractive and is experiencing a bump up in testosterone. That feels good. There is probably no olfactory factor in the mix because the subtle changes in scent related to her cycle would be overpowered by the dabs of perfume she placed behind each ear. But what else might be playing out here?

Men are more likely to be interested in looking for short-term sexual partners than are women. In fact, when they are asked how many sexual partners they would ideally like to have over varying periods of time (from one month to a lifetime), men indicate they would like to have more sexual partners for each time interval than do women. Men are willing to have sexual experiences after knowing a woman for much shorter a time than are women. An interesting study using young and attractive male and female experimenters demonstrates this point. The experimenters approached students of the opposite sex on a college campus and posed one of three questions: 1) "Would you be willing to go on a date with me?" 2) "Would you be willing to come to my apartment?" 3) "Would you be willing to have sex with me?" Here's how the responses went: About half of both the men and women agreed to go on a date with the experimenter, but then the numbers diverged. Only 6 percent of the women said they would go back to the man's apartment and none of the women said they would go to bed with the man that night. Now let's look at how the men responded: 69 percent indicated their willingness to go back to the woman's apartment and 75 percent of the men said they would go to bed with a woman that same day.

What can we conclude here? Pretty much what we already know. Even though a man might be good-looking, women don't feel comfortable having sex until they know a good deal more about him. Would Charlie sleep with Cate this night after their dinner if she were willing? If he's like 75 percent of the other men, the answer is yes. Is this going to happen? Probably not. Before they agreed to get together for dinner, Cate and Charlie indicated their interest in a long-term relationship. For serious relationships, women and men tend to have roughly similar requirements and standards. And for women, these remain the same even for their short-term sexual partners, while men tend to be willing to drop their standards significantly for casual sexual flings.

Dropping Hormones and Brain Chemicals into the Mix

Helen Fisher, a longtime researcher on human bonding from Rutgers University, breaks this process into three categories, each with its attending hormones:

1. Lust—testosterone and estrogen

2. Attraction—dopamine, serotonin, and norepinephrine

3. Attachment—oxytocin and vasopressin

We all have testosterone and estrogen. Testosterone increases sexual desire in men as well as in women, and some women are more sexually aroused when they ovulate and estrogen release is at its highest. Some short-term relationships can be solely about lust without any particular real attraction or thoughts of the future.

Attraction is a more layered phenomenon than lust. When we are drawn to someone in a broader way than just the thought of a sexual encounter, the stakes go up. The experience of attraction is accompanied by the copious release of both dopamine and norepinephrine. The reward system in our brain lights up with activity and the anticipation of delight. Norepinephrine is released in a fight-or-flight reaction, activating and dialing up vigilance. When we feel attraction, we also can feel a sense of vulnerability and uncertainty. Are these strong feelings we are having reciprocated? Uncertainty, of course, is unnerving for some and exciting and challenging for others. And what about serotonin? Serotonin levels actually go down in the throes of an important attraction. This dialing down of the calming influences serotonin provides may be responsible for the overwhelming feelings of infatuation and obsession that can develop. The combined feelings of attraction and sexual arousal can also have another effect. The dominance of these feelings shuts down a valuable source of feedback, disconnecting the prefrontal cortex that regulates critical thinking and rational behavior. We certainly don't get smarter during the early stages of love, for the stronger these feelings and thoughts are, the more vulnerable we are to losing access to the part of the brain most important for critical thinking and good judgment.

The next neural system that gets engaged involves a deeper bonding and attachment. This is the system that feeds what we all think of as enduring love. The chemicals that help this process along are oxytocin and vasopressin. These hormones might be thought of as the yin and yang of love. While oxytocin is released during childbirth and breastfeeding, it is also expressed during sex, particularly when it is accompanied by attentiveness, tenderness, and affection. Where a dopamine release can feel pleasureful in an exciting and dramatic way, oxytocin follows a slower, more meandering path. It stimulates feelings of ease, contentment, and safety. To illustrate, let's take something as basic as "personal space." The average distance that strangers feel comfortable standing apart is approximately four feet (intimate partners and family members stand closer together). Two groups of men were given a nasal spray of oxytocin. One of these groups was comprised of men in committed relationships with women and the other group comprised of single men. Both groups went into a room where they encountered attractive women. Interacting with the women, the men in stable relationships stood significantly farther away from the women they were talking to than did the single men.

Vasopressin, which is also released in love relationships, provides a little different dynamic. While oxytocin signals trust, safety, and contentment, vasopressin signals something more akin to "mine." The experience of "mine," of course, broadcasts a reminder of the importance of the connection, but it also can stimulate proprietary feelings as well, including jealousy and possessiveness.

With our discussion of attachment, we've gotten ahead of our story again. Charlie and Cate are probably just now finishing their dessert. What's likely stirring is estrogen and testosterone as well as a release of dopamine and norepinephrine. The possibility of oxytocin and vasopressin will have to wait for future developments. Depending upon the degree of attraction, serotonin might turn out to be in short supply should they see each other again. Perhaps it's nature's way of adding adhesive to the bond, bringing it into sharp, intense focus by disabling the brakes at least momentarily.

Here's a pertinent study to illustrate the point: You have learned how imbalanced serotonin can make a person vulnerable to developing OCD. Researchers located a group of men and women who had been diagnosed with OCD, none of whom was taking any kind of serotonin-related medication (SSRI). The researchers then found another group of men and women who had recently fallen in love, as well as a third randomly selected control group of comparable composition. The researchers took measures of serotonin density and found that the unmedicated people suffering from OCD as well as those women and men just fallen in love had significantly *lower levels* of serotonin than did the members of the control group. Why would this be? you might wonder. Nature's object of attraction is reproduction, but reproduction alone doesn't ensure that genes get passed along successfully. Real success is only when the offspring is nurtured and cared for carefully enough to pass those genes along once again. And the likelihood of this is greatly enhanced when the parents are bonded to (dare we say even a bit obsessed with?) each other. Ensuring the importance of a love relationship in a person's mind is a surer accomplishment with depleted rather than a surfeit of serotonin. Having just fallen in love, we're probably not spinning on whether we locked the front door, but we may very well be engaging in a similar ruminative process starring our love partner. And, as you might imagine, those going into a love relationship with already-imbalanced levels of available serotonin are particularly affected (more about this later).

Our Microbiome and Genes at Play

Charlie slumped into the chair, propped a foot up on the coffee table, and began: "I never thought much about being alone before I met Cate. But now the thought of being without her feels inconceivable. It's like I met some missing part of myself. It's only been a couple of weeks, but with all the time we've spent together, I feel like I've known her my whole life. When I'm with her I feel totally alive. The feel of her skin beneath my fingers, the way she smells, the tiny hairs at the base of her neck all bring up the most tender feelings I've ever known. I don't usually talk like this, but then I don't usually feel like this. She's the last thing I think about as I go to sleep and the first thoughts I have when I wake up are about her. All I can say is that I've never felt so lit up and glad to be alive. What do you think?"

What did we think? Was this budding love or some passing enchantment? Were Charlie's words evidence of a relationship that was building the early fastenings that might lead to a connection, grounded and lasting? What we thought was, Whoa! We'd heard it all before, different names, slightly different words, but the same rush of sentiment. If we had a bucket of cold water handy, we'd have thrown it on him. We hadn't seen Charlie in a while, but he was at it again, chasing the chimera of a set of feelings that burned bright as a meteor. And for about as long.

Truth is, Charlie didn't really want to know what we thought. What he wanted was some smiling head nods affirming that this time was somehow different, that Cate was "the one," that novelty and pursuit weren't once again at play here. That his feelings for Cate were real and would last. We had a lot of thoughts, but they again take us ahead of our story. Before we share them with you, let's take another step back. Let's take a look into yet another very hidden and powerful force that interacts with feelings of attraction—our microbiome.

Little is more tangled than our fascination with and need for one another. The roots are planted in our genes and we're set up for how we see ourselves and others on day one, when we glide through our mother's birth canal and are bathed in her microbiome.

There are obviously many experiences that impact us from very early on. What reserve does our mother have to love us, value our uniqueness, possess the curiosity to want to get to know us despite all our imperfections? Were we wanted in the first place? By both parents? Did we live up to the fantasies our mother had about what we would bring to her experience? Was our coming-home party from the hospital a welcome one or were we met with a jealous brother or sister? How did these earliest of days play out as the novelty of our presence turned into the challenging reality of our growing personhood? Were we colicky babies? How was that related to? And, of course, this is just the beginning. But beyond all these undocumented moments that influence how we feel about ourselves and how we are drawn to and connect with others is the microbiome we inherited from our mother. How stressed has she been? How calm? What kind of diet has she had? What history has she had with antibiotic use? All of these factors shape the composition of the microbiome she passes along to us.

Our own microbiome—the bacteria, viruses, protozoa, and fungi that reside in the dark recesses of our gut—greatly impacts how we behave. There is a gut/brain axis that creates a two-way dynamic in which our microbiome exerts an influence on our behavior and our behavior, in turn, influences their composition. For example, if you transpose a skinny rat's biome into the gut of an obese one, that overweight rat starts watching what it eats and slims down. And it goes the other way as well. The variety of what we eat, and how often and widely we travel, are examples of what we do that alters our biome.

In a recent study, researchers found that the diversity of our biome is related to the number of social connections we have; the broader the diversity of the freeloaders that live in our gut, the greater the connections. And, on the other side, the researchers found that those of us packing a biome with a narrow diversity tended to be more anxious and vulnerable to depression. This is the first large-scale study linking the composition of our biome to personality factors, and it concluded that possessing a robust diversity relates to more outgoing, social tendencies and having a more homogeneous diversity is associated with feelings of stress and anxiety. If this sounds descriptive of the biome of Swords and Shields, well, it very well might just be.

Clearly, those of us with less social anxiety and greater confidence are more at ease in the early interactions with someone new, conferring a decided edge in attractiveness. This edge is probably even more pointed in men, where confidence leads to assertiveness and assertiveness leads, in turn, to more contacts with less stress and feelings of awkwardness. When it comes to attraction, one critical element we haven't yet touched upon is how comfortable we are with ourselves. Being comfortable in one's own skin is singularly attractive. The propensity to stress and anxiety associated with a narrow microbiome makes such positive feelings about oneself more difficult. For those of you who may be concerned about the diversity in your own gut biome, you might consider the following: reducing stress, getting a good night's sleep, and exercising, along with eating a wider diet and more fermented foods and fiber with less sugar, can go a long way toward increasing diversity.

We don't go looking around for what we find attractive in another person. Our attractions find us. As you know, our brain likes to think as little as it has to because it is calorie conscious. Consider something we all have for a moment: preferences. We don't give them much thought. We don't intend them; we simply make note of their presence. Some preferences are learned by trial and error. Think of your first sip of beer or your first puff on a cigarette.

You may have liked it and started a lifelong habit or found that you just didn't care for it. There are those of us who like red wine, those who prefer white, and still others who don't like the taste of wine at all. But some preferences are built in; we acquired those preferences back in the dust of time and don't have to learn them anew, for we are born with them. Take something as elemental as food, for example. Humans across the globe prefer fatty and sweet tastes over those that are sour and bitter. Things that taste fatty and sweet are much less likely to be poisonous or toxic. And when the architecture of our brains was forming (and calories scarce), sweet and fatty foods gave us more of the calories we needed. We don't have to learn what not to eat; our noses and tongues tell us to avoid certain things because they smell and taste bad. These preferences are baked in, so we don't have to give them a thought, much less have to learn the basics by trial and error in every generation. Fortunately, our ancestors did all the heavy lifting and passed on their lessons to us.

Even though we may give great thought as to those who appeal to us and those who don't, the underpinnings of our mating preferences, as we've shown you, burble far below conscious awareness. What we notice is the finished product of our preferences, not the scheming strategies and hidden pushes and pulls that form our patterns of attraction. Let's take a quick peek at still another influence shaping our choices in love. Among the ingredients of this unconscious mix of reproductive strategies is an intuitive attraction to cues that reflect fertility and the health of our potential offspring's signals of immuno-compatibility.

As you will recall, the goal of romantic bonding isn't simply finding a soul mate (great a feeling as that is); it's making babies (or experiencing and acting on its artifacts). An interesting study suggests that we may be more attracted to those potential partners who have immunity genes that are *different* from our own even though we aren't aware of these differences. These differences occur in genes that influence our immune system's ability to stave off infections. Creating healthy children is potentiated not by similarities, but their opposite. Healthier babies, possessing strong immune systems, are produced by partners bringing different sets of immunity genes to the mix. This is why mutts are healthier than their purebred cousins. These same immunity genes are also tagged with their positive role in fertility.

For those of you who would like to know more about immune compatibility and how it works, you might look at Daniel M. Davis' book *The Compatibility Gene*. Part of the impetus for this work goes back to a study done by a Swiss zoologist in 1994. He examined a particular part of the DNA of around one hundred young men and women. The small DNA segment studied contains the coding for the body's immune system. This is the major histocompatibility complex (MHC) and the identification of its genes is used to determine who might be a compatible partner not for making babies, but for an organ transplant. These genes produce molecules that help us fight off disease and a more diverse selection of them provides a distinct benefit to the immune system.

Here's the experiment: The men were asked to wear a cotton T-shirt for two days during which time they didn't drink any alcohol or use any kind of cologne that might change their natural scent. These T-shirts were then put into boxes with holes cut in the top. The women were asked to rank the boxes by smell in terms of both pleasantness and sexiness. The results showed that women preferred the smell of the T-shirts worn by men with *different* compatibility genes from themselves.

We have no knowledge of Cate's and Charlie's compatibility genes, but there's a good chance that they could be significantly different.

So, you think you know who you're drawn to, who your type is? We hope we've muddied the water a bit and made you aware of some operative dynamics you might not have known about before. As we said, attraction is complicated. Those want-to-jump-up-and-down, exhilarating feelings are akin to an iceberg, where most of their contributing elements lie hidden beneath our awareness. Much like many of our preferences, we don't set out to feel attracted; we simply notice its presence. We've described the many ways our bodies guide us to the ones we love. Our noses, hormones, and brain chemicals help us locate our partners. And they assist us in making that partner singularly important once they are located. These same elements then kick in to create feelings of trust, safely, and contentment. And this whole unconscious progression has but one aim: to get us to stay together long enough to have and care for babies. All of this and we haven't even yet gotten to the ways in which our brain types shape our patterns of attraction.

How Our Brain Types Exert Their Sway with Attraction

Just as a refresher: Our brain types are a by-product of our relationship with arousal. Swords, having a bit too little arousal, tend to look for ways to increase stimulation in their lives, while Shields, possessing a bit too much natural arousal, look for ways to reduce it. Now we'd like to jump up a couple of levels of abstraction here, climb out of the weeds, and talk about Cate and Charlie in a little more detail.

We've known Charlie for a while. He came to us for flu shots and a brief coaching session for help resolving a sensitive conflict between a couple of the staff members at his animal clinic. Getting his degree in veterinary medicine taught him a lot about animal diseases and their treatment, but not much at all about the perils and pitfalls of office management. At the end of those sessions, Charlie brought up the fact that he had just ended a relationship, one that had fallen apart like several before. He said, "If I ever flip over the moon for someone again, I'm coming in and I want you to tell me to slow things down. I don't want to feel guilty again about moving too fast and then hurting somebody's feelings." And here he was in our office again, doing exactly that. Over the next few months, we saw Charlie first, a number of times alone, and then him and Cate together. We'd like to tell you more about them because they exemplify some of the common dynamics that Swords and Shields have as they try to move from feelings of attraction to a relationship that is more committed and lasting.

Exceptionally bright, Charlie knew what he wanted to do from a very early age. For Charlie, school came easy, but his homelife was a very different story. His mother had poor boundaries, tended to share too much with the boy, and used him to fill in the gaps of her disappointment with her husband. Charlie was her protector, but also something more. His father drank too much and was always in AA, but despite his attempts to stop drinking, his alcoholism only progressed. "My mother came to despise him," Charlie told us. "We were pretty much secondary to his bourbon. All I wanted to do was get through dinner and go to my room with my dog. What I hated most was feeling like I had to protect her and make up for everything she needed that she wasn't getting from my father. To get away from him, she used to come into my room and just want to hang out. I wanted to scream. I never did. Instead of going places with my father, she would drag me along. It didn't matter that I didn't want to; I had to go with her."

According to Charlie, high school and college were a bit of a blur. After lots of girlfriends and drama, late nights, and a few too many excuses to use Adderall, he cruised through his training to become a vet. As you will recall, the woman Charlie was involved with before he met Cate was one who, during the early months of their relationship, he had similarly strong feelings for. And the women before that followed the same patterns. Charlie pursued these women with great interest and passion, as he had girls in high school and college. And each time as they settled into the less frothy routines of spending time with each other, he lost interest and moved on.

Charlie knew that his Sword brain type posed certain issues in how he managed his staff, but he wasn't clear about the ways in which they had shaped his love life. And complicating this blind spot was the residue from his relationship with his mother, whom he continued to avoid other than at holiday or birthday gatherings he couldn't muster an excuse to cancel.

"What do you want in your relationship with Cate?" we asked Charlie.

"All I want is to feel the way I feel about Cate right now and to feel it forever."

We knew that meant trouble. Because of Charlie's challenged relationship with arousal, his cycling in and out of relationships was at least in part an unconscious strategy to modulate the discomfort around feeling flat or bored by employing his tried-and-true strategy: the pursuit of a new romantic partner.

We had Charlie rank-order the following list in terms of being *most* emotionally important to *least* important in his relationship with Cate, with 1 being most important and 16 being least important to him. The following is how he ordered these emotional qualities:

Approval	8	Validation	13
Good for my ego	9	Security	14
Equality	11	Acceptance	5
Challenging	6	Freedom/independence	3
Aliveness	1	Contentment	10
Trust	4	Safety	15
Feeling completed	16	Excitement	2
Predictability	7	Social status	12

Looking at Charlie's top five choices, it was clear that he's in love with being in love. He likes the way dopamine and noradrenaline makes him feel, although describing his pattern in this way obviously didn't sound very romantic to him. Charlie is a smart guy and knew enough about brain chemistry to understand that dopamine and noradrenaline are released as "motivators" of behavior rather than "appreciators" of the goal of the action once it has been accomplished. In other words, the experience of pleasure is connected to their anticipation of the goal and not the goal itself. Often, dopamine-hungry people (Swords like Charlie) conflate the heightened emotions connected to longing with the milder feelings of love. His top three choices were aliveness, excitement, and freedom/independence, all feeling states associated with dopamine releases. When we cast these dynamics into pursuit and capture, he understood his connection to the hunt. He told us with great sadness and honesty, "I work so hard to get women to love me, and then when I'm successful I don't know what to do with it. It's like I get itchy, start looking around, and want to move on. The minute that happens, they get clingy and that makes me want to run even faster. Cate seems so special to me. I don't want to do that anymore."

We knew Charlie faced two hurdles. First, the necessary progression healthy relationships move through as couples get to know each other is a necessary dampener of dopamine. In addition to his motorcycle rides with buddies and his purchase of options in the stock market, "capturing" the perfect partner was a predictable source of a release of dopamine. If his experience with Cate was to prove deeper and more lasting than his other skirmishes with romantic partners, he would have to become more conscious of his relationship with arousal and learn to deal with it in different ways.

The second obstacle was his damaged relationship with his mother and how expressions of healthy growing connections in his romantic relationships set off old fears of being engulfed (his needs ignored and co-opted by his mother's hunger and self-involvement). And it certainly didn't help that Cate is a Shield and had some experiences from her past that added complexity to the mix. Cate's quixotic and likely bipolar father left her mother beleaguered and stressed, always waiting for some next shoe to drop. When Cate was eleven, he abandoned them both. The imprint these distracted and compromised parents had on Cate was anything but a secure early attachment. Unfortunately, we carry our formative attachment styles with us and they play out in our most important contemporary relationships. Having a bit too little serotonin didn't help Cate as she explored her potential love partners, and her anxious and insecure connection style soon became entangled with Charlie's issues.

What's to be learned here? For you Swords (male or female), if you recognize elements of yourself in this pattern of moving from partner to partner like Charlie, these are some things to think about. As we've described, relationships are hugely stimulating and cause the release of copious amounts of dopamine. And because of that, they can become natural go-to strategies to ramp up flagging arousal in the system. For Swords, novelty is like a candy bar. But novelty can't be sustained in a healthy intimate relationship, for the natural progression is away from newness and toward a growing sense of continuity and routine. Patterns are important, and when they are understood they can be illuminating. By looking at the patterns he engaged in and stringing together the relationships he entered with great passion only to leave, Charlie was able to see how he used these experiences with women to create drama and excitement to increase his level of arousal. What patterns can you identify in your own life?

All of us are vulnerable, at some level, to approaching relationships with mixed goals. For example, looking to find an intimate partner capable of returning enduring love while, at the same time, expecting drama and a dopamine buzz. Sometimes these goals can be realized within the relationship in a healthy and mutually beneficial way, and sometimes not. Obviously, novelty and excitement inevitably fade in healthy, sustainable experiences with partners. And getting back to what you know about the chemistry of love, dopamine and norepinephrine released in the chase have a much higher stimulus value than the feelings created by oxytocin do. For Charlie to get to the point with Cate where he could appreciate the experience oxytocin provided was going to take work. What remained to be seen was whether he was actually up to it.

We felt that despite some of their obvious challenges, the relationship between Cate and Charlie had real potential. From that first day Charlie described Cate, he never flagged in his caring for her. He had come to realize that, while it was difficult for him to stay in any relationship, running away was no longer an option he wanted to give himself. He admired so many of her qualities and was determined to try to break his familiar patterns.

Charlie's task with Cate was twofold. First, he needed to broaden his comfort around arousal and this required building into his life some regular contemplative moments. What he took to was a mindfulness meditation app we suggested. And second, Charlie took on the commitment of doing something that was distinctly uncomfortable for him: learning to be less squirmy around quiet moments of intimacy and closeness. Trying to make sense of what was at the bottom of that discomfort, Charlie blurted out, "When a woman starts to need me, I feel like I have to perform. It makes me feel taken over by my mother all over again." We knew Charlie would have to learn to reinterpret Cate's affection as a gift and act of generosity rather than a demand.

As we learned over time, Cate brought some of her own mixed issues to this relationship. Possessing the hypervigilance most Shields have, she tended to personalize some of Charlie's independence as a lack of interest and investment in the future of their relationship. While she never said these things to him directly, these feelings, nevertheless, leaked out in insidious ways. They'd been together for nearly six months and what Cate yearned for was the freedom from the anxious attachment she had with her mother and the unconditional acceptance and safety she never received from her father. Cate came in one day and led off with the following: "I'm afraid I'm pushing him away. Look, as a bond trader, I deal with risk every day. I just don't feel like I want to deal with it in my love life. To avoid the questions in my head, I know I push Charlie too hard for answers he doesn't have or can't give me yet. I can feel myself crowding him, and even though I know it's not good for our relationship, I find myself continuing to do it."

Why do we sometimes do the very things that we know are self-defeating? We do them to avoid the feelings we're *having* in hopes of substituting those feelings with *others*. We are trying to regulate our emotions, trying to avoid discomfort. Uncertainty is very arousing and, as you know, arousal is something Shields like Cate assiduously avoid. We asked her if she could give us a couple of examples of when she felt most uncomfortable with Charlie. Cate thought about it for a moment and then told us, "I know this is going to sound stupid, but here goes. When he's sitting there watching TV, I like to go over and sit next to him. I like to snuggle when we watch a movie. And I'm aware that if I'm sitting on the couch and he comes in, he's as likely as not to flop down on the chair. When I ask him to come over to the couch, he does, but I can't help but feel that if he wanted to be there that's where he would've sat in the first place. Here's another example: He'll tell me he's made a plan to go for a motorcycle ride with his friends and I always find myself making some comment that I wish I hadn't. I'm perfectly capable of entertaining myself, but sometimes I don't think I give him that impression."

We asked Cate if she would be willing to try something for the next two or three weeks. Taking her two examples, we asked that she do the following: First, let Charlie come to her. Let him be the initiator of affection (he'd always been that in the past). And second, we asked if she'd be willing to not only not make a comment when Charlie wanted to spend time with his friends but also see him off with a smile. She agreed to give both a try.

While the other person is the object of our attraction, the real motivation for wanting to be in that person's presence is how being around that person makes us feel. We tell ourselves we are drawn to qualities and aspects of our potential partners, but in truth we are simply attracted to the mix of our own emotions we have in their presence.

We also sent Cate home with the same assignment that we had given to Charlie. Below is how she rank-ordered the terms she thought of as being *most* emotionally important to her in a relationship, with 1 being most important and 16 being least important:

Approval	8	Validation	4
Good for my ego	12	Security	10
Equality	6	Acceptance	7
Challenging	14	Freedom/independence	16
Aliveness	9	Contentment	1
Trust	3	Safety	5
Feeling completed	11	Excitement	13
Predictability	2	Social status	15

As you can see, she prioritized her emotional needs in quite a different way than did Charlie. This was not a big surprise in that Cate's Shield-like nature is more safety oriented in general, which tends to express itself in mate selection as it does in other life choices. Complicating matters, finding herself in the throes of an important attraction had the effect of depleting the available serotonin she was in short supply of to begin with. Cate's level of arousal spiked and, while she loved how she felt, the dizzying intensity made her uncomfortable. Swords tend not to question intensity but simply enjoy its presence. Shields like Cate can interpret excitement as sliding into anxiety and, as a result, become hypervigilant. You've learned that attraction tends to make people momentarily less intelligent (disconnected from the prefrontal cortex, the center of reason and judgment). This dimming of rational and critical thinking has a much shorter duration for Shields than it does for Swords. Feeling in thrall with someone feels immediately pleasurable, but the depth of the pleasure (and the arousal it brings) soon turns to vulnerability, setting in motion protective thoughts and questions: What if this wonderful way I'm feeling isn't real or doesn't last? How is Charlie going to feel about me when he really gets to know me? Will he get tired of me? What if I am putting too much into this? What if I end up getting hurt?

Protective thoughts are not always protective, like when they diminish our quality of life and when their true purpose is to regulate uncomfortable arousal rather than clarify or resolve real issues. As a successful bond trader, Cate was comfortable in her dealings with the uncertainty of a sometimes-capricious bond market. She wasn't comfortable with the necessary uncertainties that inhabit all evolving romantic relationships. Shields often interpret uncertainties not as neutrals to be filled in with experiences over time, but as threats. Rather than seeing time as the friend that always reveals the truth, Shields sometimes see it more as an enemy. Cate wanted answers and she wanted them sooner rather than later. In that mode, things that are not a test become one. Believing information to be helpful, Cate found herself looking for it when it wasn't even there or, when it was there, being vulnerable to misinterpreting it. As you will recall, Shields are more likely to make certain predictable errors. They tend to make false negative errors (seeing actions as dangers that in fact aren't). In the early stages of romantic love, Shields, in a counterproductive attempt to protect themselves, can go negative, grab hold of the worst-case scenarios, and make them true in their mind, irrespective of their truth in reality. It's as if by giving words to your most dreaded fear, you feel as though you are protecting yourself. Cate gave us an example of this fairly early on. "There's nothing he's done to make me think he doesn't care as much as I do," she told us, "but I find myself looking for things as measures of his interest. Here's how crazed I can get: I like my alone time. I always have. But when Charlie wants his, I feel like I'm less important. Sometimes, I say things I'd rather not have said or ask too many questions like I don't trust him when really, I do. I'm afraid I might lose him doing some of the things I do."

Unfortunately, uncertainties tend to have a timetable of their own that may be at variance with the one in your mind. Love, the experience of it, is felt most intensely when we're moving toward someone. Men, particularly Sword men, bond in motion. The prerequisite for "motion" is that there be some psychological distance in the relationship that needs to be traversed. That requires an invisible but palpable gap. Picture two people standing a few feet apart with one moving slowly toward the other. If the other person rushes to meet the person moving forward, that gap shrinks and collapses. With little or no gap, there's nowhere to move and the feeling of motion and intensity fades. Letting Charlie come to her (which was probably the most difficult thing Cate needed to do) was the very thing that connected him most intensely to his feelings of love for her.

Cate also had a twofold task. She first had to learn that Charlie's need for solitary experiences like reading a book, wanting to walk the dog by himself, or spending time with his friends wasn't a threat. And second, she had to come to terms with the fact that Charlie's role wasn't one of completing or validating her, nor was he responsible for taking away the insecurities she brought into their times together. We are all responsible for completing and validating ourselves. It wasn't that Cate didn't know all of this, for she did. But sometimes she knew her energy around Charlie felt "insecure or, God forbid," she acknowledged to us, "needy."

Eight months in, attraction takes on a different character. Questions that could be asked and explored early on suddenly take on more personal meaning. "Are you interested in having children?" posed on the second date is a far different question than when it's posed months later. When Cate asked Charlie about his interest in having children, it took him aback. He hadn't thought much about children, one way or the other, at that point. And the way she asked the question wasn't in the abstract, but more a question about his seriousness and their future. His flustered, noncommittal response was devastating to her. For Charlie, the question set him on an "I'm going to have to think about this" journey. While she would never have been so direct with him, Cate was hoping for him to say some version of, "Of course, you're the center of my life and I would love to make babies with you." As he felt vaguely pressured, her disappointment caused Charlie to take a step back. Rather than freedom, he saw walls, and rather than commitment and safety, she saw indecision and jeopardy.

The following day, Charlie came in alone, annoyed with us. After all, they had been coming in and talking for months now, and instead of things getting better, they seemed more volatile and tense. What we told him was that this was not only predictable but a positive sign. Positive in that it reflected the fact that they were struggling with their respective issues. We encouraged Charlie to try to stay the course, to remember that time held all the answers.

He wasn't satisfied with our response. We hadn't been able to remove the conflict he felt internally or make what was going on between the two of them any smoother. But before he left, he did flash an interesting insight, saying, "Well, I guess I wouldn't be going through all this if I'd bailed out and was starting all over again with someone new." No, he wouldn't.

"I sort of feel like if I give myself one more contemplative moment, I might just jump out of my skin," he said. "I'm assuming you know sticking with all this is really hard?"

We nodded.

"I love Cate. I really do, but I feel like my freedom is slowly slipping away and like I'm going to miss having that strange encounter. How long am I going to have to feel this way?"

"How many more years do you expect to live?"

"Funny. Very funny."

As Charlie was leaving, we said, "You're letting Cate carry all the dependency here (the emotional awareness and vulnerability of 'getting' how important someone is in your life). Maybe if you picked up your share, her shoulders might come down a bit and she might feel a little safer." He gave us a long look and closed the door.

The next couple of days were difficult for Cate. And when Charlie hadn't come forward with any response to her question, she called him. "Maybe we're on different tracks here," she told him. "I think it would be good for us both to take some time apart and think about what we want." When he agreed, she wanted to take back what she had said, and only her fierce pride prevented her from breaking into tears.

Little has such momentous highs and agonizing lows as does romantic love. Freud once said, "We are never so defenseless against suffering as when we love." It wasn't just Cate feeling miserable, for Charlie was as well. Even though she wasn't depressed, we thought it might be helpful for her to get a boost in serotonin and an increase in the diversity of her microbiome. Here are the suggestions we gave to her.

Baobab fruit is one of the best sources of soluble prebiotic fiber. The fruit is hard to find, but pulp powders are available in most health food stores. Another way to increase serotonin is by eating dark chocolate containing raw cacao. Cacao is filled with the amino acid tryptophan, which is a known serotonin enhancer. Add to that some biome-pleasing fermented foods like the Japanese dish of fermented soybean natto, unsweetened Greek yogurt, full-fat sour cream, kombucha, sauerkraut, or kefir. All of these are rich in the probiotics that will help your gut produce more serotonin.

Charlie and Cate's time-out provided some real, soul-searching, contemplative moments for both of them. Both knew they had issues, some historical, some related to their brain chemistry. To override these distorting factors requires real consciousness, not for just a moment but sustained over time. It first takes an understanding of the past wounds you bring with you to your present, seeing and acknowledging the influence they have. Second, it takes an awareness of the ways your particular brain chemistry shapes both your feelings as well as your actions in a relationship. And third, it requires a willingness to reformulate the expectations you bring to the experiences with a partner. For Charlie, this meant reminding himself that Cate was not his mother, that he could let his guard down and move closer to her without being engulfed by her. And he had to do something else to be successful. Charlie had to look *elsewhere* for excitement. Cate is a real live flesh-and-blood human being to be learned about, understood, and loved, not a convenient strategy to modulate his arousal level.

To be successful with Charlie, Cate's journey was a little different. She had to learn to befriend Charlie's independent nature rather than seeing it as a threat, foreshadowing the abandonment she so feared. Cate didn't need to look elsewhere for a solution to regulating her emotions; she needed to *look inward*. These are the big questions to pose while examining the quality and value of a relationship: How do I make sure that it's not a reenactment of or reaction to some wound I still carry? And how do I make sure it's not a strategy I've learned to employ to regulate my brain chemistry?

A few weeks into their time-out, Cate and Charlie decided to take a time-out from us as well. Some months later, we heard from them in the form of a card. It contained a cheery little note telling us that they were fine and together again. And in an unsigned insert, someone had found their inner Byron. Here's how it read:

With this woman
I may always be afraid of being swallowed.
My fear is simply part of who I am,
An unintended trailing from my past,
Ancient as a boy and a needy mother,
Present as my shadow.
But because I am no longer a boy,
And because I care,
Despite my fears
I will lean forward
With love.

With this man
I may always be disappointed.
My hunger is simply part of who I am,
An unintended trailing from my past,
Ancient as a girl and an unavailable father,
Present as my shadow.
But because I am no longer a girl,
And because I care,
Despite my hunger
I will lean away
With love.

Their note made us smile. Something was working. It's not necessarily going to be easy for either of them. Insight is evanescent and hard to hang on to. Given the smallest crack, habit wants to seep in, widen the crack, and take over. Charlie and Cate are both young and have very different brain chemistry types. There will be temptations along the way, frustrations, crises of faith, expectations conscious and otherwise, and, of course, inevitable misunderstandings and hurt feelings. We hope that little aspirational meditation they penned is an anchor they will both choose to come back to. As we said at the outset, attraction is complicated. Sustaining it, even more so.

Here are some things you might consider before moving onto the next chapter:

1. Looking back, can you identify any early family circumstances, events, or interactions that have influenced your choice of romantic partner?

2. Are there similarities that comprise your "type"? If so, what are they?

3. What are the common patterns, feelings, or dynamics you've noticed in your past romantic relationships?

4. Can you identify any common conflicts or circumstances leading to the endings of these relationships?

5. Knowing what you know now about brain chemistry and your brain type, what impact do you see that having on your romantic relationships?

6. What are the most important things you've learned about yourself from past relationships?

7. In terms of your personal brain type, what issues can you identify that you might take on to try to override in your romantic relationships?

8. List five of the most important ways you would like to feel in a romantic relationship. Now list five important ways you, in fact, felt in your past romantic relationships. Make note of how many are the same and how many are different. How do you account for those differences? How do you understand your responsibility for them? What role do you think your brain type plays in these differences?

CHAPTER EIGHT

Marriage: What's Running the Show?

How the Partners We Choose and
Our Interacting Brain Chemistries
Create Conflict, Promote Balance, or
Amplify Our Unconscious Brain Type Issues

WHILE MARRIAGES TOO OFTEN END in epic battles and acrimonious divorce, they most often begin with a kiss. So, what takes us from sweet kiss to family law court so often and so easily? Studies of modern American marriages are replete with statistics and predictions. Elopement is the single greatest predictor of divorce. The number of people attending a wedding ceremony seems to predict its success; two hundred appears to be a very good number, six not so good. Divorcing men don't feel *appreciated*, while their female counterparts don't feel *listened to and understood*. Reciprocal validation is a pretty good predictor of success, while poor communication skills signal failure. Money is the most frequent source of conflict, and infidelity draws the most common kill stroke. When asked who is responsible for the failure of the marriage, most people blame their spouse. But do we get better with experience? Unfortunately, no. Fifty percent of first marriages end in a divorce, 60 percent of second marriages, and 73 percent of third marriages. And woven into all of these issues, of course, is the role our brain chemicals play in the stability and pleasure or rockiness of that journey.

Marriage, or some sort of bonding ceremony or ritual, appears across cultures. As we described, the experience of attraction and desire is our emotional reaction to a release of hormones and brain chemicals. The net effect of this wash of dizzying feeling is a temporary disconnect from the brain's prefrontal cortex. Old Mother Nature wants babies to be made and that rational part of the brain only gets in the way. It's all about babies. Attraction ensures their creation and marriage provides their protection and nurturance. The brain, having kept the prefrontal cortex silent long enough for bonding to occur, gets reconnected as soon as the honeymoon is over and we unpack our bags.

Enter the Prefrontal Cortex

The brain has finished its time-tested job of seduction successfully and we've gotten married. Already, testosterone levels have fallen and testosterone suppresses oxytocin, the hormone that enhances bonding. The brain has been careful to lay down all the best circumstances for making and protecting those babies until they can go on to make babies of their own. We've talked about how complicated attraction is and how the prefrontal cortex is MIA during this phase. What happens when—slam, bang—suddenly that critical and judging part of our brain wakes up once again? We see and hear things we didn't before and we have expectations we've often not fully articulated even to ourselves, let alone put into words with our partners.

Marital expectations are cobbled together from bits and pieces of our past: how we saw our parents treat each other at home as well as aspirational models of the love we wish for and hope to find; our insecurities, fears, hopes. Folded into that soup are our values and attitudes, our past romantic relationship experiences, and myriad other shapers, along with our brain type. And all of these expectations coalesce around our potential partner during the attraction phase of love, the phase where our prefrontal cortex is conveniently muted.

Expectations are deeply human. We all have them. There's but one problem. They are rarely put into words and expressed. There are two contracts in a marriage, one *explicit* and the other *implicit*. There is the obvious legal contract that is augmented by either traditional vows or ones you've written yourselves, designed to be the promises for your marriage. But there is something even more impactful at work. It's not that our marriage vows aren't important, but it's the implicit, largely unarticulated contract that becomes operational at the end of the ceremony. And this contract comprised of our expectations (usually assumptive and unnegotiated) exerts great sway on the experience of the marriage and can be a source of future conflict.

Now, with the prefrontal cortex reactivated and our brain working on all cylinders, these hidden expectations bubble to the surface. At first, they are subtle—something small misses the mark, a hidden wish not fulfilled, some trivial disappointment. We are let down, nevertheless. Consider the syntax there: *we* are let down. Someone *else* is the culprit—our partner. Something in what they said or did was at variance with an expectation of what we would have liked them to have said or done. Frequently, these letdowns are the by-product of our hidden expectations, the implicit contract we've never really talked about.

When the prefrontal cortex is hooked back up, we sometimes realize we've fallen in love with only a part of our partner and that there are things about them we've ignored, discounted, or assumed would change in their love for us. Perhaps the most insidious and common tenet of our implicit contract is who we put in charge of our happiness. Too often, instead of looking to ourselves as the essential fount of contentment and satisfaction, we look to our partners. We would be just a little bit happier if they were just a little bit different. This might be a good time to take a look at the implicit contracts that exist in your marriage. Yes, contracts plural—*yours* and *theirs*. If you give your invisible contract some thought, you might discover some of the things you expect of your partner that you've never put into words. What are those things? Make a short list, no more than five. Now it's time to take back some control. We all like control, right? How can you steal some back here? You do that by assuming more responsibility for your own satisfaction. What items on your list would you be willing to take on? Where can you take your partner off the hook for that fulfillment and put yourself on it?

And what about your partner's hidden contract? What would your guess be for a short list of their unexpressed expectations? Jot some of them down, no more than five. Without having any conversation about this with your partner, try doing the following as best you can for the next month: Take at least two items from both lists and keep them in your head. The exercise is about acceptance, responsibility, and generosity. Try silently accepting your partner for who and what they are. Free them from the way you would like them to be. Assume responsibility for your own happiness. Take those items from your list and think of the ways you can create your own satisfaction. And finally, practice generosity. Without calling attention to them, take a couple of items you've guessed are on your partner's list and see what you can do to move in that direction, the more specifically the better. Maybe your partner will read this chapter and put in a little work as well. Be the model. Give what you would like to receive.

Marriage is experienced from the inside out. We've found that it's helpful to take a little more objective look at how that relationship is put together and functioning. To sharpen your understanding of yourself, answer the following questions as specifically as possible:

1. What value does your relationship have in your life? How central and important is it, independent of convenience and habit?

2. What model of marital/intimate relationship did you see growing up?

   > What role did your mother play in the family?
   > What role did your father play?
   > How do you see the success of your parents' marriage?
   > If not successful, how do you make sense of the root problem?
   > How do you see your parents' relationship informing your own?

3. What sacrifices (if any) have you made to maintain the relationship?

   > If there were sacrifices, were they understood and discussed before you were married?
   > What sacrifices do you see your spouse having made, if any?
   > How transparent have the sacrifices been?
   > Were they made with love, guilt, or resentment?

4. How would you characterize the current state of your marriage? Circle as many as apply and give specific examples.

Loving	Stable	Critical and judgmental
Supportive	Boring	Anxious and uncertain
Accepting	Distant	Angry and resentful
Encouraging	Distrustful	Other (describe)

5. What qualities do you most appreciate in your partner?

6. In what ways do your differences impact the relationship?

7. Who, on the outside, influences your relationship?

> Friends   Family
> In-laws   Religious affiliations
> Work   Other (describe)

> How would you characterize that influence? Positive/
> negative?

8. Which of your needs are met in the relationship?

9. What (if anything) do you need from your partner that you don't get?

> How clear have you been about what you need?
> What sense do you make of not getting what you need?

10. What are the strengths in the marriage? The weaknesses?

11. How is money structured in the relationship?

> Who handles the money?
> How are financial decisions made?
> Are there any financial agreements (pre- or post-nups)
> in place?
> Are there any conflicts related to money?

12. How important is sex in your relationship?

> How satisfying/dissatisfying is the sexual relationship
> to you? To your partner?
> Are there any particular conflicts?

13. How trusting are you? How trusting is your partner of you?

14. List any conflicts/issues in the relationship from most to least important.

15. What issue(s) would you be willing to work on?

16. What issue do you think is most important to your partner?

17. How constructively is anger handled in the relationship?

18. How do you show your support, interest, empathy, and love?

19. How does your partner show theirs?

20. What role does your or your partner's brain chemistry type play in your marriage?

Those of you who chose to dig into these questions in any depth have just created an up-to-date snapshot of your marriage. It's most helpful if you and your partner both respond to these questions. For some of you, your responses might be upsetting to your partner. If you're comfortable doing this and your partner has gone through the questions as well, the two of you might share notes. This is an exercise in communication. Communication is about sharing information, *not about defending it.* The trick here is listening. Flip a coin to see who goes first. One of you says something like, "This is how I answered question one." The other just listens, no comments or follow-up questions. Then it's the other person's turn. Again, no reacting, just listening. Information can be illuminating and it can sometimes be uncomfortable. But it's information your partner has chosen to share with you. The greatest gift you can give them is to listen and understand that it reflects how they see things, their interpretation, their summing up of the relationship. Your task here isn't to agree or disagree with anything you've just heard, simply take the information in. Then, instead of talking about what you've just heard, we'd like you to do something really difficult: just sit with the information for a while and digest it. After you've waited a day or two, sit down with your partner and use the exchanged information as a springboard for a dialogue.

If you've thought about your expectations and the questions we have posed, you've constructed a way of looking at some of the elements that affect the feeling tone and quality of your relationship. Feeling tone is how you experience the relationship, your emotions associated with it. Emotions are contagious and no-where moreso than in our intimate relationships. When emotions and the actions they influence run in a similar vein, they tend to have a magnifying effect, so you can imagine that in marriages between two individuals with like brain types emotions are amplified, particularly when stressed. The net effect of a same-brain-type relationship is that instead of providing a kind of balancing ballast, there's the danger of exaggerating each other's brain type tendencies.

Marriages that combine opposing brain types pose very different sets of potential issues. The upside is that, given a high degree of acceptance and reciprocal control, a marriage between two different brain types can balance and smooth out tendencies that might be self-defeating. But where acceptance is marginal and one person carries the stick, colliding brain type expressions can easily become sources of conflict as well as targets of blame, guilt, and shame. Let's take a look at how these permutations play out in real life.

Health and a Little Help from Our Friends

Her name is Mackenzie, but forever she's been known simply as Mac. It was pouring rain. She was lost, trying to find her way to the clinic for her Prolia shot—monthly medication to treat osteoporosis. When she finally found the clinic, she was a half hour late. Standing under an umbrella in the rain, she knocked on the window to get the nurse's attention. Previously, by phone, they had agreed to give her the shot outside due to her fears of being exposed to Covid indoors. The nurse kept pointing to the door. Mac continued to implore her to come outside. It was a standoff.

Frightened and frustrated, Mac turned around and left. Because of Covid restrictions, she'd already missed two injections—a dangerous lapse, given her level of osteoporosis. Even though she was fully vaccinated, Mac was extremely cautious, ever worried about contracting the virus. However, the bubble she created around herself had become a prison.

As an inveterate Shield, Mac is stressed, hypervigilant, and has long suffered hypochondriacal tendencies. Her wife, Kaitlyn (also a Shield), while disappointed that Mac hadn't gotten her Prolia injection, told her how relieved she was that she hadn't gone into the clinic, possibly exposing herself to one of the "variants." Kaitlyn, too, was fully vaccinated, but, like her wife, was also deathly afraid of getting sick. A match made in heaven? Maybe, but their similar Shield tendencies were doing them no favors.

Together, they'd spent the last year isolated in their apartment, seeing no one other than delivery people. Given their health concerns, they were fortunate to be able to work from home. But unfortunately, the pandemic did nothing but reinforce and reify their aversion to arousal. They had gotten no natural sunlight for a year, and the only exercise they had was walking to their car, driving to a Whole Foods, and popping the trunk for the clerk to put their order in.

What do you do if you find yourself in a relationship where each amplifies the other's fears instead of providing some sort of reasoned, calming influence? The first thing to consider is that although the internal aim of hypochondriacal tendencies is to protect health, its effect can be exactly the opposite. In that hypochondriasis is driven by fear and Shields tend to be avoidant, they often ignore real symptoms for fear of finding out what they might mean or put off critical screenings that are anxiety laden.

Also, the stresses that Mac and Kaitlyn's illness fears place upon them may very well have hurt them. Bottom line: the combination of a Calamity Jane and Jill is unhealthy. Recognizing and acknowledging that is a big plus.

The second step is much more difficult. It would be helpful if both assumed responsibility to offer up some cogent, "Yes, buts," instead of the usual, "Yes, ands." Illness is obviously different from one's fear of it. Mac and Kaitlyn, who were together 24/7 during the pandemic, tended to curate their news sources similarly, and each inadvertently amplified rather than calmed the other's fears. While folie à deux isn't listed in the fifth edition of the *Diagnostic and Statistical Manual of Mental Disorders*, emotions are contagious. The emotions bouncing around in their apartment during the year of the lockdown were most certainly not the calming variety. Even though their relationship was strong, instead of helping, they frightened each other into a dark vortex. Support and validation are two strengths in a marriage, but it's important to be discriminating about *what's* supported and validated. We've explained to you how Swords tend to indulge in their impulses. Well, Shields can be equally indulgent. The difference is that their indulgence is inverted. Instead of a reward-driven "I want," it's a punishment-avoidant "I don't want." Mates who support and validate "I don't want" in a hypervigilant partner can facilitate worry and somatic concerns. Mac and Kaitlyn supported each other too much. And for some of the wrong things.

What we had them do was agree to form an alliance on the side of "high-probability" safety instead of the bulletproof kind they were trying to achieve. They started by going for walks (masked of course) together and worked up to going grocery shopping in a market. They made a commitment to try to offer each other calming rather than alarming feedback. Mac, who had been a bit of a medical news junkie, agreed to cut back on her consumption, and both signed on for a regular meditation exercise.

If you and your spouse are both Shields, here are some questions to answer and discuss with your partner:

1. "Do I help calm your health concerns or do I fan them? Can you explain?"

2. "What can I say or do that would be understanding but also helpful in tamping down your worries when you have them?"

3. "What doctors in our lives do we agree to trust?"

Had either Kaitlyn or Mac been a Sword, their reaction to arousal might have been a little less anxiety provoking. Swords tend not to focus on somatic symptoms, bringing us to a different kind of danger: denial.

Cheryl and Ward, both Swords in their late forties, each have their own issues. Two years ago, Cheryl had a treatable breast cancer. She has always had trouble maintaining a healthy weight, and following her surgery and radiation treatments she put on pounds she hasn't been able to lose. Ward, who has a family history of heart disease and has had three stents to widen his arteries, also struggles with his weight.

As you know, a risk factor for Swords is that they tend to not notice—or to ignore—physical symptoms that could be troubling. It was only when Cheryl's mother (who also had breast cancer) pushed her to get a long-overdue mammogram that Cheryl's tumors were discovered. The trip to Italy she and Ward had planned last year took precedence over the surgeon's recommendations as to the timing of the surgery.

Ward was very supportive and helpful during her prolonged recovery and treatment. It felt like a time for them both to take stock of all that they had and to be a little indulgent. Probably a little too indulgent. Cheryl's recovery segued into the pandemic lockdown, with her gaining thirty pounds during that time and Ward twenty.

As we've explained, those of us who are Swords tend toward symptom denial, dichotomous/fast thinking, and eating to stimulate or as an antidote to boredom. Cheryl and Ward watched each other get fat without daring to say something for fear that the finger would be pointed right back at themselves. Cheryl, in particular, didn't like what had happened to her body and twice went on a diet. Each time, Ward managed to sabotage it by adding cheesecake to their food delivery order, her known weak spot.

Diet undercutting is not uncommon. Even when partners complain about their mates' weight gain, when that person demonstrates some healthy resolve it is sometimes received as threatening.

Unfortunately, "Oh, come on, one little bite isn't going to hurt you!" is a common and distinctly unhelpful sabotage.

What would have been helpful would be for Ward to have celebrated Cheryl's wish to lose weight and had the thoughtfulness to be a better model of restraint himself.

The challenge around health in a Sword/Sword marriage is in spotting tendencies to downplay or be in some denial of health issues. If you see evidence of symptom denial (not being proactive with their health) in your partner, be willing to speak up, be the voice of reality, risk being reminded of your own blind spots. There's only one thing worse than falling into denial about your own health and that's having a loving confederate who inadvertently supports you looking the other way. Take some responsibility here.

If you happen to be married to another Sword, ask each other the following questions:

1. "How do you see the ways in which I relate to arousal interacting with my health issues and the decisions I make about them?"

2. "Are there things you see me not taking care of that might hurt my health?"

3. "How can we remind each other about these things in a way that we pay attention to?"

So, what happens in a Sword/Shield relationship? As a Sword, Todd practices a kind of magical thinking when it comes to dealing with his medical issues. The magical thinking goes something like this: If I don't go to the doctor, I can assume everything is all right, but if I make an appointment, I have a whole list of things I know they will find that are wrong. One of those "things" he was worrying about was a growth on his arm. Only after a lot of prodding from his wife, Amy, did he make a telemedicine appointment with a dermatologist, where he was told he would need to come in for a biopsy. It had crossed Todd's mind that it might be melanoma, but just as quickly he said to himself, No, it's probably nothing. He never made an appointment to get a definitive diagnosis. Todd is also three years late on getting his first colonoscopy even though his mother died of colon cancer.

Amy, a Shield and a bit of a germaphobe, had a hard time pushing Todd to go to the doctor because of her own fears of Covid. She worried about crowded elevators and having to sit in a waiting area before going into an exam room someone just vacated. After she and Todd were both fully vaccinated, her anxiety ebbed enough for her concerns to be focused on Todd's health. When a little nagging wasn't productive, she went into action herself. "I've made two appointments for you," she told him, "one with the dermatologist and another for a colonoscopy, and I'm going to go with you to make sure you go."

We are all responsible for dealing with our own health. But that said, one of the tangible benefits of having a partner who knows you and loves you is that they not only see the tiny cracks in your system; they also point them out and push you when you need pushing. It's having another pair of eyeballs to make sure you take good care of yourself. Sometimes we all need a little help from our friends.

Money: Who's Got the Stick and What They Do with It

Sandy and Mike just filed for bankruptcy. In the past two years, they've teetered on the edge of financial crisis but were always able to balance, juggle, and move money around to keep minimum payments afloat and bill collectors from burning up their phone lines. Both strong Swords, they met in college, fell in love, and moved to Los Angeles to pursue their dreams. Sandy worked her way up through the system to become stage manager for a large downtown theater and Mike was successful selling and leasing commercial real estate. Between the two of them, Sandy and Mike were doing quite well financially. The only problem was that even though their income went up each year, their expenses ran even higher. Much higher.

Sandy, a bit of a fashionista, had a penchant for vintage jewelry and art deco furniture she bought to furnish a string of houses they bought and sold. While she made a respectable living, it was Mike's commission checks they used to support their expensive lifestyle. Rather than saving, they continued to borrow and spend, living on the edge, pretending they weren't in danger.

The year 2020 was a sobering one for them both. Sandy's theater shut down and commercial real estate hit a sudden wall. In the early days of the pandemic, they came together and tried to lay out a financial plan that would enable them to outlast the crisis. Mike was able to get a part-time job at a large home improvement retailer, and Sandy applied and was qualified for unemployment benefits. They weren't bringing home anything close to what they used to, but they put themselves on a strict budget and were getting by. That lasted until Sandy's birthday, when her parents sent her a check for $3,500. Even though her parents were living on a thin margin themselves, they understood the dire circumstances Sandy and Mike were in and found a way to send her the money. Instead of telling Mike about the money or putting it into their joint account, she cashed the check and found herself at her favorite jewelry store in Beverly Hills, laying out the cash and putting the rest on a credit card for an antique Georgian necklace.

When Mike found the box hidden away in the back of the closet, he dropped it at her feet, shouting, "How much did you spend?"

"It was my money."

"Oh yeah? What's mine is yours and what's yours is yours? How much?"

"I don't have to tell you. It was for my birthday from my parents."

"How much?"

"Thirty-five hundred dollars."

"That would have covered the mortgage this month."

"What about the koi fish you just bought?"

"It was four hundred dollars and I'd already ordered it."

"It's the principle I'm talking about."

"Don't talk to me about principles. Why with what's going on right now would you go and buy a necklace?"

"I needed it to cheer myself up."

"Yeah, well, wasting money doesn't cheer me up."

"Neither did all those expensive lunches I saw on the Amex bill."

"In case you haven't noticed, in between breaking my back at that god-awful job, I'm still trying to do some real-estate business."

"Really? All I've seen lately is money going out and nothing coming in. You're not the hotshot you think you are."

The conversation only went downhill from there.

It wasn't long before Mike and Sandy lost their house and Sandy's jewelry was sold on eBay for pennies on the dollar. With the bankruptcy, they jettisoned a lot of debt, but their self-image and their marriage were damaged.

What can be learned here? Because of their similar brain type, they had inadvertently magnified tendencies each had on their own. It was easier for Mike to indulge himself seeing Sandy doing it as well. If you're married to another Sword, be on the lookout for this kind of amplification. As you know, Swords tend to have issues around impulse control and delaying gratification. If you see this tendency, it's important for one or the other of you to adapt and play the role of contrarian. Be willing to say no. To be more prudent. Be willing to construct a realistic budget that leaves you in the black at the end of the month. Have regular discussions about money. Set some budget-appropriate amount as a cap for what each can spend without running it by the other partner. Work together and make sure you both take responsibility for your financial health.

You know Swords tend to be volatile emotionally and given to expressions of anger, blame, and accusation. These moments are damaging to the health of a marriage. Sandy and Mike nearly destroyed their love for each other by acting reflexively and indulging in their need for excitement. Shopping, spending money, and making risky investments are all cheap and easy ways to stimulate the flow of dopamine. But these actions can have dangerous and damaging consequences. Being smart requires a cold and sober look at your relationship with money, for it is identical to how you relate to arousal.

Albert and Trish have a very different relationship to money. Albert has a kitchen drawer filled with collected condiment packages. Trish, also a Shield, is even more parsimonious. Rather than viewing money as a source of potential pleasure, they see it solely as stored security to be doled out with great care, scrutiny, and reluctance. It's hard to fault a couple so personally responsible and forward-looking, and it's unlikely we'd ever have met them had they not had a child, Mark.

Trish and Albert are by no means strapped, for each makes more than a modest income. But self-sacrifice was a given and an unspoken, reciprocal badge of honor.

Their frugal spending habits take on a game-like quality, with each competing to be the one willing to do with less.

"This is entirely her money she's spending here," Albert told us, taking a seat alongside Trish. "If it were mine or ours, we wouldn't be here. Nothing against you. I just find this a colossal waste of good money. I—"

"Albert," Trish interrupted.

"I know. I know. I agreed to come. Let's get on with it."

"Let me say, first of all," Trish began, patting him on the knee, "Albert is the sweetest man I've ever known." His shoulders dropped and he took her hand. "We've just gotten off track lately and I want to get back on."

They were both in their early forties, had been married twelve years, and had a six-year-old son. Trish was an academic, taught in the University of California system, and had published a couple of books that had become standard texts, providing her nice ongoing royalties. Albert was a pharmacist with dreams of owning a pharmacy of his own one day. His hard work and rigid saving habits had been an inspiration to Trish. She'd come from a much shakier financial background than he. Unlike with her family of origin, where her alcoholic father was likely to be jobless and their electric service an uncertainty, being with Albert made Trish feel safe. She thought it was smart that the only cosmetics she used during their marriage were out-of-date samples Albert brought home from the pharmacy. She found his going out of his way to buy day-old bread charming. She got him. They never owned a new car, refrigerator, or music system. She understood the reason that he missed the opportunity to buy the house they longed for, both fearing the market was going to go down further. There were no resentments. Not until Mark came along.

Trish didn't mind the hand-me-down baby clothes or the crib they found along with other baby paraphernalia in a yard sale. Mark wasn't able to see any of this as shabby, but over time she started to. She didn't mind sacrificing for herself; she did it willingly. But when it came to Mark, she started to give him little indulgences: a store-bought toy here and there, a new mattress for his first bed, a pillow never slept upon. None of this met with Albert's approval. He told her they should be saving that money and putting it away in a college fund for Mark's future. She reminded him that they were already doing that.

They argued often. One night, Trish wrote in her journal: "Something is wrong here. I don't want to be a bad model for Mark, and I'm not sure that being a martyr isn't being just that."

Things came to a head in the days just ahead of Mark's fifth birthday, when Albert brought in a used bicycle. Tears came to her eyes when she saw it. "The kickstand is bent," she said.

"I can fix it."

"No," she said firmly. "His first bike is going to be a new one. I'll pay for it."

"That's ridiculous. I—"

"No, *we've* become ridiculous."

The next day, Trish bought a brand-new bright red bicycle for Mark. She loved the look in the boy's eyes when he saw it. She would love to see that look in Albert's eyes, too. She couldn't remember if she'd ever seen it. They had been so good together, her fears so neatly dovetailed with his. Her caution synced perfectly with his natural reticence. If he didn't need anything, she would show him that she didn't need anything either. Their silent dance of sacrifice had gone on for years. Had it brought them happiness? she wondered. She thought not. What had they done to each other?

Trish recalled early in their time together, when she thought that buying a few shares of Tesla might be a good investment. Albert put out that bright little ember just as, years later, when a pharmacy came up for sale, she had thrown cold water on that idea, as she did not believe them ready to take the chance, having to borrow so much money. The light had gone out of his eyes. She remembered the look on his face, an amalgam of disappointment and relief. That's what they brought to each other: disappointment and relief, she concluded as she described their relationship to us.

That was a bit too dreary an assessment. They'd also brought a great deal of love and warmth to each other.

Albert perked up when we talked to him about the brain chemistry of reluctance, avoidance, and risk aversion. The need to challenge the discrimination between the real and the felt. We talked about balance and how courageous it was for Trish to give words to the other side, to speak up for reason, for measured risks. For pleasure. We asked Albert when was the last time he splurged on himself. He was stumped. A little smile creased his face and he said, "I haven't done it, but I keep checking out the machines that make espresso and cappuccino with the frothed milk. Someday."

Actually, that day came sooner than we thought. The first thing Albert told us on our fourth visit was that he found the perfect espresso machine on craigslist and bought it. It may not have been new, but this was progress. And last month we learned there was even more progress: Albert is currently in negotiations to buy the pharmacy he's worked in these past years.

We worked with another double-Shield couple wherein one of the partners loosened the reins on her formerly cautious financial behavior—but for a very different reason. Rob and Jane were typical Shields, ever cautious and risk avoidant. But their marriage presented a surprising twist we hadn't expected. "Look, I'm pretty easygoing," Rob began. "It's just part of my nature. From day one, Jane has always handled our personal finances. She does all the bill paying and investments. She's a detail person and much better at numbers than I am. We've been married for twenty-three years and we both do fairly well financially. Look, there's no one I trust more than I do Jane...until in this last year or so. I know we live in a community property state where everything we have is half hers, but while she was always careful, now, in my book, she's become reckless."

"Reckless" may have been an exaggeration, but Jane had changed her risk profile for investing in some dramatic ways. As a Shield, Jane had always been somewhat risk averse. What caught Rob's attention was that she'd been selling off their portfolio of municipal bonds and had started trading options. It wasn't that their net worth had changed in any significant way; it was that he lost confidence in the security of their future.

Jane was blasé listening to Rob describe their situation. "Here's my side," she said. "I've always been conservative and careful with what I did with our investments. Probably too careful. It wasn't so much an investment strategy as it was being afraid to take reasonable chances for better returns. I've just loosened up a little bit. All of a sudden, we've changed places and Rob's become the worrywart."

There was no question that Jane had changed, but why? Brain chemistry is generally stable. How to account for such a shift in risk tolerance?

As we asked questions and took a complete medical history, we found that several months ago Jane's carpal tunnel syndrome became much more aggravated and she started taking acetaminophen on a daily basis. This wasn't unusual, for many people do. In fact, somewhere around a quarter of all Americans take over-the-counter pain medication on a weekly basis. But a number of recent studies show that these medications not only numb pain; they also change the risk tolerance of those taking them. These changes aren't noticed as big aha moments; they are much more subtle and insidious. The net effect of these over-the-counter pain medications is a disinhibiting one, causing people to take chances they would normally not take.

If pain medication might have the effect on someone like Jane with her Shield brain chemistry, you can imagine the impact it could have on someone with Sword brain chemistry, where they already live more on the risk-tolerant side.

Recently, Jane had a surgical repair of her wrist and no longer is in need of pain medication. Months later, she shut down her options account. She doesn't see any connection to the medication she was taking, but we have our own suspicions.

Negative Affect, Innocent and Not So

Not all treatment goes the way we would like it to. Let us tell you about Marty, a G.I. doctor. He's been married for five years to Karen, an administrator in the hospital he's affiliated with. Marty was twice reprimanded by the hospital department head for his behavior in the ER, but it was events happening at home with Karen that got him into treatment.

How clearly do we see ourselves? How often do we see ourselves as the source of the problem? How often do we find others at fault? The answer to these questions is both symptom specific and an excellent predictor for who will find therapy a positive experience and who will not. People coming in reporting feelings of anxiety and depression tend to see themselves at the center of their issues and also tend to be Shields. And those who find themselves in therapy because of anger issues tend to look for external explanations for their irritation, holding others responsible. These people are most often on the short side of arousal, the Swords of the world. Predictions? Which group do you think gets more out of therapy? Yes, you're right.

But before we get to Marty and Karen, let's step back for a moment. As you know, Swords have too little available dopamine and, concomitantly, natural arousal. But that doesn't mean that Swords don't get aroused, and when aroused that they don't find high levels any more uncomfortable than do Shields. However, where Shields typically interpret uncomfortably high arousal as internally generated, largely about *them*, Swords can look at stress-induced arousal spikes as situational, imposed upon them by *others*.

Marty lives a stressful life. It's easy to perforate a bowel during a colonoscopy, yell at a still-green intern doing something stupid in the ER. When stressed, Marty gets arousal spikes. Against everything Karen, a Shield, felt comfortable with, Marty managed to take them both into a highly leveraged lifestyle. While Karen managed their money carefully, she had little control over the credit card in Marty's wallet and his reckless spending habits were a frequent source of their arguments. While money was often the context that set off one of their spats, the greater concern was his increasingly abusive behavior. In fact, it was during a recent argument that Marty got physical. Shocked and speechless, Karen chalked it up to a malpractice lawsuit he'd recently been named in. But, not a week later, Marty didn't simply shove her again; he grabbed Karen by the neck and hit her.

That event precipitated an ultimatum. For months, Karen had asked Marty to go with her to couples therapy. He had refused. Now she was no longer interested in seeing someone with him. She told him that unless he was willing to get into therapy and learn to control his anger better, she was done. It was under these circumstances that we first met Marty.

We learned a lot during that first session. He'd had a difficult upbringing—a single mother and men he never came to know in and out of the home. He never knew his father and wasn't sure his mother did either. He'd joined the Army right after high school and went through Ranger school. While still a resident, he married someone he'd known less than a month and divorced a year later. Marty married Karen the following year. As a child, he had taken Ritalin for a couple of years after an ADHD diagnosis. In terms of anger, he had a quick temper; he had gotten into fights in school and lately was given to bouts of rage while driving. He told us that Karen didn't like to be in the car with him when he was at the wheel. Marty was perfectionistic and as brutally critical of himself as he was of others. He took no medication.

The next sessions with Marty proved to be unproductive. He was always on time, but he was constantly looking at his phone. While in the first session he had been fairly responsive, he now lapsed into withholding silences or one-word responses. Every inquiry led to an unsatisfying dead end. Therapy is a two-way street, not someone simply responding to a stream of questions.

"Look, I said I'd come and I'm here," he said as he checked his email.

"Showing up is not being here, Marty," we told him. "Being here requires a willingness to explore the reasons for why you come in the door."

"I told you, I'm here for Karen."

"That's not enough. We can see you're angry…hurt…in a lot of pain."

"The pain is in having to drive over here and do this. What do you want to know? Work some of your magic."

"There's no magic here, just hopefully some honest dialogue."

Silence. Marty started scrolling through Facebook. "What?"

"Maybe we can begin with your filling us in on your experience with the meditation and breathing exercises we gave you."

"You know what? I breathe just fine."

"Did you try either of the exercises we suggested?"

Silence. You get the idea. By the fourth session it was clear that while Marty was going to show up for these meetings, he had no intention of any meaningful participation. At the end of yet another unproductive hour, we told him that we weren't going to keep meeting with him just so he could give Karen the appearance that he was in treatment.

"Thanks for nothing," he said as he stormed out of the room.

Sometimes therapy doesn't work out, isn't helpful. A couple of months after that last meeting, we got a short note from Marty. It read as follows: *Hope you're satisfied. Karen filed for the divorce. MK.* In the envelope, pounded flat with a hammer, was his wedding ring. Could his marriage have been saved? Might we have done something different, been more effective? Perhaps. We'll never know. What we do know is that under the circumstances, Karen is safer without having Marty in her life. We do hope Marty will get help, for as we told him in our short time together, he's in considerable pain.

Anger is a secondary emotion, a more tolerable cover than the pain that is its trigger. Here's how it works: Anger releases the hormone norepinephrine that acts as an analgesic agent, creating a distraction from the hurt. But in addition to the numbing provided by norepinephrine, anger also releases the stimulant epinephrine, creating a flood of energy.

As you know, Swords like Marty are drawn to arousal and the surges of both numbing and energizing agents can be addictive. Although we never got to know Marty very well, we suspect that his painful early experiences led to feelings of powerlessness that his anger blunted and protected him from—a dysfunctional storm of chemically induced self-empowerment.

Here's another story: Van sits with his back to the wall, glancing around at the crowded restaurant. Facing him is his wife, Chloe. A waiter nearby tips another few sips of red wine into their glasses. Both on the Shield side of the brain chemistry divide, Van and Chloe are hardworking and tonight they are treating themselves to a well-deserved meal away from the house. Pleasant night out for a happy couple? Not quite.

Some dimensions of behavior are influenced by imbalances in brain chemicals, while other dynamics are not. Some are simply equal opportunity traits co-opted by Swords and Shields alike. Control is one of them.

In his mid-forties, this is Van's third marriage; it is Chloe's first. A couple of years younger than Van, she found him kind, generous, and respectful. Growing up feeling as though she was plain and ordinary (she was neither), Chloe was swept up by his attraction to her and the sweet romantic gestures he made in the months before their marriage.

Many of her friends commented on their similarities and how much they seemed to have in common. However, the compatibility they seemed to share in the first months of their marriage faded quickly. At first, it was Van checking on where she was going and whom she was going with. These innocent curiosities soon morphed into subtle admonitions about her whereabouts and company, followed by more direct controlling behavior. In the beginning, Chloe thought his inquiries were protective and reflections of his caring. Now, three months in, she was told when they were out to dinner that she had to sit facing the wall so Van could be sure she wasn't making eye contact with some man or another across the room.

For men like Van, marriage releases a strange artifact, a possessive entitlement that it is his right to control Chloe because *she is his wife*. Chloe told herself that going along with his requests would be reassuring to Van, that it would assuage his sexual trust concerns. We told her that indulging in his insecurities only served to validate his fears and confirmed in his mind that she needed to be controlled.

A good marriage is never about control. It is about freedom and rooting for your partner's growth and happiness. Trust never grows in the soil of distrust, only in the incremental gaps opened that freedom fills and confirms. We must all learn how to deal effectively with our own relationship with arousal. Van's level of arousal (interpreted by him as anxiety) needed to be dealt with by him. Instead, his strategy was controlling, directing, and changing *Chloe's* behavior to mitigate *his* discomfort.

"But what if I'm doing something that makes him act this way?" Chloe asked. Typical Shield question. That's how Chloe reduced her own discomfort with arousal, thinking, If there's something I do that makes him feel insecure, I can control the situation by changing it.

We are all responsible for the integrity of our own actions. What we are not responsible for is modulating our partner's discomfort with arousal. Van was using control as a strategy to tamp down the unpleasant thoughts that his heightened arousal led to and Chloe was using compliance to accomplish the same ends. To have a healthy marriage, she was going to have to learn to do something all Shields hate—give up avoidance as an arousal-regulating strategy.

It took time for Chloe to see the part she played in the well-choreographed dance she and Van did with each other. We knew we were making headway when one day she came in and said, "I sat down with Van and told him a couple of things. I said, 'I love you and I want to be married to you, but some parts of this aren't working. If you need someone you can micromanage, I'll understand. But that's not me. I'll never go out to dinner again and have to face the wall because you don't trust me. Not ever.'"

We asked her how Van responded. "I was really scared when I said that to him, but I was totally shocked by what he told me. He said he didn't want to lose me and then he said, 'It's me. You've never given me any reason to distrust you. I don't want anybody else. It's not your problem, it's mine, and I'll try to work on it.'"

It remains to be seen whether Van can learn to tolerate his spikes in arousal without making Chloe's actions the solution. In couples therapy, Chloe learned she should have been more inquisitive about his relationship history and have seen the same damage that insecurity-driven control had exacted on his previous marriages. Such patterns are habitual and not easily surrendered. Those unconscious strategies don't simply disappear in the honesty of a single conversation. However motivated Van is, there will be slips.

Chloe needs to set and police the kind of healthy boundaries of respect and trust that define a loving relationship. If there's a silver lining here, it's that success will require her to be less avoidant and self-blaming, not mollifying her own discomfort with the ease of compliance. This isn't an easy task for a nonconfrontational Shield, but Chloe's understanding of the ways in which her brain chemicals shape her feelings and influence her actions has led to freedoms she hasn't experienced before. "If I'm not going to let Van push me around anymore," she said, "I'm sure not going to let myself get pushed around by my own brain chemicals."

Sex: From "Oh, This Feels So Good" to "Oh, This Feels So Bad"

Love possesses the wondrous power to assure, elevate, enliven, as well as to crush and devastate. Curiously, among the by-products of love is stress. Yes, stress. Among the great stressors in life are the loss of a loved one, moving to a new city, going to jail, divorce... and *getting married*. Stress of course is physical. When we are stressed, we spill cortisol into our systems. This is particularly impactful to Shields because cortisol depletes serotonin, leaving them more vulnerable. This effect no doubt has evolutionary value in that stress and its cortisol release are designed to prepare us to meet some danger. When getting ready to either run or fight, the last thing the brain thinks is needed is the calming influence of serotonin. Being in love should feel safe, but our body plays a kind of cosmic joke on us: just when we need the tempering influence of serotonin the most, it turns off the spigot.

Mason and Holly came to us as newlyweds. Both Shields, they were college sweethearts, just having graduated. Mason had been offered a job in Los Angeles as a software engineer, an opportunity he wanted to seize. Holly, with her degree in physical therapy, was confident she could find work anywhere. Neither wanted to experience a long-distance relationship and they decided to relocate from South Bend to the West Coast. After a slightly hurried wedding with friends and family, they drove across the country.

A move, a wedding, new jobs, and one more thing: neither had had any real sexual experience before getting married and their attempts had not been successful. The failure hadn't been due to a lack of interest or trying. Mason suffered from premature ejaculation.

Because Shields are so sensitive to the physical and emotional effects of arousal, they are more prone to having sexual problems than are Swords. For men, the manifestation can be premature ejaculation (the spike in arousal related to sexual excitement paired with the dimmed effect of too little available serotonin creates a situation where very little physical stimulation can result in an ejaculation). Another manifestation can be difficulties in getting an erection (feeling anxious and anticipating failure, they release cortisol, triggering a fight-or-flight reaction that causes the blood to run to the arms and legs and away from the very spot it needs to be).

Although it was painful and embarrassing for them to share, they both had a strong determination to make their relationship work—all of it. Both agreed to spend twenty minutes a day doing a mindfulness meditation, and we prescribed Mason an SSRI designed not only to address his anxiety but also as an antidote to the premature ejaculation he experienced.

Holly had never taken a prescription medication other than a rare antibiotic. Rather than prescribing an SSRI, we gave her a list of some of the ways she could increase available serotonin other than taking a prescribed medication.

Sexually, Holly was essentially without experience. The first thing we did was give her a little a little rudimentary sex education. You might be surprised to learn how many people think they know all the basics (even though they don't) or are afraid of feeling embarrassed to ask real questions they have. That done, we encouraged Mason and Holly to engage in sex play with an emphasis on *play* instead of outcome.

Somewhere around six months in, Mason could maintain an erection for several minutes with considerable stimulation from Holly. And, for the first time in her life, Holly was having orgasms herself. Sometimes therapy is a slog and sometimes it's like watching a flower gather its strength and bloom. You don't want to do too much or get in the way, just stand back and watch. Holly and Mason were like that. By the time we ended our work together, about a year after our initial meeting, they were enjoying a loving and sexually fulfilling relationship.

Being in therapy certainly doesn't create love, but sometimes it can keep love from becoming damaged or even repair damage if it's not too deep and extensive. We'd like to tell you about a couple that faced a crisis in their marriage. Cara and Jim have been married for six years and have two small children. For five of those six years they had a pretty strong marriage. Jim, a Sword, has a karate studio for children and adults and Cara is a social worker at a children's hospital. She is a Shield.

Cara struggled with a mild depression following the birth of her second child but over a few months had pulled herself out of it. What she was having more trouble working her way through was the painful nature of her job. Cara was brought in any time a child was in the ER and abuse was suspected. Over her two years there, she had seen more bruised and battered kids than she ever thought possible. She would be the first person to acknowledge that all too often she came home in a mood that was anything but upbeat.

Jim, is, by nature, more outgoing and optimistic. His first serious girlfriend had been into partying, which he enjoyed himself. Both had enjoyed the buzz of Adderall, Ritalin, and various other stimulants they could obtain. Athletic and daring, she got him into rock-wall climbing and was mouthy and careless about who she offended or challenged when she was high. Jim first got into karate to feel more confident dealing with some of the dangerous situations her loose lips more than occasionally created. When she suddenly took up with the drummer in a local bar band, he was as relieved every bit as much as he was hurt.

A few months later, Jim met Cara. In contrast to his background, she came from a stable family and her parents were still married. It may be of interest to learn that the offspring of divorced parents have an elevated risk of divorce themselves. Having no historic model for lifelong marriage, they can have a weak commitment to enduring the struggles that are often a requirement for maintaining a long-term relationship. Cara was everything Jim's ex-girlfriend wasn't—curious about him, shy, and contemplative. While it was a little intimidating for her, she looked upon his outgoing energy in awe. He was exciting, even a little bit dangerous, to her. Jim thought Cara just needed a little push to open herself up more to life—something no one in her family ever did. He was willing to give her the encouragement and enjoyed seeing her step into things that were unfamiliar and that brought along a smile and newfound confidence.

Cara flourished with the balance Jim brought to her life, until the babies arrived. Along with the children came the swift return of caution and a growing reason to say no to activities, events, and new situations. Choosing the perfect babysitter was torturous and Cara was always glad to get home after the occasional movie nights she and Jim built into their relationship. When finally she agreed to a long-planned vacation and a few days away from the children, Cara insisted that she and Jim fly on separate planes in case one crashed.

Jim was every bit as connected to the children as Cara was. Every morning he would get up early to make breakfast for the family. His kids' favorites were the purple, red, or green pancakes shaped like animals that he made by adding a little food coloring to the mix. Cara was in charge of the bathing and teeth brushing after dinner, but then Jim would read them their favorite books.

Over time, Jim and Cara's conversations centered more and more on the kids, their activities and concerns. Both felt a bit separate. Neglected. Neither talked about it. It was Jim who strayed. The relationship started innocently enough. She was the mother of one of the kids in his karate studio, divorced, attractive, and curious about Jim, and he enjoyed her sense of humor and the ease she had about herself. He found himself looking forward to the chats after class when she picked up her son. There was a lightness about her that was appealing. Enlivening.

After he lived a life of deception for a couple of months, guilt overtook him and he told Cara about the affair. She was devastated. Terrified. "We can't be together," she told him, "not ever, not after that."

Jim slept on the couch in the following days. He told a friend what had happened and that he had ended it with the woman. He loved Cara and was afraid he'd ruined everything. It was at his friend's suggestion that he came to us.

What seemed clear from the outside was that despite the betrayal, and hidden in the hurt, there was still love.

"I lost Cara as my best friend, and I want to get her back," he told us in that first joint session.

"You don't betray your best friend," Cara said.

"No, you don't," we agreed. We suspected their relationship was strong enough to try to save, but trust had been damaged. Trust is an asymmetrical phenomenon—it's knit together incrementally over an extended period of time and experience and ripped away in an instant. To help them build it back was going to take effort and patient caring.

Our goal for anyone we work with is to expand the sweet spot of arousal they are comfortable dealing with. That means Shields must take on the task of getting familiar with and tolerating slightly higher levels of arousal, while the task for Swords is just the opposite.

Feeling slightly overwhelmed, Cara had resorted to a classic Shield trick: she tried to reduce the arousal/stress she felt by pulling inside. She had fixated her anxiety on the children and deployed her natural avoidant tendencies as a strategy to regulate her emotional discomfort.

Jim had complained loudly at first about the narrowing of their lives and then, an odd thing. He started spending less time with his male friends, stopped going to the biweekly poker game he enjoyed, even said no to a salmon-fishing trip to Alaska he was invited to that Cara had encouraged him to accept. Although he never told her, he secretly held her responsible for the nos he himself wanted to say. Wives often become convenient excuses husbands use to get out of activities with their friends, but then the men forget the distortion and hold their wives responsible.

Cara and Jim had forgotten how to have fun together, how to have the heady conversations about politics and the foibles and struggles of everyday living that they'd loved. They forgot how to ask each other for what they needed.

"Jim stopped nudging me to go on more adventurous outings. I needed that and I never told him," Cara told him.

"I didn't think you were interested."

"I wasn't disinterested. I was scared. Big difference. Why did you stop?"

Jim just shrugged.

We see this a lot with couples. Using the other as an excuse without ever copping to it. Let us be clear, Jim is responsible for the excitement in his life, as well as the normal and predictable dips in arousal he experiences. He needed to reconnect with his friends and start doing the things that brought him pleasure—with Cara if she wanted to go, or on his own. Cara needed to stop assuming and start talking, to stop using the kids as the reason for her anxious feelings, and to challenge some of her indulgent avoidant tendencies.

And what about sex? It had long ago become routinized. Assumptive. Both looked to the other for signals of interest. Both misread them, held inside their silent hurts and rejections, their wishes. Subtle resentment built up on both sides, and resentment is the killer of love. Jim found Cara vaguely withholding and she saw him as on the edge of indifferent. Neither was, but each could be easily interpreted as being so. Neither said anything. They both just went on with their days, and each laid down one more layer of resentment.

"I felt like I'd become invisible," Cara said to Jim.

"I thought you enjoyed hiding in plain sight," he responded.

This was a natural setup for one or the other to stray. Being the riskier partner and having less impulse control, Jim betrayed the relationship and destroyed the trust built over their years together. In truth, they had both inadvertently abandoned the connection, stopped making it a priority. The science suggests that we have an unconscious bias toward looking at our partners' behavior rather than our own as the primary ingredient of happiness—our happiness. This creates a tendency toward becoming "other" oriented—"it's his/her responsibility to make me happy." We encouraged Jim and Cara to shift to a more proactive (less other-dependent and grievance-oriented) relationship where they both assume responsibility for making themselves happy.

At the outset, we'd established that they wanted to make the marriage work. The first order of business was to begin healing the damaged trust. The obstacle for Swords, assuming all the best intentions, is impatience. They've made their mea culpas and are ready to move on. This is usually expressed by wanting to resume sexual activity before their partner is ready. This is particularly important if the damage to trust was the result of an infidelity. The offending partner frequently gets tired of having to offer repeated reassurances, even when those assurances and time are what is most needed.

Jim was challenged in both those arenas. He needed to let Cara set the readiness timing for the resumption of sexual contact and he needed to be receptive and responsive to as much reassurance as she needed. A tall order for him.

Cara's hurdles for regaining trust were different. When Shields are hurt, there is an unfortunate tendency to brood, hiding the pain away in a protective shell. Cara needed to learn that the expression of her feelings was her friend and a necessary ingredient for healing to occur. Feeling vulnerable was frightening enough for Cara, but putting it into words with Jim was much scarier. She needed to challenge her discomfort with risk and to take more chances with him. Not only did that mean communicating more honestly; it also meant not falling prey to the temptation to check his phone or scroll through his emails. Trust is rebuilt only by opening up gaps and having those gaps filled. It's by the closing of those gaps in a reassuring way that trust is reestablished, increment by increment. And only she could open those gaps.

What's important in the sexual domain is an ongoing willingness to talk about one's sexual feelings, sensibilities, and needs. Too often, those conversations don't happen or, when they do, happen at the height of when one or the other partner is hurt or angry. Sex should be fun and a playful way to stay connected and express affection. The danger is in letting one's relationship with arousal get in the way and botch things up.

Shields tend to make sex too serious, too symbolic, too comingled with issues of body embarrassment and prowess or worries about attractiveness. Instead of fun, it becomes a test and frequently a test where one's partner doesn't even know they're being tested. Shields need to learn to embrace the arousal (interpret and reframe it as excitement and not as anxiety), get out of their heads and into their bodies. Take some risks. Risks are what opens up those gaps in trust, ease, and acceptance. Take the chance that your partner might actually fill them and you might just find that you even enjoy them.

And you Swords who tend to be a little more comfortable with yourselves—be the model for openness and enjoyment. Your tolerance for risk confers upon you a privileged place in the relationship. And along with that special position comes responsibility. In bed with a Shield, it's important to know that your words carry weight. Swords' chops are often sharpened by having a bit of uncertainty or danger in the mix. Intimate relationships aren't designed to provide that. Get over it. For excitement, take up skydiving or bungee jumping. Your partner isn't responsible for your need to bump up arousal.

And how about novelty? Intimacy of course is the antithesis of the new and unfamiliar. It doesn't take long to have heard all of our partner's stories and share all our personal issues and themes. If it's novelty you crave, marriage isn't the place to look for it. Continuity and the comfort of the familiar are elements that can be mined in an intimate relationship, not newness. For those kinds of fresh and unchartered experiences, look elsewhere and you won't be disappointed.

Growth and Discomfort

Among other things, acting smart means exerting the effort to override the subtle influences of your brain chemicals that don't serve you well. It requires being and staying awake, something that's hard for us all. Part of the reason it's difficult is because being awake can be uncomfortable. We learn to steer away from emotional discomfort as children, and by the time we are adults we've gotten good at it. Often, too good. It's not easy to check anger, inhibit impulses, be patient when you're feeling anything but. It's not easy for Swords to embrace some amount of sameness, boredom, and predictability, to remain faithful. And it's not easy for Shields to be more social, to be more outspoken when it's appropriate and a good sport some of those times when they'd like to say no. It's not easy not letting anxiety guide your decisions, not easy releasing secret grudges, remaining faithful.

Ease and comfort are pleasant but not particularly intelligent. Instead of allowing comfort to run the show, allow your highest self to step up and make the decisions. Your life will be fuller. Comfort will catch up.

Growth does have its signals. Often, when we are growing the most, we feel confused, hostile, anxious, weepy, even depressed. Whenever we grow and change, we feel anything but comfortable. Butterflies feel the restrictive and crushing pressure of the chrysalis before they break free. Maybe, just maybe, if you're feeling a little edgy and strung out around the complexities of a close relationship, it's not a bad thing. Those feelings may just be growth, a fertile period preparing you to better engage in a clearer way for the changes and demands that lie ahead.

A last challenge—go back to that question we posed earlier in the chapter about the role your brain chemistry plays in your marriage. See if you can come up with two or three ways/dynamics in your relationship that are problematic and that you see are related to your brain type. These should be things you do frequently to regulate feelings of emotional discomfort that affect the relationship in some negative way. For each item on your list, write out how you might go about addressing this issue in ways that would be healthy, constructive, lead to less conflict. Look for one of the strategies we've described earlier that fits your particular issue. Small steps are perfectly acceptable, for they accumulate and can lead to larger ones. What's important is the consciousness that you are taking these steps and your commitment to their continuance. We've found it helpful not to make a big announcement that you are doing these things. If your partner notices, they notice, and if not, they don't. What's of value here is that *you* notice. You are doing these things, these difficult things, because they are healthy and generative to do. You are doing them for yourself. And we hope your partner might also be reading this chapter and have the willingness to put in the effort as well.

Is taking on this challenge easy? No. You've been doing things this way for a long time. But is it a smart thing to do? Yes. The small price to pay here is manageable discomfort; the gain can very well be the critical difference that sustains a successful and enduring marriage.

CHAPTER NINE

Calming: A Parent's Central Organizing Task

A Calm Child Grows into a Healthier and More Successful Adult. Diagnose Your Kid's Brain Type and Explore the Toolbox.

"WE'D TAKEN THE CLASSES, READ all the recommended books, Kelly had chugged down her daily handful of prenatal vitamins, and I strapped this twenty-pound contraption around my belly to get a taste of how awkward and uncomfortable it is in the last weeks of pregnancy. Oh boy, that was something. Pretty awful! If I were Kelly, I would have complained a whole lot more. We were prepared. Even her mother thought so. Hard to get a kudo out of that one. Baby showers behind us, tiny clothes neatly folded and hidden away in drawers, I'd managed to unbox the crib and somehow get the thing screwed together. Kelly and I stood looking around at the not-yet-occupied little room when she said, 'We're done. Let's go to a movie.'

"After the movie we went to a coffee shop for burgers. Kelly grinned at me across the table. I grinned back. Then I saw her eyes suddenly widen and her mouth gape open. 'What?' I asked.

"'I'm having a contraction.'

"I knocked over my glass of Coke reaching for her hand, asked her if we shouldn't go to the hospital. Pulled out my phone to call the doctor.

"Kelly shook her head no. 'Let's sit for a few minutes and time the contractions,' she said, losing the color in her face. 'Maybe I was wrong and that was something else.'

"'Like what?' I asked, glancing at the time on my phone.

"She shrugged and took a bite of French fry and then . . .

"Wham! She grabbed my hand, grimaced in pain. I looked at the phone. Two minutes. Two minutes?! 'Let's get out of here!' I yelled.

"The ride to the hospital was eerily quiet aside from her re-strained moans which were coming more frequently. Once we got there, I pulled up in front and helped Kelly inside, calling out for help. They sat her in a wheelchair and told me I couldn't leave my car parked in front of the hospital. I watched as she disappeared into an elevator then jogged back to the car, so I could bring it to the parking lot. By the time I got back inside, I realized I had no idea where they'd taken Kelly. Eventually, someone directed me to the labor and delivery floor. The elevator was taking forever so I rushed up the stairs. The only thought going through my head was, Oh my God, we're really going to have a baby.

"When I got to the L&D unit, I looked around frantically for someone I could ask about Kelly. A nurse told me to wait and he'd see what he could find out. I'm not sure how long I waited; it felt like an eternity. But then I saw the nurse approaching, a big smile on his face. 'Congratulations! It's a girl.'

"And then it happened. We were parents. I felt like we weren't prepared at all."

Joe was right. He and Kelly weren't prepared. None of us is really, despite all the books and classes. Certain aspects of becoming a par-ent are instinctual, augmented by the hormones the process stimulates. But the actual day-to-day practice feels like a learn-as-you-go, trial-by-fire experience fraught with uncertainty and self-doubt. The parent/child relationship often wants to go in its own direction in spite of all the best intentions. It can be frustrating or disappointing or surprisingly easy and successful. Parenting is a chance for some to re-create pleasant and healthy childhood memories. For others it's an opportunity to understand and forgive the foibles of our parents, recognize them in our own repeated missteps, a way to get it right this time around, a way to embody necessary corrections. Either way, the challenge can be difficult and complicated to pull off. And, for most of us, there isn't a particular plan or well-marked path to follow. We just bump along in a reactive mode simply doing the best we can, responding to the myriad issues that come along.

The broad sweep of parenting is beyond the scope of this book. What we would like to give you here is twofold. First, we're going to help you determine your child's brain type and provide some tools you might use to help ease the self-defeating tendencies that may accompany your child's brain chemical imbalances. And second, we are going to share some thoughts on how your own brain type tendencies interact with those of your child. But before we dive in, here are a couple of questions to roll around in your head: Do you see how your brain type influences your parenting style? How it may influence your thoughts about your child? What do you think about your ability to blend your patterns of parenting successfully with those of your spouse or co-parent, if you have one? Do these patterns conflict, support, or amplify one another? How do your brain type leanings enhance your understanding of your child or, maybe, sometimes get in the way of your child's development?

How do we prepare ourselves for what may be the most important undertaking we will ever have—to help guide the tiny creatures we bring into the world from the helpless potential of their beginnings to the greatest fulfillment of their unique capacities? Truly, what parents want most for their children is for them to be able to recognize and express their gifts with the greatest confidence and freedom. And the best way to accomplish that is by understanding the kind of obstacles that stand in the way of achieving these goals. As you know, the obstacles that a child with imbalanced serotonin has are different from the challenges that come along with a bit too little dopamine.

You know your own brain type and probably can make a pretty accurate guess about that of your child. But to refine that guess, fill out the following questionnaire .

Assessing My Child's Neurotype

My child—

1. Is outwardly expressive in nature.	T	F
2. Can imagine threats that really aren't there.	T	F
3. Is very sensitive to disapproval.	T	F
4. Is game to try most anything.	T	F
5. Tends to be on the shy, contemplative side.	T	F
6. Is pretty unfazed by punishment.	T	F
7. Has a cheery, optimistic outlook.	T	F
8. Tends to hold on to negative memories.	T	F
9. Tends to blame others when things go wrong.	T	F
10. Is someone who wants what they want—right now!	T	F
11. Has a very hard time hearing the word "no."	T	F
12. Tends not to be very aggressive.	T	F
13. Seems to have good impulse control.	T	F
14. Typically holds anger in.	T	F
15. Seems to almost enjoy taking unnecessary chances.	T	F
16. Seems to worry a lot about getting sick.	T	F
17. Tends to be cautious and nervous in new circumstances.	T	F
18. Is easily distracted.	T	F
19. Follows routines pretty well.	T	F
20. Tends to be risk averse.	T	F
21. Seems overly concerned about making mistakes.	T	F
22. Is a bit of a daredevil.	T	F
23. Has a hard time delaying gratification.	T	F
24. Tends to avoid social challenges.	T	F

Scoring

For every answer marked as true, fill in the circle corresponding to the question number on the graphics of the brain below. Whichever brain has more circles filled represents your child's brain type—Shield or Sword. There will likely be circles filled on both images. That's because there are no pure brain types. As you can see, Swords tend to have some Shield tendencies within them and vice versa.

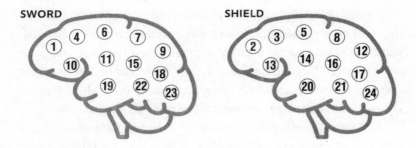

With regard to your child's brain type, the most far-reaching impact you can have is in helping them learn how to be calm. Yes, to calm themselves. To be focused and at peace in their own bodies. Calming is a skill set and a teachable one. If this sounds simple, it is not. If you set in place the foundations for self-calming in your child, the bounty of your guidance will follow them for the rest of their lives.

Earlier, we talked about an arousal sweet spot. This sweet spot is a subjective level of stimulation or arousal in the central nervous system that, when we are in it, provides the emotional comfort to express the highest degrees of freedom in our actions. Being outside that sweet spot, we become more constrained and start exhibiting the narrower, more patterned behaviors characteristic of our brain type.

While swimming around in our sweet spot, we are calm and free. Knocked out of that place of equilibrium even a little bit, not so much. Think "Goldilocks and the Three Bears." Anything not "just right" produces discomfort. Shield children typically feel anxious with too much arousal and Sword children feel bored and restless having too little. Calming your child means helping them tolerate spikes or dips in arousal, expanding their sweet spot. Calming Shields allows them to be less avoidant, not quite so cautious, and more comfortable socially. Calming Swords allows them to be less impulsive, more sensitive to downsides/dangers, and better able to delay gratification.

And as you know, Swords and Shields have strengths as well as vulnerabilities. Calming preserves all of the strengths and reduces the weaknesses. Predictable stress-induced brain type traits (the weaknesses) are compensatory strategies in services of one goal: self-calming. The good news is that they work. The bad news is that they work too well and don't always support good health, relationships, accurate threat assessments, not even general well-being.

As if helping your children navigate their unique arousal issues isn't complicated enough, folding in how you understand and relate to your own brain chemistry adds additional layers. Sometimes empathy and seeing yourself in your child can be as much a hindrance as a help. Similarities and identification with your child's brain type or tendencies can result in being overly protective on the one hand or blind to some of the self-defeating traits your child may exhibit on the other. And conversely, parenting a child whose brain type is the opposite of yours can leave you baffled by some of the choices they make that would be at variance to the reactions and choices that feel most natural to you. Having a child will test the limits of your boundaries and demand every bit of personal clarity you can muster.

Understanding your own brain type gives you an enormous leg up in fine-tuning your parenting style. You will know much more clearly when and how to commiserate and when and how to nudge. You've seen firsthand how our brain type gets insinuated into how you feel and the decisions you make. Let that personal knowledge become an integral part of the mindset you bring to the ways in which you parent your child.

Calming a Shield Child

Being the mom or dad of a Shield child has unique challenges. These children can be sweet and affectionate, smart and capable, as well as baffling to many a parent. Let us tell you a little bit more about Kelly and Joe, the couple you met earlier. Kelly is a writer. She grew up in the Midwest as the third child of five. Her parents have a good marriage and still live in the same house in Indiana where Kelly grew up. Embedded deep in the mix of her siblings, Kelly was shy and contemplative as a child, likely to hole up in the farthest corner of the house reading as her four brothers stomped around downstairs. The house was always astir with their endless arguments and friendly roughhousing.

Where Kelly is soft-spoken, gentle, and cautious, Joe has a voice as big and booming as his body. A partner in a law firm, he is a litigator. Having played basketball in college, Joe stays in shape racing mountain bikes and exercising his special passion: snowboarding. As you may have surmised, he is a pretty straight-up Sword, while Kelly has distinct Shield leanings.

After telling us the story of Logan's birth, Kelly and Joe went on to describe some of the issues they were having with their eight-year-old son. It didn't take much digging to see that Logan was a Shield.

"Joey and I get into it when I see him pushing Logan too much. He compares him to himself when he was that age and I don't think it's a fair comparison. Logan always comes up short."

"Not always," Joe piped in.

"You're right. Not always. But most of the time you are critical of him. I think you're a really good father and I know how much you love him. But you don't show him. I can't think of anything that would make Logan happier than to feel like you were proud of him. There just has to be a way for him to earn that based on who he is, not who you expect him to be."

"I don't think I'm all that critical," Joe said, turning to us. "I'm disappointed. For him. Couple of examples: We gave Logan a really great birthday party at our house and he spent most of the time in the bathroom hiding. And a couple of years ago, I took him snow-boarding. He fell a few times, got a little snow down his back, and said he didn't want to do it anymore. Look, I'm pretty physical and competitive. It's a tough world out there and I think it takes some grit to get by. I just want to prepare him the best way I can."

"You left out the wrestling," Kelly said.

"Yeah, well when I was a kid, I used to love getting down on the floor and wrestling with my father. He always let me win, but not by much. It was one of the things I missed most when my parents divorced and my father moved away and started a new family. But when I try to re-create that bond with Logan he just starts crying."

"Look, I know the touchy-feely, tender expression of your emotions is really hard and I get it. But there have to be other ways to get physical with Logan. How about just a hug? He's terrified when you start up with him," she said, looking our way. "How would you like to get down on the floor and wrestle with that body?"

Good point, we agreed. But we wanted to key in on Joe's discomfort around closeness. As we explored it, what became clear was that although his discomfort was never talked about, Logan and Kelly were certainly aware of it. Subtle as it was, Joe's discomfort was one of those family secrets everyone knows, is affected by, yet no one steps up and acknowledges. The famous Scottish psychiatrist R. D. Laing put it this way: "I have never come across a family that doesn't draw a line somewhere as to what may be put into words, and what words it may be put into." This unspoken rule always works best when it's observed without calling attention to itself. In Laing's words, "If you obey these rules, you will not know they exist."

There's a downside here. These rules may ignore the elephant in the room, but they don't make it vanish.

Some recent research may give a bit of insight into Joe's issue. Studies have shown that childhood experiences such as the death of a parent or the parents' divorce are associated with anxiety and depression in teenagers and, later on, parental insensitivity, reduced warmth and affection, as well as the increased use of punishment.

Research has also shown that adults whose parents divorced when they were young children have lower levels of oxytocin. As you will recall, oxytocin is a hormone made in an area of the brain called the hippocampus and is released during childbirth and breastfeeding, enhancing the bond between mothers and their babies. Often referred to as the "love hormone," it is released during orgasm in both women and men. Oxytocin has the effect of strengthening emotional bonds, trust, and openness. It allows people to feel more outgoing and sociable.

Joe had heard of oxytocin but didn't know much about how to interact with it or its inverse relationship to stress. We explained to him that as oxytocin goes up cortisol and stress go down. That got his attention. He was very familiar with stress. We told him how easy it was to increase oxytocin simply with some physical touch: a massage, a pat on the back or handshake, petting his dog, and yes, a hug. We talked about some of the foods that contain oxytocin, including anything with vitamin C, D, or magnesium, fatty fish like salmon, mushrooms, spinach, avocados, and tomatoes.

Returning to who Logan is and some of the more granular details of what life was like at home, we learned a lot more. Logan was clearly one of those children whose amygdala had been screaming in his ear from early on. As we explained some of the brain chemistry issues Logan was struggling with, Joe sat back in his chair for the first time and uncrossed his arms.

As is not uncommon for Shield children, Logan was easily aroused, anxious, and hypervigilant. He had a habit of chewing on his pencil. After watching some new story on the cancer-causing effects of lead in paint, he became worried that he was going to get cancer and die. When he was told that pencil lead wasn't really lead at all but simply graphite and some wax to hold it together, he wasn't convinced.

Living through the lockdown has been a difficult time for them all. Both Kelly and Joe began working from home, and both tried to help Logan stay organized with Zoom school. They were all in one another's hair. During that time, Logan's anxiety bounced around from target to target. Just when one got knocked down, it got attached to another.

By the time in-person school started up again, his anxiety had shifted around once again and got attached to reentry worries. As you know, Shields contend with consistently heightened levels of arousal. Logan, as do many Shield children, conflated excitement with fear. At a physiological level, they are essentially identical. Logan missed seeing his friends and was looking forward to being with them again in person, but instead of those feelings being interpreted as exciting and pleasurable, they felt similar to plain old raw arousal and got misidentified as fear or washed out entirely.

All of us tend to label our feelings, sorting them into good and bad piles. This automatic sorting process begins when our body reacts to an emotion and ends when we see how we experience and express it. In talking to his mother about going back to school, Logan told her he didn't think he was going to have any interesting stories to tell and was worried that the kids he was most interested in seeing again wouldn't remember him even though they'd all been Zooming throughout the school year. Logan was also afraid he might forget some of the things he wanted to tell his friends when finally he was able to see them.

So, how can you help turn situations that feel vaguely threatening into experiences that feel more like opportunities? Logan's worries were really his form of negative self-talk. We gave Kelly and Joe some simple tools designed to flip negative talk into something more positive.

Logan's worries number one and three were essentially the same. He wanted to have something interesting to say in those first times back in touch with his friends. After a little poking around, Logan remembered that he and his parents had gone to the mountains, played in the snow, and seen a bobcat. They even had a picture of it. Joe and Kelly teased out a couple of other experiences the family had had in the past few months, including the most memorable one where Logan and Joe built a treehouse in the backyard. Logan did have stories.

Kelly helped him reframe his second worry by reminding Logan that if he remembered all of his classmates, they would also remember him, that his feelings about his friends were really about excitement and how much he was looking forward to being with them again. Kelly also gave him three words to say when he was aware of "those feelings and thoughts." The three words are, "I am excited." Studies show that for something as universally anxiety provoking as test taking, simply saying those three words in the drumroll up to the test increases test scores significantly. Anxiety is something we want to get away from; feeling excited is engaging. Simply reframing anxiety as excitement creates the more positive experience of engagement.

We also gave Joe and Kelly a fun mindfulness meditation for the family to practice together. Sitting in comfortable chairs, each blocking one nostril with an index finger, they all did an inhale for a count of four. Then, switching fingers and blocking the other nostril, they exhaled for a count of six. This was a ten-minute drill and the object was to get through it without anyone laughing. Even when someone laughed, the experience was a success and a bonding one.

Logan returned to school and is doing well. Joe has a lot more understanding about the differences between his brain chemistry and Logan's. He developed a newfound respect for some of his son's traits that were strikingly different strengths from his own. "I saw him work on something: a kit where he built a solar-powered clock," Joe told us. "It was really complicated, but he stuck with it. I would have thrown that thing across the room. He made it work. I was very impressed."

"He didn't just tell Logan that," Kelly chimed in. "Joey gave him a huge hug."

We were moving in the right direction.

We all talk to ourselves, only most of the time we don't move our lips. Internally oriented Shield children naturally engage in self-talk. Unfortunately, these verbal observations tend not to be simply neutral snapshots of events, experiences, or states of being;

they tend to be negative. Why? Shield children can see threat when it's not really there and when it is there magnify its danger. This threat assessment leads to Shields' go-to control strategy, which is avoidance. It goes something like this: "If I can control myself, I can change and control the way I feel." Take particular notice here that this goal isn't changing the way a person *behaves*; it's a control strategy directed to regulate the way they *feel*. Too often, negative self-talk leads to decisions where an action is avoided when it might have been more positively engaged.

Here's an example of how this can play out: A couple of kids are paired to work together in a schoolroom project that is presented to the class. Kid A, a Shield, lets kid B dominate the presentation, largely taking credit for it and using the "I" pronoun rather than "we." And after, kid A watches as other children come up and say nice things to and ask questions of kid B, who did almost all of the talking but clearly no more than her share of the preparation, maybe less.

Here's a little sneak peek into kid A's head: I did most of the work on this project and she took most of the credit. Maybe I think I did more than I really did. No, I know what I did. I just couldn't open my mouth. I didn't talk. I should have talked more. More? I barely said a word. What's wrong with me? I hate not being able to say the things I know. I knew this was going to happen. I hate myself.

Shield kids direct anger and disappointment inward. Kid A had a high level of arousal going into the presentation and speaking up was seen as only increasing that uncomfortable feeling. She controlled the arousal by avoidance, keeping her mouth closed. But this strategy comes along with a noticeable price. The price is the depreciation, the negative self-talk that kid A knew she would have to pay, and yet she paid it anyway. That's how odious the power of arousal and its interpretation as a threat can be.

The most useful gift parents can give Shield children is to help them expand their tolerance for arousal. Using a school presentation as our example, what might a parent do that would be helpful?

Let's dig into this a little deeper. There's no better antidote for performance anxiety than preparation. We're going to call this child Molly and she, like most Shield children, put in the work (if for no other reason than to avoid the anxiety she would feel if she didn't). Where Molly let herself down was in indulging in her old standby strategy avoidance. This habitual ploy to modulate discomfort is unfortunately the lead-in to negative self-talk. Children who employ avoidance are hard on themselves. They attack their self-esteem and image rather than attacking the avoidance.

We're going to roll back the clock—it's now a few days before the presentation. Here is something Molly's mom or dad might have helped her with. We call this game Bring on the Dragon. Shields have a dragon and it's healthy to acknowledge its presence. The trick isn't ignoring it but changing its valence from negative to positive. The dragon, of course, is arousal and it can be seen as either dangerous and overwhelming or alternatively as a friendly source of energy and excitement.

Days before the presentation, Molly's parent might say, "Let's play Bring on the Dragon. Are you were going to be standing or sitting for your talk?"

"Standing,"

"Okay, so you stand here and I'll sit over there and pretend like I am one of the kids you're going to be talking to.

"Ready? Everybody will be looking at you. Did you and your partner discuss who's going to talk first?"

"No."

"Good idea to do that. Ask her if it's okay if you go first."

"Why first? I don't like to go first."

"It's always better to go first. Waiting to go second makes the dragon feel scary. The game here is to make the dragon feel like it's your friend."

"You want me to talk first?"

"Yes. Thinking about that right now, how are you feeling?"

"I'm really nervous."

"Yes. I know you are and that's okay. It's natural and normal for people to feel exactly that way when they're either unprepared or excited. Are you unprepared?"

"No."

"Then you're probably excited. When we're really excited, our body is filled with lots of energy."

"Yeah, it's like I'm about to explode right now."

"Good, that means you're really excited and have lots of energy. Go ahead and let the energy build. Let's see if you can explode."

An eye roll.

"Let's try something else to see if we can make the dragon bigger. We're going to take five big breaths. Each time, I want you to pretend that you're blowing your breath into the dragon and keep on blowing until your breath is really all gone. Okay, a big breath.... And that's five. Were you able to make the dragon any bigger?"

"No. It's the same. Still scary."

"No explosions, I take it. Okay, here's the truth: Dragons are exactly what we make them. That scary dragon is really an excited dragon in disguise. The dragon is here to help you. It can never hurt you. We're going to do something now. We're going to flip the switch. We're going to be taking some more big breaths and slowly blow the air into the dragon again. We don't want the dragon to go away because you need the energy. So, when you take in the big breaths, I want you to call the dragon by its real name. You're used to calling it *Scary*. Its real name is *Excitement*. And it's part of you. So, with every breath, I want you to think to yourself, 'Excitement is what I'm feeling. I'm glad you're here and I'm excited.'

"Okay, let's start.... And that's five. How does the dragon seem now?"

"I don't know. Maybe about the same."

"That's okay. You've been used to calling it by the wrong name for a long time. We're going to play this game every day until the presentation. And every time we do it and you call it by its real name, *Excitement*, it's going to feel a little bit friendlier."

Anxious kids feel out of control. They mistakenly believe that they will feel more in control by trying to avoid and get away from the arousal they feel. Paradoxically, the surest way to dampen the effects of the arousal is to accept its presence, even invite it. The minute the arousal is accepted, it loses its fangs. A child's terror around arousal is in their impossible fight to try to rid themselves of it. The moment they realize it is a normal and natural part of them, the power to frighten them begins to fade.

Let's look at another example. Jeannie is fourteen and in the full blush of adolescence. Although she has had scrimmages with them before, the anxiety attack she had recently was the one that caught her parents' attention. Anti-vaxxers in her extended family had warned her about getting a Covid vaccine. As a Shield, Jeannie, with a history of asthma, sat down for the shot with a pounding heart. Simply remaining in the chair waiting after was torture. Her mind was trying to sort out her racing thoughts and the internal chemical storm that was brewing. She stood finally and told the nurse she thought she was having an allergic reaction. She wasn't. What Jeannie was having what was a panic attack.

Here is something you parents can do to help your child if they are experiencing anxiety and it even works for panic attacks. Acupuncture and its needle-free version, acupressure, have been used for centuries in Eastern medicine to create homeostasis or balance. What follows is a technique you can do along with your child until they know it by heart and can do it on their own.

Using the index and middle fingers of your right hand, tap the outside edge of your left hand (for about ten seconds). Now tap your forehead, just above your left eyebrow (same ten count). Continuing with that count of ten, tap your temple next to your left eye. Now tap the area right under your left eye. Move on and tap your upper lip right under your nose. And now your chin. Tap the left side of your collarbone. Now tap the top of your ribs under your left arm. And finally, tap the top of your head. You can repeat this if necessary to enhance calming.

Calming a Sword Child

The English language has a lot of phrases that are unidirectional—
"fix up" or "tumble down," for example. We never hear "fix down"
or "tumble up." "To calm" fits into that same directional paradigm.
We only think of "calming down" because that's the phrase in the
vernacular. "Calming up" should be there as well, for that is exactly
the correct term for making a Sword comfortable. But beyond comfort, calming Swords frees them to be their flexible best and helps
them expand the sweet spot in their relationship with arousal.

Jennifer's relatively few years on the planet have led her to one
stark conclusion: "I will never be able to keep up." She is seventeen
and a high school junior. When she was in elementary school, her
third grade teacher brought up concerns about Jennifer's distractibility and lack of focus. By the fourth grade, her parents were given
the suggestion that medication might be helpful in regulating her
moody, distracted behavior. Jennifer's mother chalked it up to the
family going through a stressful time

When Jennifer was nine, her parents went through a messy and
acrimonious divorce. Their marriage had been marked by complaints hurled at each other, and now those same gripes continued,
in the third person, in rooms with only Jennifer there to hear them.
In the often questionable wisdom that only divorcing parents can
muster, they chose to split up the children. Her brother, Josh, went
to live with his father and Jennifer with her mother. Weekends, the
kids were together, alternating between their mother and father.
Jennifer was devastated. Her mother told her they would learn to
get along better together. She wasn't concerned about getting along
better with her mother. She missed her father and Josh terribly.

When the family home was sold, Jennifer and her mom moved
into an apartment complex along the 101 Freeway. The next few
years were sour and troubling. Jennifer watched a trail of unknown
men come in and out of the apartment. They largely ignored her,
which was just as well; she didn't want any more to do with them
than they with her. Retreating more and more often to her room,

she took solace in being alone. Concentrating on her homework for any length of time was still difficult for her. Instead, her evenings were more often spent laying in her bed, earbuds in, rocking to the music, a thumb in her mouth.

Jennifer loved the weekends, particularly when she was with Josh and her father. She idolized her brother and followed him around anywhere he would let her and he let her more often than not. They spent hours skateboarding together until it got dark, and later she stood hunched over his shoulder in the room they shared as he played Fortnite online. Jennifer was captivated by the game, and sitting next to her brother she imagined the moves she would make if she were playing the game herself. She watched, listened, waited. One night her chance came. "Take over for a minute; I gotta pee," Josh said. When he came back a few minutes later, Josh became the observer, watching her play. After twenty minutes, the game ended and his teammates complimented him on his play. All he could do was mutter, "Holy shit." Soon, Jennifer was on Josh's team using the handle LooseShoelace. Josh never told anyone she was a girl. Gaming had all of the elements she loved: the exhilarating feeling of risk along with a sense of uncertainty despite how many times she played the game.

Jennifer, if you haven't yet surmised, has imbalanced dopamine. The allure of novelty is a hallmark for Swords and it can have a devastating impact. Novelty seekers like Jennifer glom on to an activity, a project, most anything that carries along with it the expanse of newness. Gaming provided that oomph until Jennifer entered her adolescence and it was taken over by the interactive swirl of Instagram, Snapchat, and the incessant monitoring of her Facebook page. Unfortunately, the feelings of accomplishment and mastery she received from her gaming abilities faded as she followed her new interests.

Jennifer's day began and ended with the phone through which she managed (if you can call it that) her social media presence. Her connection to her phone had the effect of disconnecting her from her schoolwork. She had an increasingly difficult time paying attention and completing assignments. For a lot of us, an online identity carries with it some sense of its being optional. Not for Jennifer. Not for a lot of kids. Checking, posting, rechecking became a growing necessity. Her social media platforms were managing her and she was paying a terrible price. That price was stress. She no longer had face-to-face time with friends and became progressively more isolated. One night while checking her Facebook page, she realized she had lots of Facebook friends but almost no one in real life, that she'd gotten really good with her thumbs but had sadly lost her ability with words.

A girl who'd always had a surplus of energy now felt sapped and in a constant fizz of agitation. But as exhausted and restless as she was, had Jennifer been given the choice between abandoning social media and her phone or losing one of her hands, she would have to give that decision real thought. Dr. Jean Twenge, a psychologist who has long studied generational differences, has found that digital natives like Jennifer tend to be more conforming, less happy, and lonelier than earlier generations. Being connected with their devices leaves kids today less connected to the analog world of conversation and face-to-face contact.

Unfortunately, Swords tend to have difficulty with moderation. If a little is good, more is a whole lot better. Jennifer's phone pinged with every notification, and each ping could mean some bit of information that was absolutely necessary to check out. She'd become a slave to the tool she held in her hand.

By the time her mother brought her in to see us, even Jennifer knew that her connection to her phone wasn't healthy. "I've tried sticking it in my closet, but I hear it in there and I have to go in and get it. It gets in the way, I'm not studying like I should and I know this sounds crazy, but I feel like if I don't have it in my hand, I'm going to miss something. I used to be able to play my guitar for hours. I don't even touch it anymore." Rachel, Jennifer's mother, added, "I'm just like her only I don't have to worry about getting into college. After work, I'm watching television, on Facebook, and googling people half the night. I have a hard time asking Jen to do something different when I am as hooked on my phone as she is."

Maybe we could do something that would be helpful to both Jennifer and her mother. We'd learned some important things in our conversation with them. Clearly, they were both Swords and both competitive. We look for any little edge that we can find and proposed to the two of them a game to wean Jennifer from her phone.

What we designed for them was pitched as a progressive digital cleanse. Here's the way it works: Jennifer and her mother are, as are many Swords, early-to-bed people. (Does that sound paradoxical? Swords tend to go to bed early and rise early, whereas Shields tend to be night owls. Evenings tend to be a time of lower stimulation and arousal. Shields often treasure this time of greater comfort, while Swords like Jennifer and her mother simply get drowsy as arousal wanes. For week one, they both committed to turning off their phone for one hour a day between 11:00 PM and midnight, by which time they were likely to be asleep anyway. They agreed to change their passwords and exchange phones during that time so that neither could "just check," if tempted. It may have been pushing it, but we suggested that if they were still up, they might use that time to catch up with each other's day, an experience long forgotten.

The second night, Jennifer went into her mother's room and said, "Okay, this really sucks. Give me my phone and I'll give you yours." Rachel's refusal was met with, "Well, don't expect me to talk to you," as Jennifer left, slamming the door.

Week two, we upped the ante to an hour and a half a night, a stressor that nearly blew the game apart. We were trying to help Jennifer expand the sweet spot of her arousal. As you've learned, Swords, short on arousal, calm themselves by foraging for stimulation. And, often in the restless hunt, they overstimulate and exhaust themselves. For Jennifer to surrender her phone for a period of time provided an opportunity for her to challenge and redefine her relationship with arousal.

We had described this digital break as a body awareness plunge. We explained to Jennifer that when we are a little short on dopamine we can feel sensations in our body that have solely to do with our brain chemicals. That these sensations can make us feel as if we should *do something*, like check our phone. We explained that when we feel these sensations we get used to acting on them because the actions stimulate our nervous system and make us feel better, more normal. That these inner sensations serve no better purpose than to get us to try to get rid of them. That she would feel freer and more in control if she could learn to tolerate the sensations, not think of ways to make them stop. We asked that she simply make note of the sensations and allow them to be there without having to do anything with them.

For the second week, in the first phone-free hour and fifteen minutes, we told them they could do anything they wanted to do so long as it didn't involve screens. During the last fifteen minutes, we asked that they find a quiet place to sit. "What? And do nothing?" Jennifer asked, horrified. We nodded and told her that doing nothing was really a big something. That *something* was an intimate introduction to the inner world of her feelings. We asked them both that during that last quarter hour they observe the feelings and thoughts they had with curiosity and without judging them as either good or bad.

Contemplative moments for Swords can be very difficult and uncomfortable. The skill set here is accepting these denizens of the inner world as benign and seeing them as your own. This exercise in acceptance is best accomplished without fidgeting and while keeping your hands still.

At week three, we added in a reframe. "I keep wondering what's going on and thinking I'm out of it," Jennifer described her phone-free experience, "that I need to make sure I'm not missing something."

"Here's what you might try telling yourself when you get those feelings," we told her. "'I'm not missing anything that I can't catch up with later. There is nothing I need to do now other than be with myself.'"

Weaning Jennifer from her phone was a gradual process. The goal was to get her to completely log out of her social media accounts for a day at a time. The road to getting there was bumpy, but over time she learned to translate her distractedness into focus through the mindfulness exercise that made her better able to tolerate the silent gaps in external stimulation, or contemplative moments as she learned to call them. During our time together, we also gave her some apps (Luminosity, Elevate, and CogniFit) designed to increase concentration and focus.

The second part of the program we designed for Jennifer was a little more complicated. The goal was to help her find ways to "calm up" by raising her level of arousal. As we've described, children (doubtless Swords) identified by teachers and diagnosed by pediatricians as having attention problems and being overly active (ADHD) are often prescribed stimulants. These children look for ways to stimulate themselves through restless behavior to, in essence, calm up and feel more at peace internally. That's why, if given a stimulant that raises their level of arousal (and dopamine levels) pharmaceutically, they can drop the compensatory foraging for excitement behavior.

Jennifer didn't need medication; she just needed to start doing some things that were absorbing, because such activities are rich sources of arousal and would increase the time she spent in her relative sweet spot. Exercise, particularly the kind that is filled with as many challenges, uncertainties, and mastery rewards as skateboarding, was a great candidate. It didn't take much coaxing to get her back on board.

Children need to know the purpose behind the things we ask them to do. We reminded Jennifer that the modified mindfulness meditation drill that she was doing had some very interesting science behind it. Becoming more mindful has been shown to increase different types of attention, including alerting, orienting, and executive control. Simply listening to a brief ten-minute audio-guided mindfulness meditation has this same effect. We explained that there were even things that she could introduce into her diet that would be helpful. For example, a well-controlled study showed that a mixed-berry smoothie enhances attention for over six hours. Flavanol-rich cocoa (chocolate) has been shown to greatly increase the oxygenation levels in the frontal cortex, a brain area responsible for decision-making and planning. And as a bonus, chocolate even boosts our endorphins. For a less sugary alternative, beetroot juice does the same thing. About six ounces of this earthy-tasting drink has been shown to increase the oxygen levels in the brain significantly. And we also encouraged Jennifer to spend a little more time out in nature. For reasons that are still poorly understood, doing this has been shown to provide real cognitive benefits, including better attentional control and working memory as well as enhanced cognitive flexibility.

In that Swords tend to be externally oriented and prone to blaming others for issues, controlling anger is a common problem. One thing we found helpful is to have them make a "Things That Make Me Mad" list. For each item on the list, have your child tell you whose fault it was, either *theirs* or *someone else's*. Use the items listed as *someone else's fault* to explore the possibility of what role your child might have played in creating the issue. The goal here is to question blame and to encourage more appropriate personal responsibility.

The healthiest way to help your child regulate negative emotions like anger is to be willing to do yourself what you are asking your child to do. Kids certainly know their parents get mad and may have witnessed them having difficulty containing hurtful expressions as well. "Do as I say" is a long-standing parental control model. Sword children, as you know, are not very sensitive to the punishment that is the typical sledgehammer that follows: "Do it because I said so and if you don't…" As children are natural mimics, they are inclined to do what we do instead of what we tell them to do, if the actions are incongruent.

We saw this at work when a couple came in wanting to talk about their preschooler, Jonah, who'd been sent home for using "bad language." The schoolmaster repeated some of the words and phrases Jonah had been using. This precocious four-year-old was communicating with the same emotionally laden words his parents use at home. "We told him," his mother began, "not to use certain words at school. He just doesn't listen to us."

Jonah was showing some of the early signs of anger and impulse control issues. We thought it would be easier for him to regulate negative emotions if he could find other ways to express his anger. In fact, it might be helpful for the entire family. "You guys are the ones who taught Jonah how to talk. You taught him the words to use when you're frustrated or irritated or mad. If you want him to be more discriminating, be the model. Come up with words and phrases that communicate the feelings, but translate them into words that pass muster in a Baptist preschool."

Jonah's father leaned in, "I don't want to have to change the way I talk. The words just come out. I even like the way I feel saying them. I know it's supposed to be a good school, but maybe it's just not right for him."

"We can't speak to the rightness of the school fit, but we can for Jonah," we told him. "You're asking him to give up how he's learned to talk and express his feelings. To exert a kind of control of his speech that you're not willing to do. That's a big ask. Jonah is going to talk like the two of you do. Maybe not in front of you if you make him really afraid of the repercussions, but everywhere else. Are we talking about wanting to do something that would be effective and helpful to Jonah or what's easiest and most comfortable for you?"

We don't always get an honest answer here, posing the question of effectiveness versus comfort. But this time, we think we did. Their greater concern landed on Jonah. We had Jonah's parents make a list of his spicier vocabulary. It was actually a shorter list than they thought, a less daunting redefine.

We asked them to sit down with Jonah and say some version of the following: "There are some words that we all say that can make other people uncomfortable. Here's what they are.... We are all going to try and find other words than these to tell how we feel. And if we mess up and forget and say one of these words, we're going to remind one another and ask, 'Is there some other way you can say how you feel?'"

The parents told us a little bit about how it went on their next visit. "I say 'shit' a lot," Jonah's father said to his wife and Jonah. "I'm going to try and say 'shoot' instead."

"Can I say 'poop'?" Jonah had asked.

"We'd rather you not," his mother told him. "How about just 'I'm mad and let me tell you why'?"

This discussion with Jonah proved to be pretty productive. This family participation exercise gave him the opportunity to learn to better describe and express how he was feeling, an invaluable Sword skill set. Jonah found as many opportunities to ask his parents if there was another way to say how they felt as the question was posed to him. This nonjudgmental modeling took on a game-like quality that not only taught him to think before he spoke but also had the effect of expanding Jonah's vocabulary. He even managed to graduate from his preschool.

Whether you're calming your child down or up, that process expands the sweet spot of their arousal. And that expansion preserves all of the strengths conferred upon each brain type while reducing their weaknesses. Shields become less anxious and avoidant and more sensitive to enjoyment and pleasure, increasing the variability of their behavioral repertoire. Swords become more attentive to detail and better able to delay gratification. They lose their blindness to negative possible outcomes, having a similar outcome of freeing up choices and decisions. Shields can let go of their hyper-vigilance and laser focus on what "might happen." Swords are able to rely less on their compensatory, foraging behavior. In doing so, both brain types become more present, having freer access to the best of themselves.

Having an only child can make our parental strategies more clear-cut and easier to apply. Having multiple children adds layers of complexity, especially when one child is a Sword and the other is a Shield. What takeaways do you have from what you've learned about how to calm up or down your child? The process of putting this into words makes these nuggets of knowledge much more accessible. How can you personalize one of the strategies we've discussed to fit the needs of your child or children? How can you make these approaches specific? Set some reasonable goals, making your child an active and informed participant.

One last thought: Since these tendencies are baked in and the habits you are trying to help your child override are ingrained, this reshaping is a process. What makes it a successful process is clarity of goals and your staying power. Starting something is relatively easy; maintaining the course, with its frustrations, lapses, and temporary failures, is much harder. Patience, along with a generous dollop of tolerance for imperfection is what it takes. We encourage you to be as kind and compassionate with your child's struggles as we hope you are with your own.

CHAPTER TEN

Bring Your Brain Type to the Table

Using Your Unique Brain Chemistry to
Make Healthier Food Choices

EVEN THOUGH STACY IS NEARING her fiftieth birthday, she hasn't lost a beat. Sure, she has suffered some knee damage and had to stop running—which, in turn, was part of the reason she gained thirty-five pounds, but she keeps up with her two teenage children. Stacy is married, very passionate about traveling, and a bit of a foodie. Jeff just turned forty-eight, has been divorced for twelve years, and lives alone. Although he and Stacy don't know each other, they work on different floors of the same high-rise office building in downtown Los Angeles and share many similarities. They are both bright, ambitious, and doing well in their careers. Even their risk for developing age-related illnesses is similar. Both are significantly overweight, feel chronically stressed out from work, and lead largely sedentary lifestyles. Both have joined gyms over the years, but let their memberships lapse due to various personal explanations and excuses. And both Stacy and Jeff have been on and off a variety of diets, losing weight only to gain it back plus a few pounds each time.

Stacy has never met a piece of chocolate she didn't like and is on her laptop until the wee hours of the morning. Suffering from insomnia, she has tried a myriad of sleep aids with little success, and nods off midway through a late-night movie. Her idea of stress reduction is scrolling through Facebook. She has a family history littered with atherosclerosis, high blood pressure, atrial fibrillation, stomach ulcers, and ADHD.

Jeff is a smoker and has a family history of spastic colon, depression, OCD, stroke, type 2 diabetes, and dementia. Jeff also has sleep problems. Either he can't get to sleep because he's ruminating on an ever-changing list of nettlesome thoughts, or if he does fall asleep, he often awakens within a few hours, his thoughts spinning once again.

Both Stacy and Jeff had a grandparent die from cancer, and Jeff's father died of complications from diabetes. Neither has given much thought to the health issues in their family trees, but from genetics alone, each has some significant risk factors.

Why Have We Gotten So Fat?

America has never been heavier. In 1990, only 15 percent of the United States population was obese. By 2010, that number had risen to 25 percent. Today, a staggering 36 percent of American adults are obese (the number for children and teens is now 17 percent). This obesity epidemic has placed a severe strain on our healthcare system, spawned a $66 billion weight loss industry, and prompted a National Institutes of Health–funded research effort that has spent upward of $1 billion looking for ways to better understand and attack the problem.

The *why* of the epidemic is as vexing as the *what* to do about it. Genetics clearly plays a role in the metabolic process, but our genetic composition is perhaps the one constant in the equation; there is nothing new there to account for the additional poundage. What is relatively new is our love affair with inexpensive fast foods—and the industry's ever more sophisticated production of energy-dense processed foods filled with hidden sugars and an excess of salt. We love our sugary drinks, but the more we drink them the thirstier we become because sugar disrupts and fools our body's regulation of thirst. And even "healthy" alternatives have their downsides. What makes those flavored seltzers taste so good? Flavor essences, mainly fruit acids, which can soften and even dissolve tooth enamel, particularly when combined with carbonic acid, created through the carbonation process.

Further, the host of chemicals to which we are exposed daily disrupt and mimic hormones and interact directly with how we store and burn fat, and those chemicals are garnering attention and concern among health scientists. Ten studies with sample sizes from 888 to 4,793 subjects found a positive correlation between the level of BPA and obesity risk. This chemical is used in everything from plastic water bottles and canned goods to soaps and shampoos. It is even found in dust and the air we breathe. BPA is thought to mimic the hormone estrogen and the greatest risk is exposure during childhood. Along this same vein, another study, out of the Ohio State University, concluded that the city air pollution we breathe leads to weight gain, particularly belly fat. And a Swedish study measuring human fat mass found people with the most pollutants in their blood were 10.6 pounds heavier than those with less pollutants in their blood.

Despite the fact that 70 percent of us are overweight, a new study in the *Journal of the American Medical Association* (*JAMA*), an international peer-reviewed journal, reports an increasing number of people giving up on losing weight and that Americans are more sedentary than ever before. Stress also plays a part. The *Journal of Neuroscience* recently reported that chronic stress and anxiety act to disengage a region in the prefrontal cortex critical in decision-making. (This is why you may eat that big handful of peanuts or corn chips even though you're about to sit down to dinner.) Sleep deprivation, too, is more than a bit player in this complex drama. It leaves the brain unable to tell the difference between what's important and what's not, which is why you may be more apt to give in to food cravings when tired.

What We Know So Far

Here is the stripped-down version of what we know so far about weight loss: No diet—from low carb and Paleo to low-fat and vegan—will work for everyone. And exercise alone is not a guaranteed strategy for keeping body fat at bay over the long haul. The way our brains are wired and the chemicals that activate that wiring serve to make sustained weight loss difficult. And even when we lose weight, most of us gain it back. In fact, dieting causes the body to lower its calorie burn rate to mirror the calories taken in. A new study from the University of Cambridge finally points to why: the same group of neurons in a region of the brain called the hypothalamus that light up and make us eat if food is available also signal the body to go into energy-saving mode and stop us from burning fat when food is scarce.

The bottom line? Losing weight and keeping it off is difficult. It is achievable but requires thoughtful effort. So, what do those who lose weight and keep it off have in common? According to the National Weight Control Registry, those who have maintained weight loss for at least one year share certain behaviors: they weigh themselves a minimum of once a week, eat breakfast, have modified what they eat in some way, watch fewer than ten hours of television per week, and do some form of exercise daily.

The most potent obstacle to sustained weight loss is the way the brain works to sabotage whatever weight loss we *can* achieve. In fact, being overweight seems to make your body continue to be overweight. A recent study from the Washington School of Medicine reported that while our preference for sweets usually fades as humans age, this is not true for overweight men and women, who continue to show a strong preference for sugar as they grow older. Is it simply a cruel twist of fate? Hardly—the reflexive brain is greedy. It does not have the capacity to look at the body and conclude that it has stored enough fat to last through the next famine; it just says, "Bring it on" when it comes to sweets.

Most of us, at one time or another, have made a resolution to eat in a healthier, more intentional way. And unfortunately, many of those resolutions were abandoned shortly thereafter. Sure, we start out with the best intentions, but invariably something sabotages us—an unexpected stressful event, a holiday or celebration, or simply life being too busy. We also share the awareness of how important the fluid and foods we put in our mouths are to our general health, so we try yet again and vow this time to stick to the next "best" diet.

In this chapter, we're going to explore the link between your brain type's relationship with arousal and the sabotage of controlled eating. Do any of the following statements apply to you?

- "I have tried but failed to stay on at least two diets in the last three years."
- "Unexpected stress has derailed my attempts to lose weight."
- "I eat when I'm anxious or worried."
- "There are certain foods I just can't seem to stop eating."
- "I eat when I'm alone or bored."

If you identified with any those statements, you may need a little help with maintaining healthy eating. In truth, as straightforward and simple as eating appears, it presents some real challenges to most people. Why? The simple answer is that we are often in a battle with our brains and don't have the tools to win that fight. In nature, eating has a singular purpose: to provide the healthy calories we need to survive. Most of us are fortunate to have enough food available to us and we don't just eat because we are hungry. We eat out of ritual, socialization, and habit. And more importantly, many of us eat to comfort ourselves. Never before has there been such easy access to unhealthy food or more chronic stress built into our daily lives. This presents the perfect storm for the activation of self-defeating brain chemical imbalance tendencies. Shields and Swords alike can fall prey to using food as a self-soothing strategy.

But there are some solutions.

Let's talk leverage for a moment. Personal leverage. By personal we mean learning to work *with* your brain instead of *against* it. Think of it as your very own form of jujitsu, where you employ the momentum created by an understanding of what propels your motivation and the day-to-day decisions it shapes. This leverage is built in, comes along with nature, and is effective because it combines what you feel at the moment with your thoughts and intentions—emotion *and* thought. We need that multipronged combination to fire and sustain change. That leverage is infused in the very imbalances we have in our brain chemicals—embedded in our brain types.

The dynamic here, or course, is your relationship with arousal. You've learned how the pesky tendencies it creates can cause you trouble. We're going to show you how to use these same tendencies to your advantage. Leverage for a Sword is different from that of a Shield. Shields will learn how to use their antipathy to arousal as a tool for positive change, and Swords are going to learn how to take advantage of their attraction to arousal. The reason why healthy eating is so hard is that we are asking a brain designed millions of years ago to help us survive in a fast-food, sedentary, screen-dominated world. That three-pound miracle in your skull was developed during a time when nutritional food sources were scarce and you had to cover a whole lot of ground to find and hunt it down, or dig it out of the earth. Our brains were wired when there was nothing to do at night except find safe shelter, rest, and conserve calories to meet the next day's challenges. This brain of ours and all its ancient circuits thinks it's gone to heaven—it wants to eat far beyond its needs and tells us to sit down and save energy if we don't need to move.

The truth is that *we* may want to change, but our brain doesn't. To do that, to challenge the dictates of our unconscious habits, takes every bit of leverage we can muster. We are going to show you some ways to put to use the inclinations that come most naturally to us—the inborn tendencies of our brain type.

The Hidden Factors That Influence Eating Behavior

Fortunes have been made exploiting our indulgences around eating and our wish to lose weight. Frank J. Kellogg—not to be confused with William Kellogg of corn flakes fame—created a line of Professor Kellogg's Brown Tablets, marketed for use in weight loss. Kellogg promised to send anyone a one-dollar's-worth package of his weight loss pills along with a book of photographs and testimonials for a mere ten-cent investment to cover his costs for shipping and to "show good faith." Kellogg's success in marketing a bogus product unfortunately exceeded his accomplishments in helping people lose weight. And those Brown Tablets are now just one item on a long list of magical cures resting in the diet graveyard.

If there is any magic to be found, perhaps it is in the cooking labs of today's large food manufacturers. In an interesting head-to-head study, dieticians constructed two diets, one consisting of unprocessed foods and the other highly processed. Each diet was matched for calories, carbohydrates, proteins, salt, sugar, and fiber content. Participants didn't have any preference of taste for one diet over the other. They ate either the processed or unprocessed diet over a two-week period and then switched diets for another two weeks. They were told they could eat as little of the food or as much as they wanted, irrespective of the diet they were eating. On average, they ate about five hundred calories a day more when they were eating highly processed foods and gained two pounds in the two-week period.

Researchers concluded that when given the opportunity to eat processed food, we quite simply eat more of it. Why? They suggest that metabolic signals the stomach sends assessing the energy density of what is being eaten may become garbled by the "unnatural" combinations that comprise processed foods. Most of the time, in their natural state, carbs come along with fiber and are rarely accompanied by fat. Processed foods scramble these combinations, ripping out the fiber and tossing in some tasty fats.

Imagine the following: Our brain has a dialogue with our gut every time we choose to introduce food to it. It goes something like this.

> **BRAIN:** Hey, stomach, got your message. I'm hungry and I'm about to eat.
> **STOMACH:** Got it. I'll get things prepared down here.
> **BRAIN:** Okay, here we go. Let me know when to stop.
> **STOMACH:** Will do.

Sometime later...

> **STOMACH:** Hey, I don't know what to make of the combinations you're dropping down here. I can't get a read on the metabolic load. Something's missing. You better keep eating.

And that's exactly what we do; we keep on eating. It would appear that when we present highly processed foods to our stomach their composition and unnatural combinations are not accurately recognized. Confused, the stomach says keep it coming.

Swords and Shields are both vulnerable to such miscommunicated signals for different reasons. Shields see food consumption as a useful tool to modulate stress and tamp down arousal. Food is perhaps the most primitive form of being comforted. First, we are calmed and comforted being fed in our mothers' arms and then later, we find comfort in raiding the fridge. If Shields lack better strategies to reduce arousal, the availability of food (particularly tasty, processed edibles) becomes an all-too-easy, albeit self-defeating, balm.

Swords have their own unique challenges with habitual food choices. Highly processed foods have significant "reward value" for reward-sensitive Swords. They tend to eat to excite. The beginning of the habit chain of behaviors that gets acted out automatically is the thought of some tasty treat. When Swords run low on arousal, they bring out their deck of arousal boosters. There is little more easily attainable or stimulating than a go-to morsel to give them the dopamine release they crave.

Satiety, or "feeling full," is related to a small pocket of neurons deep in the cerebellum, a part of the brain long thought to be primarily involved in motor coordination. When these neurons are activated, we feel full and when they are silent, we feel hungry. There is no way to magically activate these neurons, but we can show you some effective ways of dealing with their silence.

Eating without Thinking

Repetitively employing food as an arousal-modulating strategy takes on unconscious, habitual qualities. Neuroscience shows us how these habits form. Behavior we repeat creates a loop in the brain that memorizes the whole chain of microbehaviors, forming these separate parts into a single chunk. Accompanying these noted repetitions is a release of dopamine to facilitate the process (and yes, Shields enjoy a small hit of dopamine just as Swords do). Repetitive chains of behavior can supplant what we think of as intentional, purposeful behavior (aka choice).

Habits become our own autopilot chunks of behavior simply because they are rewarding—the results of how we've learned to get by in the world. Neuroscience has discovered the circuits in the brain that correspond to the reinforced chains of behavior. When we reach for that bag of chips, the circuits in our brain that re-inforce the action light up even when *we know* this habit doesn't serve us well or is self-destructive.

As an example of how much our habits are on autopilot, once a habit has been established, only the beginning and end of that chunk of behavior is noted by the brain. The middle part, in its en-tirety, is dropped out in terms of energy expenditure—acted out automatically without thought. We see the corn chip and eat it with-out thinking.

That doesn't mean that we aren't aware of reaching for that chip, for the neocortex is watching and choosing the moments and cir-cumstances to fire off the circuits and the habit. We just act it out automatically.

So, are we just stuck with our habits? Maybe yes and maybe no. We know that habits that have long been reinforced become semi-permanent. We don't really get rid of bad habits so much as we cover them with new, healthier ones. To meaningfully suppress a bad habit and establish a new one takes time—three months, give or take, of consistently performing their new routine. We won't go into the weeds of the brain regions involved, but "suppress" is the right word. Until that new habit is firmly established, stressful mo-ments, thoughtlessness, or excuses all too easily expose the old habit once again with all its old autopilot power.

This is where understanding your brain chemistry comes in handy. To suppress a bad habit requires reinforcing a new one just as systematically and consistently as you did the old one. The most effective reinforcement is receiving something rewarding in a pat-tern that is hard to predict—just frequently enough to keep it going, but not so frequent that you'll stop if you don't get rewarded even over several times. (This is exactly the way the slots are pro-grammed in Las Vegas.) For Shields, the unhealthy eating habits are reinforced by their ability to tamp down arousal, and those habits are reinforced by their ability to excite and stimulate arousal for Swords.

A Word about Conflict

Once we've packed on the pounds and stored them as fat, the body views this fat depot as a treasured asset, necessary for survival, and increasingly is reluctant to surrender it, making losing weight difficult. If weight loss is an issue, this process takes patience and persistence. To energize and mobilize these qualities along the timeline required, motivation is the necessary fuel.

The problem is that the wish to change creates a conflict. We know we should lose a few pounds (approach or engage an experience), but we don't want to go through the discomfort accompanying the changes necessary to accomplish that goal (avoid or say no to an experience). Swords and Shields have unique vulnerabilities to this form of conflict and often succumb for different reasons. How we can be helpful here is by changing the form of the conflict itself. The advantage of knowing your brain type makes it possible to, in effect, game the system. We do this for Shields by shifting the conflict from approach/avoidance to avoidance/avoidance (making one side worse than the other) and for Swords by loading the approach side (making it more attractive). We've found this shift and loading leads to much more successful outcomes.

An avoidance/avoidance conflict is where neither choice is a desired one—choosing which is the worst of two bad outcomes. Shields are most sensitive to this conflict construction, and we use it to leverage their unique motivation to shape desired outcomes.

Sometimes the approach side of an approach/avoidance isn't quite strong enough to tip the balance consistently. Swords are particularly sensitive to highly loaded (rewarded) conflicts that allow them to focus more closely on upside outcomes. This is the kind of conflict that we gamify to take advantage of Swords' distinctive motivational leanings.

We call these shifts Leveraged Change Strategies. Here's how these strategies work.

Step 1: Setting the Goal (for Swords and Shields)

Journeys that are measurable are more easily accomplished. We suggest a weight reduction of 10 percent of your body weight. What is your target?

Step 2: Food Choices

There is a wide variety of diets to choose from. They all work well, so long as we work along with them. We recommend finding one that isn't super low in calories or eliminates certain food groups completely. These tend to be unsustainable. Instead, aim for a moderate calorie deficit, and be sure to include adequate amounts of protein, fiber, fat, and carbohydrates. Our favorite eating plan is one consisting of primarily "low glycemic index" foods. What diet suits you?

Step 3: Dealing with Arousal (for Swords Only)

Swords eat to stimulate and excite. Because of this, eating less and more carefully has the net effect of removing a strategic source of arousal, creating a predictable dip. Swords don't like dips. In the days leading up to your start date, think of some ways to compensate and increase your levels. Taking on a challenging project, planning some social activities, exploring places you haven't been before, shaking up your route to work and back, finding a new hiking trail, or buying that book you've been wanting to read are some examples of increasing *novelty and uncertainty*, having the effect of increasing arousal. What are some of the ways you can build novelty and other sources of stimulation into your life throughout this period of preparation and new habit building?

Step 3: Dealing with Arousal (Shields Only)

Because of Shields' surfeit of natural arousal, they are less sensitive to the stimulation and excitement rewards promise. Taking on the emotional state of altering long-standing habits is arousing and uncomfortable for Shields, even before the process has begun. Changing how one eats is vulnerable to early failures because of this. To compensate, it's helpful not to begin a process of change during the time of other acute stressors and to give yourself a couple of weeks for preparation.

Use this time to tie up any loose ends that might be stressful and reduce your natural level of arousal. Soaking in a warm, relaxing bath most nights might be one way or committing this two-week time to daily mindfulness sessions another. Day one will be an emotional challenge. We want you to be right in the middle of your sweet spot of arousal on the day you begin. Use this time wisely; it will pay off handsomely in days to come.

Step 4: Loading the Conflict (for Swords Only)

For those of us a little low in natural arousal, food, along with its visual and gustatory cues, is a highly predictable anticipatory reward. To be successful in giving it up, we suggest that you replace that food reward. Reward and the orbiting thoughts that surround it are a primary motivating force for Swords. A reward is quite simply getting something you want. Here is something that you might try: Come up with sixteen small but important treats, gifts, or indulgences that appeal to you and that you would like to have (or maybe eight that you would like to repeat). These should all be as easily accessible as pulling the trigger on an online cart. Write out your list and assign each "reward" a number from 1 to 16, reflecting its desirability. Now think of one more, this one even more important and desirable. We'll use this later in Step 5.

You will need two decks of cards for this next part. Here's the way it's going to work: Day one of your eating plan you're going to shuffle the two decks of cards together, including the jokers. Put the stack of cards facedown in some prominent place, easily seen (creating a visual cue is actually very important). Before eating anything, look at that stack of cards. At the end of each day, return to the cards. For every day of controlled eating, turn the top card faceup. Take a moment and remind yourself that you had a successful day, saying to yourself, "I am one step closer to my goal" (the internal reward). Every time you turn over either an ace or a 2, say to yourself, "My eating plan is paying off," and indulge yourself with one of those rewards, beginning with number 1 (the external reward).

When one of the jokers comes up, take the next day off and eat anything you want.

What happens if you miss your mark? Instead of turning a facedown card over, you take the top faceup card and stick it back somewhere in the facedown pile. To make this even more motivating, add in a time factor. The goal here is to get all the cards turned faceup in 120 days.

Step 4: Shifting the Conflict (for Shields Only)

Here's the rub: you want to develop healthier eating habits but that transition feels distinctly unpleasant. You are about to open that bag of corn chips. It's uncomfortable to say no to yourself, so what stops you? Coming up with something that competes directly with that discomforting no. What that requires is making saying yes to those chips even more uncomfortable than saying no. When saying yes is worse than saying no, what we have is a winnable avoidance/avoidance conflict. We've found that setting up this sort of conflict to be effective for Shields given their exaggerated sensitivity to avoidance. We're going to show you exactly how to do this.

Choose sixteen things you can and would like to avoid (or again, eight that you will avoid repeating). These avoidances can be anything from not throwing a party for your least favorite relative to not sending a sizable contribution (say $200) to the political party you vote in opposition to. Be creative here. Now choose a seventeenth item even more odious and uncomfortable. It might be something like, "Increase my risk of dying of a heart attack like my father did." Rank-order the items from 1 to 17 with 17 being the avoidance most important to you.

Take two decks of cards (jokers included) and shuffle them. Place the cards facedown in some visually prominent place where they can be easily seen. For every day of controlled eating, turn one card faceup, saying to yourself, "I'm on track to building a healthy and lasting habit. I was successful today."

Every time you turn up either an ace or a 2, say to yourself, "Not only am I on track but I can also cross off one of those items on my 'Things I'd Prefer to Avoid List.'" On the days you turn up a joker, take the next day off and eat anything you want.

If you have a "bad day" of poorly controlled eating, take the top faceup card and stick it back in the middle of the facedown deck. The goal, of course, is to get all the cards turned faceup and every item on your list crossed off.

To make this really motivating, add the following constraints. Take two of the items, mid-list, and commit to doing them both if you haven't turned all the cards up in 120 days.

Step 5: Accountability (Swords and Shields)

To bolster the "inner" accountability provided by the cards, it's helpful to build in some "outer" accountability as well. Studies show that the more public the commitment we make to an action, the more likely we are to honor it. Buddy up. Whether it's family, friends, or coworkers, take some into your confidence. Tell them what you are trying to accomplish. Be willing to broadcast the specifics of your plan to at least two or three people (the more the better). And yes, we all have two or three people we can let in, even if they are a next-door neighbor or the pharmacist who fills our prescriptions. No excuses. Tell them what you were doing, your target, and here's the hard part: Ask for their help in keeping you accountable. Something like, "I may not want to bring it up, but an occasional 'How's that plan of yours coming along?'" would be helpful.

The day you Swords turn the last card faceup, treat yourself to number 17 on your treat list, the richly earned reward you've been waiting for, signaling your success. And after turning that last card over, you Shields can cross off that most powerful/meaningful avoidance, breathing a big sigh of relief.

Step 6: Continuing Your Newly Developed Habits and Your Journey to a Healthy Life

For some, this is easier said than done. If you find yourself having relapsed and acting out old unhealthy eating habits, try a restart. Get out those decks of cards and bring a renewed commitment to the process.

Stacy and Jeff

You remember Stacy and Jeff, our Shield and Sword patients? Let us tell you a little more about them and how they leveraged their brain type for healthier eating.

As we've said, neither of them has paid much attention to their genetic landmines that house the risk factors for their unique predispositions. But whether attention is paid or not, how we eat interacts with those factors in predictable ways. Being overweight potentiates the vulnerability to our genetic risks, and Stacy and Jeff both had them. Stacy tended to downplay these glaring health connections and seemed more concerned with what was going on with her knees and how she felt in her clothes. Jeff was stunned when confronted in blunt terms what his genetic risks were. Pointing out what predictably lay ahead for him if he didn't get some of that weight off worried him. We were going to take advantage of that, while something else would have to be employed to get Stacy's attention.

Experts agree that even a 10 percent sustained reduction in weight produces significant health benefits. Stacy and Jeff both committed to that number as a reasonable goal and both signed on to a low glycemic diet.

Predictable forward and backward movement are a natural part of the road to sustained changes. Rarely do we see uninterrupted forward motion, even in the best-intentioned plans. For most people, the strongest variable is motivation, a complex set of issues also colored by one's unique brain chemistry. Interacting with Stacy and Jeff's wish to lose weight was the drag exerted by their brain chemical imbalances. Let's look at some of the ways they have managed to sabotage their wishes.

Stacy is a *binge eater* who has a hard time passing by a pizza joint and is capable of polishing off a can of potato chips without much thought as she watches television. Eating fires our reward circuitry, shifting the process from energy needs to pleasure. Food can cause a release of dopamine directly into the brain's reward center, reinforcing eating for the sensation of the experience instead of subsistence. This kind of signaling in the reward circuitry overpowers the feelings we have of fullness. As you know, impulse control for Swords is not a strong suit. We asked Stacy to download a game like solitaire on her phone for those uncontrollable moments when she gets that urge to binge, to momentarily distract herself and override the impulse to make an unhealthy choice. The games need to be regularly changed to give Stacy the variety she needs. Her attempts to lose weight in the past had all been thwarted by her inability to delay gratification, a common obstacle for many Swords, for they tend to be impatient and bore easily. Stacy regulates her stress and itch for arousal with potato chips, too many cups of coffee, or the extra Adderall her doctor gave in to prescribing because of her problems concentrating at work. The stimulant medication did, in fact, improve her focus, but she abused this because she knew it was arousing and gave her the energy to multitask better than ever.

In contrast, Jeff can delay gratification like a champ, but his tilt toward feeling vaguely anxious most of the time provides so little pleasure that an extra slice of cheesecake and glass of wine before bed are seen as a scant reward for his stressful life. Jeff self-soothes with food and alcohol.

Maintaining schedules is problematic for Jeff to begin with, and living alone has made it all the more difficult. We had Jeff commit to stop eating three hours before bed to reduce his sugar spikes and allow his metabolism to begin to slow down and prepare his system for rest. We also asked Jeff to prepare a daily calendar for his meals, planning for five or six small meals a day, which would keep him more in a grazing mode and help him avoid snacking on carbohydrates throughout the day.

We also asked Stacy to stop eating three hours before she went to sleep to prevent the roller coaster of glucose levels into the wee hours of the morning. As her blood sugar would dip, she would unconsciously need to refuel to maintain a level of increased arousal. This late-night eating pattern contributed to her esophageal reflux because her stomach acid was on a constant drip to help metabolize the steady arrival of treats and snacks.

Sleep—or the lack thereof—is a big problem for Stacy. She told us that on a good night, she's lucky to get five hours of sleep. Sleep deprivation has long been known to stimulate appetite as a natural response to stimulating wakefulness by adding a drive toward calorie-rich carbohydrates. Have you ever wondered why, when very tired, you unconsciously gravitate toward carbohdyrates? Additionally, studies have shown that getting more sleep naturally resulted in eating fewer calories. We gave Stacy some specific ways of addressing better sleep hygiene, which she incorporated into her plan.

We suggested that both Jeff and Stacy include "cheat meals" in their plan (in addition to the free eating days they enjoyed when they pulled a joker from their deck of cards). A recent article in the *Journal of Consumer Psychology* showed that integrating cheat meals into one's program can help people lose weight over the long term, and these findings were validated in several other well-vetted studies. There was clear evidence that people who follow a laxer eating schedule on weekends coupled with a more restrictive eating style during the week are more likely to sustain long-term changes in their weight.

For Jeff, even the thought of a cheat meal made him anxious; cheating felt vaguely dangerous. Fearful as he now was of the health consequences his weight posed, he bridled at first. We asked that he build in that indulgent meal despite his discomfort. We wanted him to hang onto his very real health concerns because they were the leverage he was using. He learned to use those once-a-week less stringent meals as potent reminders to how easy it is to damage one's health if they are not limited to a rarity. Remember, it's the rules that dictate the accumulated effects of our behavior, not the exceptions, and Shields—fearful as they are of health consequences—tend to indulge less and less over time.

For Stacy, cheat meals provided something entirely different. She came to think of these meals as a wonderful reward for a week's self-discipline. They also provided her with a hit of the stimulation and variety she craved.

In line with our holistic approach, we evaluated Jeff medically. It was clear that he was a prediabetic from his latest A1C hemoglobin level (Jeff's result was 6.8 and normal values are under 5.7). Weight loss alone can often bring these metrics into a normal and protective range. Jeff was not surprised by his results, as he saw his own widening girth and sedentary lifestyle as foreshadowing his future. Shields often have a predilection to carbohydrates, as these foods provide a boost in serotonin, but they also get converted to sugar, which only adds points to Jeff's already-elevated marker for diabetes. He was advised to incorporate more protein in favor of the carbs. Jeff felt a familiar combination of fear and hopelessness when we first discussed his need to lose weight—a conversation he had before with other practitioners. His feelings were soothed, however, when he was for the first time presented with an individualized strategy that was based in his unique brain chemistry and the reflexive behaviors that had created a cycle of failed attempts to comply.

We asked both Jeff and Stacy to take two easy-to-find supplements. The first was garcinia cambogia, which tamps down appetite and increases leptin sensitivity (and quite possibly activates those neurons in the cerebellum we mentioned earlier). Our brain has an intimate relationship with our stomach. After we have not eaten for a while, the brain secretes the hormone ghrelin, which stimulates our appetite. And as we eat, the second gut–brain pathway is activated, releasing leptin and insulin into our systems. Leptin is the signal letting us know we are full (if it's not overwhelmed by simply eating for its own sake). The second recommended supplement was white bean extract, which reduces carbs' ability to turn into sugar.

There was a third supplement we suggested: berberine. Let's talk about fat here. The human body has two kinds of fat: a brown and a white variety. Brown fat burns calories rather than storing them the way white fat does. We have a lot of brown fat when we are babies, but most of it disappears by the time we become adults. And even though brown fat accounts for less than 5 percent of all our fat, it burns 70 percent of our overall caloric expenditure. White fat, the kind that accumulates in our bellies, upper thighs, and love handles, burns almost no calories. Researchers from the University of California found a way to transform white fat into brown by boosting a particular protein, and as a result create weight loss. Berberine activates this particular protein, allowing one to "brown" portions of their fat. And do you know what else browns fat? Exercise. Much more about that in the next chapter.

Metformin, a common medication to improve insulin resistance in obese and diabetic persons in addition to curbing one's appetite, was added to their programs. There are also new dietary pharmaceuticals with FDA approval that work on multiple organs and are proven to help with weight loss. They work on the brain to release more leptin (the hormone that tells you to stop eating), the stomach to keep it distended longer to make us feel full, the pancreas to create more insulin to grab the sugar in our system, and the liver to inhibit the hormone glucagon, which is the storage product for sugar. These new prescription products can be costly, so it is important to engage your doctor to advocate to your insurance provider for the approval of these medications when appropriate. It's important to remember that whether they are prescription medications or supplements, pills can only be part of the answer. Lasting success requires the addition of the real magic: your motivation and commitment to maintain healthy eating patterns. And the best way to achieve that is to employ the leverage of your own brain chemistry.

Before modifying what Stacy and Jeff ate, we had each go through a weeklong series of "I can, but I don't have to" food/eating simulations that involved their favorite food impulse items. Seeing the process of eating as less reflexive and more intentional is essential.

During this prep week, they both set up a Healthy Habit Chart that included the goals of meeting a daily water intake of two quarts, adding leafy green vegetables to their meals, and taking a daily thirty-minute walk after their biggest meal (the best time to burn calories). They also got some very different assignments. Jeff was asked to construct his list of things he would like to avoid (to leverage his Shield tendency toward avoidance as a reinforcement). Stacy, to leverage her Sword tendency to be reward sensitive, put together a list of items that she would like to give herself.

During their first week of exercising healthy eating, they both agreed to eat only half of what was on their plate and put the remainder in a warming oven for twenty minutes. The strategy was to slow down their eating and give the satiety hormone leptin a chance to kick in. By the end of the week, Stacy was putting part—and one night all—of the delayed portion into the refrigerator. Jeff also reported eating a bit less.

A second "trick" we used for Stacy was designed to address her habitual eating of potato chips. This trick takes advantage of Swords' low pain threshold but is equally effective for avoidant Shields.

Stacy felt that nothing wrung out the tension of the day quite like canned potato chips. Never a fan of eating a small handful, she found herself devouring whole cans watching the evening news. She signed on to try a low-tech but surprisingly effective intervention.

- **STEP 1:** Stacy got a quarter-inch rubber band and put it around the wrist of her nondominant hand.

- **STEP 2:** Her first thought of potato chips struck when she turned on the news. Stacy reached down and gave herself a snap with the rubber band (Swords tend to have a low tolerance for pain, so doing this was very unpleasant). What Stacy noticed was that along with the first snap, the desire for those chips vanished (sensations compete for attention and, as she sat rubbing her wrist, the lingering sting was all her brain was pondering).
- **STEP 3:** Ten minutes into the news, she found herself up and grabbing the can from the cupboard. Another snap.

Breaking a bad habit into its component parts is an important aspect of this exercise. The thought of munching on a chip got a snap, grabbing a new can from the pantry a snap, opening the can a snap, and a snap after each chip eaten. It's imperative to follow this plan for at least a month. In Stacy's case, she keeps an unopened can of chips in her kitchen "for security," she tells herself. But now every time she thinks of chips a snap comes to mind.

So how did they both do? Somewhere around month six, Stacy relapsed and was once again mindlessly munching her beloved potato chips. She has lost twenty-six pounds and told us she is going to find that rubber band and repeat the drill of snapping it. She has been sleeping better, clocking almost eight hours, on average, a night. She got through her two-deck card stack successfully in just over 108 days, and other than the potato chips, she has maintained her healthy eating plan.

And how about Jeff? It took him two rounds with the cards, but he completed the second round much quicker than the first. And despite the predictable hiccups along the way, Jeff has managed to lose thirty-two pounds and cap his wine intake to a single glass, weekend nights only. He's also managed to spruce up his social life a bit. He showed up the other day with a new puppy, something he'd wanted to have for a long time. He's going to be a busy guy taking care of his newfound friend.

Even though we all have a predominant brain type, most people can see aspects of both types in how they behave and what motivates their decisions. For those of you who see your Sword-like or Shield-like tendencies as more subtle than those of Stacy and Jeff, you might use a hybrid version of the leveraged change strategy should you want to lose weight. The hybrid strategy looks like this: Make a list of eight rewards you will give yourself as well as a list of eight avoidances. The rewards should be things you would not normally give yourself but would bring you pleasure. The avoidances should be things you will commit to doing that you would strongly rather not, such as offering to mow the lawn for that annoying neighbor or clearing out the garage like you've been promising to do for the last five years. For every ace or 2 you turn over for a day's controlled eating, you can give yourself one of those rewards or cross out one of your eight avoidances. One of our patients had his wife put together his avoidance list. Let's just say it was really rewarding for him to cross items off that list. To up the ante, come up with a special reward or a particularly odious avoidance that you gift yourself if you complete the two-deck process in 120 days. If you don't make it through the decks in three months, you forfeit the remaining rewards and pay off the avoidances that you haven't crossed off.

How long and how healthy do you want to live? There's no better time than right this moment to answer that question. It's pretty easy to get a hold of some cards and make a commitment to your future. We're rooting for you.

CHAPTER ELEVEN

Moving and Resting: Gaining Greater Control

*Understanding How Your Brain Type
Interacts with Movement and Sleep Patterns
and Learning How to Change Them for
More Healthful Outcomes*

LET'S TALK ABOUT AGENCY, OR free will—our ability to consciously sort through our options and make the decisions and choices that construct our lives. Having agency would mean that we can intentionally intervene in the cause-and-effect linkage to choose our actions instead of them being a simple by-product of our past experiences. If this book is about anything, it is about agency and its constraints. How free are we to make the decisions we do in our lives? Or, how constrained? We've explored one of the constraints we face in these pages: the effects of the subtle imbalances in our brain chemistry and the unconscious influence exerted by our relationship with arousal. But of course there are many more constraints: our DNA, the parents we inherited, where in the world we grew up, our education, the environmental pollutants we were subjected to, our nutrition, sibling experiences, our cultural and cognitive biases, and on and on…and on.

Agency. If there ever was a need for it, exercise sustained over time calls for it. It's not easy to get a body to do something that's uncomfortable and then ask it to do it again and again. If you peek in on hiking trails, beaches, and gyms, you might get the impression that everyone is getting exercise and doing it easily. Sadly, that fitness dream is far from the truth. We know we should move more. We've been told often enough. Most of you already know the overall benefits of exercise, but the following is a bare-bones primer of the specifics. Regular exercise slows aging as well as the development of all chronic diseases, including dementia. Exercise enhances positive emotional regulation and serves to maintain our cognitive skills. How does it accomplish all this? We ask our body to engage in an activity it may be disinclined to do at the moment. This focused activity increases blood flow and oxygen, creating neurogenesis (the birth of new neurons in the brain). That phenomenon, in turn, increase the strength and integrity of neural circuits (neuroplasticity) and decreases the stress-related chemicals in the brain (cortisol and adrenaline). Exercise upregulates important neurotrophins (growth factors) that are critical to the survival and differentiation of neurons. This chained process results in actual brain growth, particularly in the area around the hippocampus (center of memory) and the prefrontal cortex (center of executive functioning). Yes, we get all this from moving.

So, there it is. Few things in life offer such a bountiful upside with virtually no downside. Possessing so many clear benefits, why then is it so hard for many of us to actually do it? Yes, we're back to agency. Free will. Does it exist or not? Philosophers brought its presence into question long ago, and more recently neuroscientists have shown pretty conclusively that it's largely illusory—that our conscious deliberations and decision-making are a by-product of unconscious brain activity. In essence, the science suggests that we don't make our decisions, but rather our brain does some time before our conscious awareness of having made a decision. We won't get into the weeds of the neuroscience, but we can say it is pretty robust.

So, what are we to think then? Are we simply the robotic accumulations of the ways the neurons in our brains have learned to behave? And coming around to the subject of the chapter, if you are largely sedentary, are you being held hostage by a brain that has already decided that the couch beats the hiking trail? We think not, but demanding choices from a brain that prefers to function on autopilot requires special effort.

Anyone who has ever tried to change a bad habit knows how hard it is to accomplish that goal. Understanding your relationship with arousal gives you an important leg up here. This understanding allows you to leverage your brain type tendencies to intentionally alter the calculus of your decisions, and provides an important degree of freedom.

There is a large body of psychological research that shows that intentional, purposeful reasoning does alter what we do in our lives. Here's an example: Dieters were asked to list the tempting foods that led to their weight gain and were then assigned to two different groups. One group was simply given the goal of losing weight while the second group was instructed to use what psychologists call "implementation intentions." They were asked to formulate conscious intentions to ignore their thoughts about the foods that were tempting to them. Simply using these intentional strategies resulted in this group eating significantly less of those tempting foods on their lists than the group not armed with conscious intentions. Other studies show that conscious reasoning helps people to learn from past mistakes and to reduce impulsive behavior. "Reframing," a strategy used in cognitive behavioral therapy, allows individuals to free themselves from negative emotional responses and learn to reinterpret signals from their bodies in more positive ways. But divergence from unconscious behavior exerts a price. That price is being present and effortful.

It is possible to override our reflexive default tendencies. Your brain may be telling you to sit down while you open your mail, but you can stand if you choose. Your brain may direct you to the elevator, but you can, using conscious intentions, choose to take the stairs instead.

Let's make one thing clear: We all have at least some agency. But freedom of choice is the antithesis of succumbing to our default settings. Agency is about being awake, being active rather than passive, and acting in proactive rather than reactive ways.

Because it's been among our easiest choices, we've become increasingly addicted to comfort. And exercise, maintained over time, is never going to be as comfortable as lounging around on the couch scarfing down popcorn. To override that seductive tendency and your autopilot brain requires effort and a willingness to say no to the indulgence of comfort. For far too many of us, the unconscious habits of comfort have trumped the health-giving benefits of movement. But it wasn't always this way.

When Comfort was a Luxury

Evolution is parsimonious. That stingy, snail's-pace process adds in traits or abilities over time that have survival advantages and drops out those no longer necessary. At one point in early evolutionary time, our ancestors were able to make their own vitamin C, but when it became so easy and prevalent a part of their diet that capacity vanished. Nature's evolutionary dance is replete with such examples. We, as *Homo sapiens*, have been configured with upright, bipedal locomotion and big brains. Science suggests that this is more than an accidental connection—that our ability to run while carrying killing tools allowed us to exhaust and outrun our prey. Human legs are filled with slow-twitch fibers, the muscle construction associated with endurance. There are many creatures faster than our ancient human hunters, but those stealthy forebears of ours possessed the stamina to keep going while their prey eventually tired and became vulnerable. In fact, science would suggest that our ability to move over long distances created the food-source nutrients that led to the massive brain growth that characterizes our species. But that success came with a cost. The moving machines that we are *need to move* in order to stay healthy.

Other species near us on the tree (chimpanzees, bonobos, orangutans, gorillas) were not designed to move in the ways we do. Theirs is a largely sedentary existence even though they have little body fat or evidence of metabolic or cardiovascular disease. In essence, they can sit on the couch and not pay for it. In contrast, studies show that the hours we sit around result in predictable minutes subtracted from our longevity. One study suggested that watching the entire *Game of Thrones* series would cost us somewhere in the vicinity of a day of our time on the planet. Our big brains have created the technology that allows us to move very little if we choose. And those indulgences are killing us. Unlike the other cousins on our branch of the tree, we need to move. Exercise is not a choice. It is a necessity.

Shields Often Don't Like Moving... and Pay for Their Indulgences

Let us tell you about a couple of Shields we worked with and what we found helpful in getting them to move more vigorously, more often. Marcy, forty-seven, and Sheila, fifty-two, both had Covid very early in the pandemic. As partners, they couldn't help sharing the virus. Marcy and Sheila are both considered clinically obese. Marcy is on the borderline of having type 2 diabetes, which complicated her recovery. She was hospitalized for almost two weeks, and luckily avoided a respirator, but couldn't avoid her persistent fatigue and night sweats. She has chronic anxiety and low-grade depression that was magnified by the frightening hospital experience. Both she and Sheila worked from their home during that protracted isolation—Marcy as an accountant and Sheila as a high school algebra teacher who Zoomed with her students.

This couple's first medical appointment after their isolation was disconcerting to them. Marcy's A1C (blood sugar level) of 6.7 placed her in the prediabetic category. This prompted a discussion of some recent findings concerning the aftereffects of Covid and type 2 diabetes. Doctors are finding that people even with normal insulin sensitivity are developing diabetes several months after recovering from Covid. The association here is the inflammatory cytokine storm triggered by the virus and the response of the immune system. The recommended treatment is exercise. Exercise is the enemy of systemic inflammation. Marcy was at risk. It was clear that she needed to start moving if she wanted to avoid a progression to full-blown diabetes.

Marcy had insomnia and complained of lying awake into the night anxious about her lingering Covid issues and how these would impact her quality of life. She also worried about Sheila, who had been experiencing lower-back pain and spasms, and was concerned about the possible problems that could be driving these symptoms. With all of this on her plate, Marcy's serotonin-imbalanced reflexes had kicked in, with enough fear of needles that she was now motivated to engage the lifestyle changes that just might turn her situation around.

Sheila is also a Shield. In many ways she mirrors Marcy, and not all of their similarities are mutually beneficial. They both grew up reading Judy Blum, *As Good As It Gets* is their favorite movie, they're both only children, they are against pharmaceuticals, they've both been diagnosed with fatty liver disease, and they consider exercise a four-letter word. The last exercise Sheila did was in junior high school, and she did so with great resistance. She told us that she is starting to forget little things—where she put her keys, some names, and some friends' birthdays that she always took pride in remembering. This is particularly scary for her because her mother has Alzheimer's. Sheila has osteoporosis but refuses medication, so some resistance exercising would be a helpful alternate prescription. Motivating this couple will be challenging, and critical to successfully transforming their lifestyles.

Like her partner, Sheila also had problems sleeping. She admitted to watching television into the early morning to distract herself from her worrying about what was really causing her back pain, and the gnawing fear that she would need back surgery. Despite her worries, Sheila agreed to getting a lower-back MRI to better understand her spinal issues. We told her that based on the description of her symptoms, her back pain was likely to resolve with weight loss and an exercise program (her subsequent imaging study was in fact negative).

Fatigue was an issue for both of them. Marcy nodded her head in agreement when Sheila complained of being totally out of gas by four in the afternoon. They both smiled and held hands at this point when acknowledging that this was probably the most peaceful time of the day, when they were forced to lie down and take a nap together. It was clear to them how important it was to make the lifestyle adjustments involving their weight, exercise, and sleep.

Homework for Marcy and Sheila

Since Marcy and Sheila were going to be a tough sell on the exercise piece of their lifestyle program and both were detail friendly, we decided to have them gather information on the benefits of exercise that might relate to their weight-loss program and Marcy's blood sugar issues. We've found that homework assignments help people get more actively and positively engaged in their healthcare. Not only do they learn pertinent information but they also see clearly the critical component they are responsible for. A week later they delivered the goods, with a very positive attitude for getting moving. Here are the headlines they discovered:

- Overwhelming evidence that exercise—150 minutes a week, with a combination of aerobic and resistance training—improves type 2 diabetes.
- Anandamide, an endogenous cannabinoid in the brain, can be supplemented in one's diet with certain CBD preparations and is also found naturally in chocolate. This substance has been shown to motivate us to exercise and control our eating behaviors.
- A single bout of aerobic or resistance exercise is proven to provide pain relief during the activity and for some time afterward. Studies have specified exercise as advantageous for those with chronic back pain and fibromyalgia.
- Exercise is proven to elevate levels of brain-derived neurotrophic factor (BDNF) and increasing this protein through intense aerobic exercise and resistance training in the brain can improve memory, depression, anxiety, insulin sensitivity, and SAD (Seasonal Affective Disorder); decrease obesity; and slow the aging process.
- Exercise slows cellular aging by increasing AMPK (AMP-activated protein kinase), especially relevant in type 2 diabetes, where cellular aging is accelerated. Fasting also increases AMPK, as do omega-3s and cinnamon. Supplements that contain the bacterium G. pentaphyllum have also been shown to increase AMPK activity.
- Mindfulness, or present-moment awareness, is associated with greater exercise motivation.
- High-intensity training promotes better adherence to exercise programs.
- Studies demonstrate that long-term motivation depends on how much you enjoy the type of exercise you're doing. If walking is pleasant, you're more likely to keep doing this than another exercise you don't like.
- The effects of aerobic and resistance exercises have proved similar benefits in treating neurodegenerative (Alzheimer's

and Parkinson's) and psychiatric conditions (anxiety, panic disorders, and depression) as a nondrug treatment.

- Yoga and meditation (regulating posture, breathing) have, in some studies, compared well to active physical activity and also to pharmacologic treatment for depression and anxiety.
- Physical exercise, specifically resistance training, has proved beneficial in osteoporosis by improving bone mass and limiting its progressive loss.

We discussed their best options for an actual program that would benefit their specific issues, including problems with anxiety, depression, Marcy's A1C issues, and Sheila's bone density and future cognitive functioning. Our first concern for this couple was how they adhere to a schedule (not a Shield strong suit). We asked Marcy to create a calendar for the scheduled activities. We had her paste a piece of clip art of an insulin syringe on the top of each month's page as a not-so-gentle reminder of what was at stake. Then we laid out a plan that combined daily walks (ten minutes away from home and ten minutes back), a yoga class online, and twice weekly resistance training starting with light weights and bands, and progressing to a more intense program. This was particularly appealing to Sheila given her mom's Alzheimer's and the literature supporting this as a possible preventative measure, and an alternative to the Fosamax her doctor recommended for her osteoporosis. They also committed to a daily meditation (ten minutes sitting straight in a chair, eyes closed, breathing in through the nose and exhaling through the mouth) as a non-pharmacologic approach for their depression and anxiety issues.

To raise their BDNF levels, in addition to the exercise routines, we recommended sunlight, a keto or paleo diet, and intermittent fasting (restricting eating to within an eight-hour window). Intermittent fasting alters the gut's microbiome to increase the production of butyrate, a metabolite known to increase the production of BDNF and neural cells in the brain. This restructuring of the microbiome also helps convert white fat (stores sugar for energy) to brown fat (breaks down blood sugar) and has been shown to improve retinopathy in diabetics. We recommended they add certain things to their diet, like coffee, dark chocolate, blueberries, extra virgin olive oil, supplements like cascara, zinc, magnesium, curcumin, resveratrol, omega-3 fatty acids—all proven helpful in a holistic program of weight management and promoting exercise.

Using Your Relationship with Arousal as Leverage

Few things are more difficult to accomplish than challenging deeply entrenched habits. Committing to and actually doing new and healthy activities for a brief time is easy. Making those changes stick is much harder. For these two women, the goal of increasing their fitness and losing weight wasn't simply cosmetic. These changes were critical to their future health and longevity.

For Shields, avoiding something bad is rewarding in that the action has the effect of reducing arousal, leading to greater emotional comfort. As we've told you, for Shields, we use their penchant for avoidance to leverage their motivation in a positive direction. Based on what we learn about them, we work together to construct a potent conflict. Not just any conflict, but one developing an avoidance/avoidance dynamic. For Marcy, we pitted the threat of potential daily injections against her discomfort with regular exercise. We are searching for something she can avoid that is more potent (rewarding) than the physical challenges of moving. With weight loss and the increased sensitivity to insulin that can occur with better fitness, she might be able to avoid the prospect of having to be on oral medication or, her greater fear, injections.

For Sheila, we did something different. She showed us a picture of her mother, now in a memory care unit of a nursing home. Although still lovely, her eyes were vacant. "She doesn't remember who I am," Sheila told us. With tears in her eyes, she continued, "It's hard to look at this picture. This is the first time I've pulled it up since the day I took it. It makes me so sad and frightened. I don't want to end up like her. To forget Marcy." Marcy threw her arms around Sheila saying, "I don't want you to forget about me either, or have that scared, empty look I see in your mother's eyes." She slowly rocked Sheila, patting her back.

As poignant as that moment was, we knew we had found a powerful counter to work against Sheila's resistance around exercise. Because we knew it would be difficult, we devised a plan to take advantage of her natural reflex toward the avoidance of negative outcomes. We asked her to have that image of her mother printed as an eight by ten photograph and place it on the front of the refrigerator. We then asked Sheila to search through her photos for a second image, one of her and Marcy in a tender moment. We asked that she cut Marcy out of that image and tape that to the pantry door. This was a reminder of the memory of Marcy she didn't want to lose. We provided a third photograph, to be taped to the bathroom mirror, one that depicted the unique changes seen on a brain MRI of a patient with advanced Alzheimer's. The photos were to stay in place for three months. Sheila looked at the image of her mother and turned to Marcy who nodded and said, "I'll help you. We can help each other. Let's get healthy, together."

Accountability is another tool in overcoming resistances to needed lifestyle changes, and essential to maintaining motivation. Once again, our brain chemistry orchestrates this by driving us toward either arousal or hiding from it. Shields, being internally oriented, do best when they partner with someone encouraging (and sometimes pushing) them into these behaviors. Fortunately, Sheila and Marcy have each other to keep them engaged. One might also engage someone less intimate, like a reciprocally interested partner on the internet. Such options exist, both one-on-one and in groups. Your doctor's office may also be another avenue for accountability, especially if there is a dedicated nurse or nurse practitioner in the practice who might have more time for partnering than the doctor. Shields can schedule more frequent follow-up visits with their practitioner to monitor blood tests, blood pressure, and BMI to quantify their progress. Daily weigh-ins are also reminders of how you are doing and tend to keep the goals focused for fine-tuning. These weight checks keep us honest, enhance accountability, and reinforce a commitment to persevere. We suggested several wearable devices that monitor the number of steps taken in a given day as yet another metric for making them accountable.

Three months into our plan, Sheila and Marcy's twenty-minute daily walk had morphed naturally into forty-minute excursions exploring their neighborhood. We encouraged them to up their resistance training. They were both feeling more energetic, their afternoon naps had largely vanished, and they were both losing weight. What was exciting to them and gratifying to us was the positive change in their numbers—weight, BMI, and Marcy's A1C was holding at 6.7.

Not all our plans work as well as they did with Marcy and Sheila. We think of these programs as result-driven experiments simply because that's what they are—experiments. Some work better than others. Many proceed with small triumphs and backslides. We are human. The seduction of comfort is powerful. We often get discouraged. It's all too easy to limit future success by a focus on past failures. We encourage our patients to look ahead and use their brain chemical motivational styles to their advantage to take small, incremental steps. The path to success is just that—small, incremental steps that are directionally correct. If patients fall off that path, we encourage them to source the reasons why, and then without negative judgement, to get back on.

A few months later we saw Marcy and Sheila again. Marcy's A1C had gone down and was now 6.4. Her sensitivity to insulin would still have to be watched carefully, but she hadn't transitioned into diabetes. While both still had weight to lose, they were continuing with their healthy eating habits and working hard. They said they actually enjoyed the exercise and had recently added an online boxing class to their regimen. They reported that they felt more confident, less anxious, and were looking forward to the years ahead.

Where these women will be a year or two from now, we can't know. What we wish for them is that they create a clearly defined, critical path for themselves. If they find themselves off that path, they will know it. And important, they will know exactly how to get back on. Comfort is a constantly beckoning seducer. Disciplined exercise requires planning, effort, and a tolerance for discomfort. Only time will tell how lasting the changes they have made will be. You know where our hope lies.

Getting Swords Up and Moving

New York is laid out like a collection of dominoes, the short sides facing north and south and the long sides east and west. Walking from First Avenue to Twelfth, you've essentially trudged the width of the city, while striding the same number of blocks moving north to south doesn't make much of a dent in getting from uptown to downtown. There is a reason we're telling you this. His name is Morgan. Morgan sits a lot. And so do most Americans. Unfortunately, prolonged sitting is accompanied by predictable health risks.

According to a recent study of nearly 8,000 adults ages forty-five or older, the average time spent sitting per day is 12.3 hours. The researchers found that those who sat more than thirteen hours a day had a 200 percent greater risk of death when compared to those who sat less than eleven hours a day. Not only is total sit time important, so is sit duration. Those sitting more than ninety minutes at a stretch had a 200 percent higher risk of death than those who typically sat for less than ninety minutes at a time. While the reasons for this remain unclear, researchers think it may have to do with reduced insulin sensitivity and slowed metabolic activity. The bottom line is that not only do we need to move/exercise, we need to get up off our bums more frequently and not spend so much of our waking hours sitting.

Morgan, as we mentioned, is sedentary too much of his day and doesn't exercise at all. He is a very sweet and affable man who loves nothing more than chatting up strangers. Well, that's not quite true. What he loves even more is sitting at his computer (he's a freelance graphic designer) or watching a Nets game or movies into the night. And when he's not doing any of that, he is trolling around online auction sites looking to expand his collection of political banners and buttons. We failed to mention that he also has a number of food addictions (cinnamon buns, French bread, and frozen Snickers bars). At the age of forty-seven, his blood pressure has crept up steadily over the years along with his cholesterol. He is also nearly forty pounds overweight.

We had seen Morgan before, cautioned him about the pitfalls that lay ahead with his growing waistline and inactive life. This information had gotten head nods and affirmations, but little in the way of any meaningful action. Too often, foreshadowing looming health catastrophes results only in momentary anxious moments, soon forgotten. This tendency is an important Sword vulnerability—heartfelt promises slipping quietly behind the comforting veil of denial.

However, the Morgan we now saw was a different man. When he walked into the office, he plopped down in the chair and said, "Would you believe this body ever ran track? I was a halfway decent sprinter in high school. Now, I'm out of breath going down to pick up the mail. I can feel my heart pounding. Look at me. Look at what I've let myself become."

What happened? Carol happened. During one of his internet excursions through political paraphernalia, he stumbled into a chat room where he found a woman who had a similar passion for this material. Carol got his attention, and he really liked her. She seemed to like him, too, but he was afraid to meet her offline. Morgan worried she would take one look at him and be turned off. "I want to look better, so I can meet her. I want to be able to go places and spend time with her, but a girl like Carol would never go for a guy who looks like me. I went to buy a new pair of pants the other day and they told me they didn't have my size, that I'd have to order them online. Fat pants!"

Sometimes it takes more than a scary list of health concerns to spring people into action. This is particularly true for Swords. Sometimes it takes a Carol, along with some healthy pride and vanity.

We have found that people are ready when they're ready. You can't force a person to make changes. But now, Morgan seemed ready. Morgan wanted to get lean and fit, so we gave him his marching orders: move more and sit and eat less. We started him on a "half diet" where he could eat whatever he wanted, but only half portions of what he would normally consume. We also asked him to monitor and log his sit time for a week. He was astounded to learn that he sat nearly fourteen hours a day. We set a maximum daily sit time of eleven hours and told him to stand up and walk out of the room every thirty minutes. Morgan agreed to set alarms on his phone to remind him to get up every half hour. "So, if I'm going to be sitting three hours less per day, what am I going to do with that extra time?" Our answer was to learn to start moving. This is where living in New York City comes in.

We developed a progressive walking program for him. We also explained the two card decks/sixteen reward strategy described in chapter 10. On the first day, he would walk three short blocks south from where he lives on 65th Street and then walk home. We asked him to track his time for the round trip and turn the top card face up. On the second day, he was to go the same three blocks back and forth but beat his time by thirty seconds. Successful, he turned another card over. On day three, he walked four blocks and back, tracking his time, and on day four he again was asked to beat his time by thirty seconds. The goal was to increase his walk by one block every other day, and continue to beat his time by thirty seconds, until he had flipped over all the cards.

Morgan was really excited the next time we saw him. He brought with him a spreadsheet that contained all the times, distances, his body weight, the sit time totals, and the hits and misses of getting his cards turned over. Morgan could now walk ten blocks in under thirty minutes, and with his half diet he lost fourteen pounds. We were even more excited when we learned that his blood pressure, cholesterol, and triglycerides were all moving in the right direction.

Morgan told us, "I feel amazing. I've gotten my total sit time down to just under twelve hours and I've been getting up every half hour and doing a few squats, touch-down jumps, and push-ups. You guys never told me how good I'd feel after a walk. Let's up the ante."

We did exactly that and rejiggered his program, making it more challenging. Oh, and did we mention he finally met Carol in person, and they have been really hitting it off? In fact, Carol began joining Morgan on his walks. Like all of us, Morgan is a work in progress. Whether he can maintain the consistency of his exercise and sit time program remains to be seen. As you'll recall, old, long-established habits are not gone but simply inactivated at the moment. The best we can do is suppress them and cover them with a new habit. To be successful over time, Morgan will have to remain vigilant.

Keeping Swords Accountable

Swords often find accountability difficult, as they tend to be less focused beyond immediate rewards and get bored easily. Exercise, as you know, is vitally important. We get something of value by doing it, and we lose something of value by not doing it. There is nothing neutral about its absence in our life. And it requires commitment. Moving around with vigor when we feel like it is one thing; doing that same thing when it is inconvenient, too hot or cold, or when we'd much rather be doing anything else, is quite another. Clearly, being easily distracted, quick with impulse, and disliking having to delay gratification can make maintenance of an exercise habit a challenge. Swords' typically muted response to health risks can make exercise appear less critical than it is. Swords' penchant for going for the dopamine hit, however, does have an upside. They actually like routines once they are established. And once they are firmly in place, engaging the routine itself is a reward.

It's pretty easy to make Shields afraid not to do something that is integral to their future health. You show them that by doing X, they are avoiding Y. Being the cautious, easily rattled and aroused people that they are, avoiding something really bad can be worth the effort of doing something uncomfortable like exercise. But Swords tend not to be harm avoidant. So how do you keep a Sword accountable?

If you are a Sword, count on your affection for routines and keep the program on track until it becomes second nature. The trick is in doing the program (whatever it is) consistently and long enough to fall into the habitual routine category. Remember that Swords are very sensitive to rewards, and rewarding events come in myriad packages. One thing that's rewarding is information about the result of our actions, and the more immediate it is, the more effective. An option that appeals to Swords is to use a smartphone app to offer speedy feedback on calories consumed, distanced walked, or whatever may be the relevant metric. There is something vividly rewarding about immediacy. While the time required to carve six-pack abs is the opposite of immediate, specific evidence of progress toward that goal can be measured and recorded in real time. These measurements are rewarding and reinforce the routine.

Keeping motivation on a consistent track can also be enhanced by buddying up. Swords tend to like company, and knowing company is going to show up for an exercise session makes it harder to pull the covers over their heads and sleep in. Even better is finding a group committed to similar goals. That's what Morgan did. Carol had three friends who wanted to join them on their walks. The power of a group is its capacity to encourage, support, and even nudge when it's appropriate. Each depends upon the other to show up, not just when it's easy and convenient, but when showing up is the last thing you want to do.

Swords, not being particularly good at delaying gratification, should set realistic, short-term goals. Losing forty pounds may be an attractive goal but losing two pounds is a much more easily reached accomplishment. String a succession of small goals together and they accumulate. Acknowledge each as an important mini victory. Put that acknowledgment into words that you say to yourself or concretize the achievement with a chart of some kind. Don't minimize even the smallest of goals. It's the direction (one walk or one lost ounce at a time) that counts.

The Downside of Sleep Deprivation

Epidemiological research confirms that sleep deprivation in both children and adults has been decreasing over the past fifty years concomitant with an accelerating rise in obesity rates. Beyond being tired, consequences of poor sleep are insidious and dangerous to our overall wellness. Sleep loss increases the release of pro-inflammatory cytokines that promote immune dysfunction while slowing down cognitive performance. There is also a negative impact on learning, memory, pain perception (increasing awareness and reducing threshold). Chronic sleep deprivation alters carbohydrate metabolism, appetite, food intake, and protein synthesis—and not in a good direction. Your slow-wave sleep, which provides restorative functions needed to recover from prior wakefulness, is impaired, which leaves your vital organs and tissues in a trash heap of metabolites that don't get eliminated, adding a general inflammatory insult to these tissues. These inflammatory assaults are the breeding grounds for creating and aggravating chronic diseases, including cancers, and now evidence is strong for depressive disorders being directly linked to inflammatory changes in the brain. Depriving your brain of slow-wave sleep creates fatigue because energy restoration is muted.

Dysregulation of leptin and ghrelin is common with sleep disruption, which further predisposes people to obesity. A newer risk factor for sleep deprivation leading to weight problems is the use of multimedia platforms, which promotes sedentary behavior and increases calorie intake.

Sleep disruptions involve problems with certain hormones and neurotransmitters. Two with starring roles are orexin (from the Greek word for appetite) and melatonin, part of Mother Nature's neurochemical arsenal that controls homeostasis in our sleep/wake state. Exciting the orexin neurons increases wakefulness and arousal. Lower levels of this transmitter resulting from sleep deprivation are known to cause increased hunger, appetite, and food intake beyond the energy required to stay alert.

Melatonin regulates our circadian rhythm and concentrations of this hormone are ten times higher at night than during the daytime. Exposure to light will suppress the normal nocturnal rise in melatonin. Melatonin secretion plays a significant role in the initiation of sleep, as its levels in the brain increase after the onset of darkness and peak between 11:00 PM and 3:00 am, falling off dramatically before the onset of the morning light. As we age, the nocturnal concentrations of melatonin decline, and many older people develop insomnia from this deficiency. Staying up late, common to Swords, impairs melatonin secretion, as light and activity mute its sleep-inducing effects.

Getting the Rest You Need

There are a number of well-defined sleep disorders such as restless legs syndrome and sleep apnea, the description of which is beyond the purview of these pages. What is relevant here are the ways our slight brain chemical imbalances interact with how we rest and can be the culprits that rob us of getting the healthy sleep we all need. While we all have these slight imbalances, we don't all have problems sleeping. Nothing, however, can kneecap a healthy night's sleep quite like the subtle way in which our relationship with arousal works. Brain type imbalances can create predictable and differing sleep patterns for Swords and Shields that interfere with getting enough restful sleep. Below we've laid out these brain type tendencies.

SLEEP PATTERNS OF SHIELDS VERSUS SWORDS

BEHAVIOR	SHIELDS	SWORDS
What time do they go to bed?	Earlier	Later
How long does it take to fall asleep?	Can take a long time	Relatively quickly
Do they have bad dreams/nightmares?	Common	Uncommon
Do they wake in the middle of the night?	Frequently	Infrequently
How long to fall back asleep?	Not right away	Usually right away
What time do they get out of bed?	Relatively later	Relatively earlier
How often do they nap?	Frequently	Less frequently
Strategy to address sleep issues	Dampen high levels of arousal	Tolerate lower levels of arousal. Earlier to bed with the lights off

It's important to remember that we are describing Sword/Shield tendencies here, rather than absolutes. Not all Swords and Shields will fall perfectly along the lines seen above. What is to be made of these tendencies? Shields, because they are overly aroused, often use sleep as a way to zone out or mute uncomfortable signals of arousal (experienced as anxiety). In looking at the chart above, you can see how the spine of arousal can weave its way through the patterns of our problems with sleep. Arousal not only makes many Shields go to bed early to dial down the stimulation of the day, but it often makes falling asleep an arduous process. It's also the reason Shields tend to wake up more frequently during the night, have a harder time getting back to sleep, and are reluctant to pop out of bed in the morning.

What about Swords and arousal? As you know, to achieve a comfortable level of arousal, Swords have to find ways to stimulate themselves, often carrying the habit far into the night, making them late to bed. Because they are underaroused, Swords are typically pretty good sleepers. They don't wake up often in the middle of the night, and when they do, they go back to sleep fairly quickly. As natural levels of melatonin wane in the early morning hours and cortisol begins to rise, Swords often awaken early, ready to put their feet on the floor and begin the day. They usually get a good night's sleep if they can get to bed at a decent hour. This isn't to say that Swords can't go through times when they do experience poor sleep. Stressful periods can cause heightened levels of arousal even in Swords. During such times, they can have the same disruptive sleep patterns that Shields can have.

So, what can you do if you are experiencing these patterns? Other than practicing good sleep hygiene—regular sleep and wake times; a cool, dark room to sleep in; no screens at least an hour before bed; doing something calming before bedtime (listening to soft music or taking a bath); and reserving your bed solely for sleep and sex—the general strategies are straightforward.

For Swords, it usually means going to bed earlier than they are accustomed to doing, requiring them to learn to tolerate the letdown feeling of lower arousal in the evening without indulging in a stimulation fix. Nothing slams the portals to healthful sleep shut quite like Swords' late-night affection for screens. Frequently experienced as a fear of missing out, they convince themselves there is still one more thing to look at or do. The strategy for a Sword's good night's sleep is essentially a non-strategy. It's simply to set a reasonable bedtime, brush your teeth, and turn out the lights. Yes, sometimes it's as simple as that. But for Swords, a simple strategy is not necessarily an easy one to translate into a regular routine.

What about Shields? Their strategy is all about finding ways to modulate and dampen arousal. We've suggested ways to do that throughout this book. But again, the strategy may be straightforward, but the deployment requires the consistent overriding of brain chemical imbalances. Much more about emotional regulation and stress management in the next chapter.

LET'S TAKE A look at a couple of people we worked with in terms of how they dealt with sleep issues. Kevin is a retired NFL player, and the ten years since his retirement have taken a bigger toll on him than all the battering he experienced during his career as a defensive lineman. His presenting complaint was daytime fatigue, but what we saw was a man who had other lifestyle issues that included obesity and a sedentary lifestyle. He reported being tired by midafternoon, and the only defense in his playbook was a thirty-minute nap. Even the six cups of coffee during the day weren't enough to keep him as alert and energetic as he'd like to be. His favorite time of the day was 10:00 PM, when he typically jumps on to social media, keeping up with all his old teammates and rivals from his football days. You may have guessed that Kevin is a Sword.

Winnie, a thirty-six-year-old divorcée, is also sleep deprived, moderately overweight, and a paralegal. She struggles as a single mom of an eight-year-old son, Jordan. Winnie watches television in bed, often nodding off just after that last sip of her nightly vodka and tonic. But after she turns off the television and lights, she's totally awake and spinning, skittering from one anxious thought to another. When she does sleep, it is a restless sleep. She awakens with her covers in a tangled mess. Winnie is depressed, has panic attacks, and it's not uncommon for her to soothe her sadness with a large pizza. She knows she has to lose weight, but she is sleep deprived and has no willpower to diet. Winnie is a Shield.

Winnie and Kevin both had several health risks to address, but sleep was a major one. Both needed to eat less and move and sleep more. After addressing the first two issues, we turned to sleep.

We asked them both to construct sleep diaries. Keeping these diaries turned up a couple of surprises for them. They both found that they had underestimated how late they actually went to bed, and Winnie logged in an average of two drinks most nights a week instead of the one shot she described taking. And neither had accounted for the late-night caffeine intake from the chocolate/almond bars (Winnie) and chocolate-covered raisins (Kevin's favorite).

We emphasized the importance of reducing cognitive and physical arousal near bedtime (tough for a Sword like Kevin, default for Shield Winnie), avoiding all electronics that emit blue light, television, and stimulants, including reading and snacking (very difficult for them both). Avoiding light at night is recommended because of its negative impact on melatonin production. We also advised Kevin and Winnie to take 5 mg of melatonin one hour prior to their scheduled bedtime. We suggested that they might consider wearing amber glasses three hours before bedtime to block specific light wavelengths that impair melatonin production. Avoiding overhead light is also an important feature of light therapy.

Winnie found that she had a hard time not cycling around negative thoughts when her bedside light winked out. Dark thoughts that transition into negative emotions increase levels of arousal. Our suspicion was that Winnie's resting level anxiety was creating rapid and shallow breathing, which increases blood oxygen levels preparing her for a fight-or-flight response. We had her try a nightly ten minutes of slow, deep breathing into her belly—a technique that is relaxing and allows for a better oxygen/carbon dioxide exchange.

We recommended that Winnie set a defined bedtime and wake time, with the understanding that creating this habit might take up to a few months. Fortunately, Shields don't need immediate gratification and keeping her sleep diary was helpful in monitoring her progress.

Like most Shields, Winnie tends to come alive slowly in the morning, and we proposed she use morning light therapy, which would allow her to slowly shift her circadian rhythms earlier. This strategy can be done easily using light boxes, which are commercially available in a variety of wavelengths and intensities. We suggested she consider avoiding the nightly vodka. Alcohol increases onset and duration of the first and lightest stages of sleep, blocking the deeper sleep stages that are known to be restorative and to maintain circadian rhythm. Instead, we had her try taking low-dose gabapentin, a natural neurotransmitter that reduces anxiety and promotes restful sleep, if the 5 mg. melatonin we suggested was inadequate in inducing her sleep. We recommended she start with the lowest gabapentin dose (100 mg) taken one capsule an hour before bedtime and two capsules when getting into bed. Here again, to help Winnie stay goal-oriented, we discussed the plethora of wearable devices to measure her progress in prolonging the amount of restorative sleep she was getting each night. We explained to her how this would motivate her to fine-tune her new bedtime rituals, to maximize the relative time spent in deep sleep.

Kevin was wound very tightly, so we taught him a progressive muscle relaxation exercise aimed at reducing tension, muscle group by muscle group, beginning at his scalp and slowly moving down through his body to his feet. As he moved gradually down his body, we had him remind himself to relax each part, saying the words as he slowly moved downward: "I'm letting my eyebrows droop. I'm relaxing my jaw. I'm letting my chin go. I'm dropping my shoulders," and so on. We also asked Kevin to eliminate his coffee and nicotine binges late in the day or in early evening as these not only affect total sleep time, but initial sleep latency and sleep quality as well. The single most important thing Kevin needed to do was to stop his late-night habit of sitting in bed with his laptop, sleuthing around on social media. Even he was shocked looking over his sleep diary at how many hours he spent lost in his screen and keyboard. After much grumbling, he agreed to set a bedtime of no later than midnight each night, which for him was early.

Motivating Swords to change their sleeping habits is facilitated with a payoff. The payoff is empirical; it's about feeling better. We had Kevin ask himself the following questions upon rising each morning: 1) Am I more alert? 2) How do I rate my mood? 3) What is my energy level? If at least two of the questions were answered positively, he was to remind himself that feeling better was the payoff.

We then had to do what we always have to do: sit back, take a breath, and wait to see what our patients do.

Changes in Lifestyles Interact

As we all know, change over time is hard, gained only with commitment and sustained effort. We are patient when we are met with resistance. It is not unexpected. We chose to tell you about Kevin and Winnie because we encountered exactly that—clinging to the comfort of the familiar. The saving grace for them both was that they didn't hide it. After giving up her nightly vodka tonics for less than a week, Winnie told us she was back at it. Her attempts at the meditation exercise we gave her didn't fare much better. She claimed focusing her attention on her breathing made her nervous, that thinking about her breath made her feel like she was going to forget how to breathe, that instead of making her relaxed she felt more anxious.

As per our suggestion, Kevin set his alarm clock to remind him of his midnight bedtime. That he did dutifully. He would then turn it off, promising himself to shut his laptop down after just one more thing he wanted to check. And that led to just one more thing. And then another. You know how the rest of the story goes.

Sleep issues for Winnie and Kevin persisted. We regrouped and doubled down our focus on exercise for Winnie and healthy eating for Kevin. Winnie certainly could benefit from losing a few pounds and she had become largely sedentary and isolated during the pandemic. It was uncanny how crafty she was at making excuses for rarely moving much beyond the confines of her house. Until we discovered something. Learning that she played basketball in high school, we encouraged her to put up a basketball hoop on her garage and teach Jordan how to play. We also started her on an SSRI to ramp up available serotonin.

Kevin, even though gaining an enormous amount of weight in the years after his retirement, still managed to exercise regularly. His routine was to get out of bed and jump on the treadmill. Early exercise creates a higher metabolic burn for the rest of the day, but it also acts as an appetite stimulant. We suggested the half diet (described earlier) and had him shift his exercise to late afternoon or early evening.

While his sleep hadn't yet improved, he was losing weight. We were stunned when, months into the program, he told us that those late-night hours he spent scrolling through social media were about envy in comparison. As he put it, "I couldn't stop checking in to see who had stayed in better shape than I had or who was more broken down than I was. Having shed all this weight, I've lost interest in looking to see where I am and how I fit in. It just doesn't matter to me as much anymore."

Even though there are distinct components to our lifestyle, we are all whole human beings. Changes in one component results in changes in them all. We even saw some real movement with Winnie. She hadn't lost much weight, but she had retrieved her old jump shot, and was damn proud of it. She had started a Zoom yoga class and let us know she was less anxious and depressed. We were very pleased when we learned she stopped drinking entirely. "I used to tell myself that the vodka took away the edge of loneliness I felt. Now I'm spending more time with Jordan, reading books to him after dinner. I think the basketball thing got us really talking again. It's interesting. The less sorry I feel for myself, the more connected I feel to him and to life."

It's clear that Winnie is learning how to calm herself. We're hoping that as this process continues, these new skills will slowly translate into better sleep. And Kevin? He's maintained his weight loss and told us recently that he's been nodding off in the middle of the evening news. He's asleep before his midnight bedtime and still remarks about how good he feels when he gets up in the morning.

Exercise and rest. So simple, so complex. So necessary. Hiding in our comfort zone is highly overrated. Come on out; choose to get healthier. There is only an upside to becoming less reflexive and more intentional. This might be a good time to do an unvarnished review of whether you're getting the kind of exercise and sleep that is consistent with a healthy future.

CHAPTER TWELVE

Navigating the Tightrope of Stress

Living Is a Stressful Experience. How We Deal with These Unavoidable Stressful Events Is Highly Influenced by Our Brain Chemistry

NAVIGATING STRESS REALLY SAYS IT all. Each of us does that every day. No one living the complicated lives we do avoids it. Stress happens. We either manage it or it manages us. As we've described, our brain types prime us for dealing with stress in predictable ways, some constructive and others not so. When it comes to the stress, the trick is in understanding yourself and overriding those stress responses that are unhealthy and don't work for you. In these next pages, we're going to introduce you to some people who let stress manage them and what they learned to do about it.

It was a little past 7:00 PM on Sunday morning when Jeff called in a full-blown panic attack. Remember Jeff from chapter 10, who'd been struggling with his weight? He reached out to us after eight months of successfully working his new program but could hardly get his words out. Finally composing himself, he let us know that his wife, Stacy, had left him for another man. He was devastated, confused, and beyond anxious. After a couple of minutes of the deep breathing, he succeeded in telling us the crushing story of how he discovered her infidelity—along with details of his rapid descent into a relationship with his old friend, Jack Daniels. Eight months of hard work now down the drain...but not really. Like many whose behaviors find some forward progress, relapse into bad habits is always just around the corner, and the trigger is an un-anticipated huge dose of stress. But relapse is not failure, and there are many tools to help stop the backslide. We will return to Jeff and how we helped him through his crisis after a brief explanation of how stress creates bad feelings, and some brain-type specific strategies to help you fight back.

Stress is defined as any change in our biological equilibrium, or homeostasis. But homeostasis is just a concept and never a con-stant; it is a unicorn that doesn't exist. It's a notion shaded by perspective, since being out of equilibrium is relative to the person assessing it and the context it is occurring within. Someone's ho-meostasis changes on a dime when they get a call from their doctor letting them know their cancer screening was positive. Someone else is out of sorts when they waltz into 31 Flavors and find they're out of mint chip. Our reaction to these shifts is driven by our ability to tolerate the arousal created by these events that interfere with our endless and unconscious quest for homeostasis. While we are all vulnerable to stress its presence provokes different reflexive de-fenses against it depending on our brain chemical imbalance.

Mother Nature Sounds the Bugle

If you ever thought your own mother was controlling, let us re-mind you about good old Mother Nature. She will make your mom look like Mr. Rogers. Perhaps Mother Nature's loudest reveille is her alerting us to stress, the strongest of all survival warnings. This biological reflex, which happens in milliseconds, is provoked when we experience an imminent threat and involves four different but orchestrated systems—the brain, the pituitary, the adrenal glands, and the immune system—with Mother Nature as the conductor. This is an automatic response, often referred to as the fight-or-flight reaction, that is hardwired into our DNA, and whose blueprint is shared with all living creatures. Here is how she has designed these cascading events:

1. CRF (corticotropin-releasing factor) is immediately released by the hypothalamus in the brain, stimulating the release of the hormone ACTH from the brain's pituitary gland.

2. The ACTH (adrenocorticotropic hormone) then stimulates the release of cortisol (the stress hormone) from the adrenal gland.

3. This stress hormone now activates the nervous system to stimulate the sympathetic, or the activating side of the nervous system, to flood the bloodstream with glucose for maximizing energy expenditure for our fight-or-flight response.

The stress response manifests as palpitations, hyperventilation, heightened cognition, and focus. This acute release of cortisol also inhibits insulin release, which prevents glucose metabolism, making this energy source more available to our musculoskeletal system to better defend ourselves. Other nonessential survival functions are simultaneously suppressed when this alarm is sounded, like digestion, sexual functioning, reducing inflammation, creating memories, and maintaining our salt and water balance. Mother Nature's design includes a "fast track" blood vessel highway that exists exclusively between the hypothalamus and the pituitary gland in order to flood the pituitary with high concentrations of these hormones designed to activate this cascade with urgency.

It appears that an overactive feedback loop of these structures occurs as a result of prolonged exposure to stress. And studies indicate that anxiety and substance use are both related to a dysfunctional HPA axis. Substance abuse is the foremost self-soothing tool for stress-induced anxiety disorders, including generalized anxiety disorders, post-traumatic stress disorder (PTSD), panic attacks, social anxiety, OCD, and major depressive disorders. In addition to these affective disorders, we also see a relationship between an impaired HPA axis, autoimmune disorders, and high blood pressure.

A Little Arousal from Mother Nature

Stress, by definition, is an arousing event for our survival instinct. Acute stress disorder is described as a heightened stress reaction presenting within a month following exposure to a traumatic event like a serious injury, threatened death, or a sexual assault. These disorders have a significant likelihood of transitioning into PTSD and must be recognized and treated before the acute nature of this diagnosis is branded into a lifelong and life-altering condition that is difficult to treat. Related and preexisting disorders, like panic attacks, social anxiety, and OCD also escalate in their expression and also demand intervention as soon as possible. Drugs are often a mainstay of treatment—some prescribed by physicians and others obtained illegally. We now have another weapon to address these reactions: leveraging our brain chemistry to personalize a more targeted and durable solution.

When Shields experience a cortisol release, the reflex is to retreat. When cortisol meets a Sword, the unconscious reaction is approach, never avoidance. There was a recent news video of a young woman out in her backyard with three small dogs when she suddenly notices a large beast climbing over the fence. The woman, without hesitation, ran toward the offending ill-defined bully and socked it so hard it fell backward. The "it" was a huge brown bear.

The woman later reported that she had no idea it was a bear when she took off to save her mutts, and may have thought twice if she did, but her level of arousal was overwhelming and her only move was a counterattack with a right upper cut. This reflex was predictable, unwise, and driven by imbalanced dopamine. Had she been a Shield, her dogs may very well have been left to their own devices.

Most stressors are not bears climbing backyard fences and don't require a lightning-quick reaction, and both Shields and Swords need a plan when stress launches these hormones and transmitters. Reflexive responses are just that—made instinctively—and they may or may not be intelligent. For those events that don't call for an immediate reaction, try giving yourself a moment. Inhale deeply through your nose (mouth closed) and concentrate on exhaling very slowly. This strategy of focused, calm breathing could be lifesaving and allow you to plan your next move. This exercise takes some practice but pays off sooner than you might think.

The sequence for how the stress response plays out behaviorally is simple. Picture this response as an ARC, like the arc of a rainbow: *Action (the stressful event)* > *Reaction (the neurochemical response that creates a reflexive behavior)* > *Control (whether or not we override or indulge the emotional discomfort)*. Let's now return to Jeff and analyze his battle with the stress of his loss.

Coping with Loss

Jeff was distraught about the demise of his marriage. He blamed himself for not being attentive enough, for gaining weight and becoming less attractive to Stacy, and for needing to research the best deal on their last Lexus, which took far too long for Stacy's liking. He also worried and obsessed about his yet to be treated diabetes. Jeff's ruminating thoughts about his health led Stacy to bouts of insomnia. These anxious thoughts were intermixed with feelings of failure, as he had been doing so much better with his sleep and his break from alcohol, his daily walks, and his weight loss since he had started working with us. Being angry at Stacy was never in the mix of these painful feelings. He was angry at himself for his perceived deficiencies in the relationship and the backslide in his health journey.

Jeff's stress response was full-blown. His cortisol levels came in close second to his alcohol levels. Neurochemically, his imbalanced serotonin was aggravated to new lows, and this translated into worries over what was next for him. His attempts to be in control felt impossible to him in this moment. We knew he was on a slippery slope of landing back on the road to overeating, not sleeping, and drinking too much. However, where Jeff saw disaster, we saw opportunity. Learning coping skills when under duress is often the best time to practice and fine-tune your new strategies.

Jeff's paralyzing, anxious feelings may be familiar to many of you. A Shield's most natural response to arousal is to retreat. Sitting with those uncomfortable feelings upon arrival, even for a few moments, is essential regardless of our individual brain type. In this moment of discomfort, we can learn to process these emotions in more constructive ways and prove to ourselves that we can actually override Mother Nature and regain control. Mother Nature doesn't care how long it takes us to recover from a threatening event; her only mission is to sound the alert. Employing a short-term, three-part trick to get through these moments can be helpful. Try pinching yourself. Yes, physical pain creates an alerting response that breaks the chain of spinning thoughts and emotions. A second tool we gave Jeff was perspective. We asked him to think of a situation that was more troubling than losing Stacy. What came to mind was his sister's recent diagnosis of pancreatic cancer. This competing loss reduced some of the spinning anxiety around his wife. Finally, the third tool included a means to increase his serotonin levels—a carb snack or a ten-minute walk. These simple actions create a semblance of control, something you can actually do when feeling out of control—pinch, perspective, and procure (a little serotonin).

We also needed to address the elephant in the room—his wanting to numb out and drink. He instinctually understood how alcohol quickly dampened his anxiety when we began his treatment. He was just beginning to override his reliance on this self-medicating fix. Jeff had been taught early on in his treatment that alcoholism, like all addictive disorders, was a chronic medical illness, created in his brain chemistry and provoked by stress. Jeff also intellectually understood alcohol's intrusion into his sleep cycle by inducing and maintaining a relatively longer period in light sleep. He had gained an intellectual advantage over his dependency, but remained vulnerable to this destructive reflex.

Over the next few weeks, we worked closely with Jeff. His lifelong social anxiety kept him out of the AA community in the past. We connected him to a recovery advocate who accompanied him to daily AA meetings for the next ninety days to buffer his fear of meeting new people and his embarrassment over his backslide into alcohol abuse.

We introduced Jeff to an online CBT (cognitive behavioral therapy) counseling program. This form of therapy involves an interactive program designed to point out errors in logic (personal distortions) and helps create rational alternatives to these existing beliefs and thoughts. The theory is that by changing the way you think about issues you'll change the way you feel about them. After six months of this therapy the outcomes of CBT versus pharmacologic interventions favor the CBT approach. Although CBT can be administered in person or through video platforms, studies during the pandemic have shown that online interventions for anxiety disorders were equally as successful as in-person treatment. CBT has been proven successful in acute-trauma panic disorders and offers a relatively quick onset of action and long-term benefits. If initiated early, it has data supporting its ability to reduce the likelihood of developing PTSD.

We asked Jeff to begin a daily diary documenting his activities and feelings. To help Jeff with his resistance to maintaining routines and schedules, we engaged his AA sponsor to work side by side with him to create and follow a strict calendar of meals, meetings, and medications.

The Bumpy Road to Self-Soothing
with Prescription Medicines

Pharmacologic interventions have potential short- and long-term advantages in treating anxiety disorders and myriad other mental health conditions when done with precision, patience, and protection and delivered by competent professionals. Medications for these conditions were first introduced in the second half of the nineteenth century and included morphine, potassium bromide, chloral hydrate, and paraldehyde, but were generic sedatives that didn't hit the bull's-eye for the brain chemistry imbalances that were to be later identified. A hundred years went by before the introduction of these targeted medications based in our evolving understanding of the brain chemistry of anxiety disorders, which included general anxiety, panic attacks, and OCD. The field of modern-day neuropsychopharmacology, sometimes referred to as the fall of the Freudians, emerged in the 1950s with the first benzo-diazepine and Librium (a medication we gave Jeff to combat his severe anxiety during his withdrawal from the alcohol). Next came Valium in 1963 and Xanax in 1981, and then the beginning of the SSRIs in 1987 with the introduction of Prozac.

The medication that Jeff needed initially was a benzodiazepine to protect him from the withdrawal consequences of alcohol. Glutamate is the neurotransmitter released under the stress of alcohol withdrawal, creating severe anxiety and agitation. Benzo-diazepines neutralize this reaction. This phase of his treatment transcended medication and required a team approach with medical, psychological, and AA support. In addition to Jeff's Librium, he was started on an SSRI to deliver the serotonin needed to help with his depressed mood and reduce his current high level of anxiety. Most people undergoing drug and alcohol withdrawal experience sleep disturbances as the metabolites from these drugs linger in the brain for an extended time depending on the substance and duration of abuse. Jeff was prescribed low dose gabapentin, a natural neurotransmitter, designed to calm his overaroused nervous system and quiet his worrisome ruminations without the risk for dependency. Combining behavioral strategies with nonaddictive and neurotransmitter-boosting pharmacology, Jeff was able to employ new tools for managing his stress and alcohol dependency without relying on sedating and addictive substances.

Self-Soothing from Substance Abuse

Many people suffering from acute and chronic anxiety disorders, manifested as panic attacks, social anxiety, and OCD, turn to substance abuse as a way to self-soothe. But these transient bumps in selective neurotransmitters offer only temporary relief of these bad feelings. Our great American philosopher Homer Simpson has been quoted as saying, "Beer, now there's a temporary solution." An Australian study of close to nine thousand patients concluded that social anxiety is the most common anxiety disorder among individuals with substance use disorders, and patients with social anxiety are two to three times more likely than those without to become dependent on alcohol. A relevant Canadian study confirmed that individuals with OCD were significantly more likely to have a lifetime alcohol and drug use disorder than individuals without OCD. We've also learned from multiple studies that anxiety-related disorders precede the onset of substance use disorders. Remember our friend the HPA axis? Emerging data points to evidence that anxiety disorders and substance use disorders share common neurobiological relationships to the HPA axis. A hyperactive HPA axis occurs as a function of long-term drug abuse and/or prolonged exposure to stress.

Another manifestation we observed with Jeff's OCD during treatment was his reliance on social media and text messaging. Many studies have confirmed that reliance on our phones for those experiencing sadness, dissatisfaction, or loneliness is a mechanism of self-soothing and a distraction from engaging with feelings. Anxiety

symptoms are known to accelerate with prolonged social media reliance. We suggested that Jeff structure a couple of times a day for
checking social media and texting (in the morning at 10:00 AM for a
few minutes and again at 4:00 PM). This was to break his habit of
picking up his phone first thing upon opening his eyes and last thing
before he went to bed.

We are now only a couple of months into this new iteration of
Jeff's journey and at the moment he is stable and doing well.

The Moment You're Told You Have Cancer

*"Cancer didn't bring me to my knees, it brought me to my
feet."*

—MICHAEL DOUGLAS, on coping with a
life-threatening illness

Judy is a very youthful fifty-two-year-old woman who was
diagnosed with cancer after a routine breast imaging, and unfortunately it had spread to her lymph nodes. Even though she had a
strong family history of breast cancer, Judy was not very diligent
with screening methods. She never took the time to do breast self-
exams, and her last mammogram was four years ago. Perhaps she
unconsciously felt that if she didn't look for cancer it wouldn't find
her. The fear of having cancer just kept her paralyzed. We all asso-
ciate the word "cancer" with death, but the reality is that cancer is
now considered a chronic disease in at least 50 percent of patients
who share this trauma. Despite the statistics having improved dramatically over the past decade, nothing provokes the HPA axis and
release of cortisol like the *c* word.

Judy's diagnosis reactivated her PTSD, a condition that develops
in some people after experiencing an intense, terrifying, or dangerous event. Her provoking event occurred the year before when her
mother was diagnosed with acute leukemia and Judy watched her
succumb to a very ugly and rapid death. During that time, Judy also

began smoking marijuana regularly to allay her ongoing anxiety. She suffered with many of the symptoms of increased arousal and reactivity—she was easily startled, edgy, and had problems sleeping—and pot seemed to help her. She did not seek any interventions and had experienced nightmares, sadness, and even some guilt because she felt she had not spent much time with her mom during the last years of her life.

Symptoms from PTSD will continue long after the initial event and are relived as nightmares, flashbacks, feelings of detachment, sadness, fear, and anger. Coexisting conditions include anxiety disorders, substance abuse, and depression. Many cases will resolve within six months if treated early, but some people will remain symptomatic throughout their lives. There are now genetics recognized in this disorder and there is also a female preponderance. Ethnic variations have also been identified, with African Americans, Latinos, and American Indians being disproportionately affected.

Judy made an appointment with an oncologist and despite the doctor's compassion and encouraging words, she was preprogrammed to fear the worst and went online checking into worst-case scenarios. During these scary investigations, she developed a relationship with jelly doughnuts. Her sleep patterns were upset from worry, and she stopped going to the gym. We explained the negative impact of stress on her immune response, and the potential consequences for her upcoming battle for her life.

We presented Judy with the Brain type test, which confirmed her as a Shield. We armed her with state-of-the art information on breast cancer. Information is power, and power was in short supply once she got her diagnosis. We explained that her current estrogen replacement therapy, initiated two years ago when she entered menopause, would need to be discontinued given the strong association of estrogen with familial breast cancers. We tested Judy for estrogen and HER-2 markers, along with newer blood and genetic markers to offer highly targeted treatments for these diverse cancers. With this knowledge Judy was able to better engage with her treatment team with some degree of control over her new diagnosis. For Shields, information is empowering and an excellent tool for reducing the stress that accompanies these treatments.

We connected Judy to a CBT therapist. We introduced her to mindfulness therapies, including tai chi, a new tool to address her PTSD. Given her history of social anxiety, we helped her find a comforting nonhuman companion from a dog adoption at Petco, and she came home with a new roommate—a two-year-old cocker spaniel she named Kawhi (she was a Clippers fan). Having a pet to focus on helped bring Judy into the present and also gave her loyal and unconditional loving support at this critical moment in her life. She also had to walk Kawhi a couple of times a day, which gave sedentary legs a chance to move. Finally, we shared with Judy a collection of papers on the microbiome, emphasizing the adverse effect a high-carbohydrate diet has on the biome, which helps orchestrate the immune response, motivating her to ditch the jelly doughnuts. We followed Judy for a year, and during this period she developed new habits that helped position her into a solid remission following her treatment.

Is Your Healthcare Stressing You to Death?

"Medical professionals, not insurance company bureaucrats, should be making healthcare decisions"
—BARBARA LEVY BOXER

Deciphering the flood of health information and the healthcare system it depends on creates a level of stress that takes the "health" out of the equation and buries the "care" completely. Most of us, when our symptoms scare us, go directly to Dr. Internet—no traffic trauma, no co-pay, and no waiting! The perfect source for soothing our anxious feelings. But getting deeper into this virtual visit will likely elevate your level of stress, since most explorations eventually lead to serious and dire findings. Let's now examine how our

Swords and Shields could use their unique tendencies to better navigate through the medical maze.

Alan has had trouble with his male plumbing. He has to run like hell to make it to the bathroom, gets up three to four times a night to go number one, and has noticed his stream is now more like the drip system he has for his rose garden. His dad and paternal uncle both had prostate cancer, and now Alan fears he, too, shares that fate.

Alan suffers from *acute procedural anxiety*, a common problem, especially for Shields. Although Shields' pain tolerance is much higher than their Sword cousins, their pessimism and anxiety over their results outweigh this advantage. This condition is defined as an excessive fear of medical, surgical, and dental procedures that often prevents people from completing these necessary diagnostics. The stress manifests in not only the procedure itself but also in the anticipation of having to go through it. His doctor ordered a series of diagnostics. Shields only ruminate in periods of anticipation. These can be simple screening procedures, but the ten-day wait for the biopsy results seemed unbearable for Alan. The arousal of even thinking about a blood test, the claustrophobia of the MRI, or the idea of having a biopsy was paralyzing. He blamed himself for procrastinating his regular checkups, especially given his family history.

This is when we met Alan. We spent a lot of time just talking about the tests and procedures he would be undergoing. The mere understanding of what to expect, including pain and recovery, allowed Alan to verbalize his biggest fear—losing his sexual function. We explained that most men, depending on the procedure they need, won't lose sexual functioning because of the use of robotic surgical technologies and newer radiologic interventions. We also told him he would be unlikely to suffer incontinence, which Alan hadn't even considered. To add some control, we promised him that he would be able to stop the biopsy at any point if he couldn't tolerate the physical or emotional discomfort. We had him compile a playlist of his favorite songs that he could listen to during the procedure. Music therapy has been shown to help. Clinical trials have examined the effects of music intervention on procedural anxiety. The studies show that exposing patients for fifteen to twenty minutes prior to and during the procedure significantly reduced anxiety and heart rate. Meditation was also recommended. Telling Alan he could bring a close friend or a family member also buffered his anxiety. We suggested that he speak with his doctor about having a prescription of anxiolytics like gabapentin and/or a beta-blocker like propranolol, to help mute the stress of these diagnostic procedures and the potential decisions they would require. Alan repeatedly returned to the concerns over potential impotence and was reassured (three times) that this was unlikely. We even discussed a list of treatments like Viagra, Cialis, and penile injectables (yes, you read this right) if his fears became a reality.

We also spent time with Alan to modulate his arousal surrounding a doctor visit by arming him with information, including potential treatment options, as related to his current problem and obsessive concerns. Empowering any patient with information when investigating a potentially serious illness is good medicine.

Here is a list of what we recommend:

- Secure the provider list of potential specialists and review this with the doctor to determine in advance who on that list would be their best choice, and then do a search on these physicians to review their profiles.
- Review your pharmacy benefits—do brand or generic prescriptions make a difference with any of your current prescriptions?
- Investigate what happens when you need medical attention after hours—who answers your calls? Are you automatically directed to an emergency room? Is your doctor able to coordinate your care if you should need to be admitted?
- Prepare a laminated card for your wallet with all your health information, including any allergies, which medications you're taking, who to call in case of an emergency,

or any other special issues someone might need in an emergency.

- Get your medical records placed on a memory stick, since the primary care doctors can change or you might be traveling away from home and have an emergency, so a doctor evaluating you would have all of your important information.
- Put together a travel kit of medications: your regular prescriptions and any others you might need, like something for pain, a broad-spectrum antibiotic, something for nausea and diarrhea.
- For an appointment with your doctor, be prepared with a list of questions and goals. Check this list before you leave to make sure you have all your questions answered.
- Bring something or someone with you to the appointment for support, and in case there is a wait, something like a book, knowing you won't likely be able to use your phone while in the waiting room.
- Try to obtain email addresses for the office staff, nurse, and doctor so they could, if they agreed, communicate in a timelier manner.
- Seek guidance from your doctor on the best ways to become informed of your health issues.
- And, ideally, spend a few minutes with your provider to explain how you react to medical procedures and how your sleep and diet are affected, and adjust the practitioner's strategies to those behaviors. If your doctor doesn't seem to grasp this concept, send them a copy of this book!

Maria, a Sword, had a different issue with her healthcare program. She was naturally impatient and had a very hard time focusing on the details of her ever-changing insurance plans that dictated which doctors she could see; procedures, hospitals, and medications she could use; and even how to submit claims for reimbursement. Simply processing office policies was difficult, if not boring. For her to go to the doctor, she needed some type of incentive or reward and would typically plan a shoe-shopping expedition after each doctor's visit. She would scream at the doctor's automated phone systems, forever being placed on hold when she did need to connect and was especially perturbed with her insurance carrier every couple of years reshuffling the deck and reassigning her to a different primary care physician. Anyone on the other end of these exchanges knew she was pissed off. But now, at age forty-seven, she needed their help.

Maria had worked her way up to a managerial position in a large grocery chain. She was seen by her coworkers as tough, aggressive, not too interested in others' points of view, and erratic in her moods. Those around her would often delight in her rare moments of levity but knew all too well the other side of that coin and were careful not to get her upset. She was married, had two children in high school, and was an avid and daring skier who recently developed a fondness for hang gliding. Maria and her husband, Vincent, had enjoyed a solid relationship until very recently when it began to unravel. Vincent noticed that Maria had become increasingly moody, her anger was more volatile and intense, and one night on her way home from work, she almost punched a traffic cop who pulled her over for speeding. She was not sleeping well and was now beginning to have hot flashes that dampened her and Vincent's sheets and their sex life. And, as you've probably guessed, Maria was now in menopause. Maria had ignored the signs—six months of irregular periods followed by three months of no periods, a change in her sleep patterns, the not-so-subtle mood shifts, and the debilitating migraines. For the past several months she thought some of these issues were related to the Norco her doctor had prescribed for the headaches, that had now increased to six tablets a day. When her doctor refused to continue prescribing, she went into a severe withdrawal and sought our help.

She now had two battles complicating her unwelcome menopause: severe addiction to opiates and a healthcare system that was impotent in protecting her. Her insurance carrier sanctioned a 12-

step program, but it's what they didn't cover that was the problem—psychotherapy, prescription medications to safely detoxify her from the Norco, and a facility that she could easily access for help. Insurance carriers are selective as to which health problems they recognize. In the addiction world, these chronic medical diseases are marginalized. Emotional or psychological problems, like anxiety, depression, and insomnia, are not priorities and are certainly ignored as precipitating problems in the development of substance abuse. We didn't blame Maria for being angry. She blamed the doctor who was prescribing these medications for not educating her on the likelihood she would become dependent. She blamed her coworkers for creating the stress that precipitated her migraines. And she blamed her husband for not stepping in sooner. Swords like to blame others and ignore their own accountability.

We first needed to detoxify her from the opiates. We enlisted Vincent's eager help. He had no idea that she was taking these drugs, which was the first step in our treatment—full disclosure and transparency. We held a family meeting and counseled them to get an understanding of how addiction develops, the brain chemistry that undermines this disease, and the role that stress plays in promoting and sustaining these behaviors. We all self-soothe in various ways—some healthy, some not. The opiates were definitely in the "some not" list. Maria's need for immediate gratification was discussed and we explained that her Sword's reward-driven motivation would not be satisfied in this treatment, since treating addiction required a lifelong commitment. We explained how addiction was a disease originating in genetics, created in brain chemistry, and triggered by stress. We got Maria to commit to a program whereby we would take her off the opiates, transition her to an outpatient 12-step program, and seek counseling that she would need to fund. The counseling would include personal and family therapy since addiction is a family disease—everyone in the family suffers trauma when a family member battles this illness. After providing this simple outline, we withdrew her Norco, which then activated her sympathetic nervous system—speeding up her heart rate; making her sweat, not sleep, and lose her appetite, and giving her diarrhea and profound muscle aches. Nonaddicting medications were provided that mitigated each of Maria's symptoms. She had a low pain tolerance, so we encouraged her to keep an eye on the rewards of getting through this difficult two weeks. Besides her sobriety, Vincent threw in a one-year membership at an exclusive health club.

We initiated a sleep program that included strict sleep hygiene and healthy self-soothing techniques. We gave Vincent a nurse's cap and taught him how to monitor her blood pressure, pulse, and temperature. As a Shield he had no problem keeping a very strict diary of her symptoms, her vital signs, her complaints, and her response to the treatment options we provided. We promised Maria we would initiate the behavioral therapies once she felt better from the detox, and would then begin restabilizing her brain chemistry with safe and targeted pharmacology for her dopamine imbalance. We selected these pharmaceuticals from a list of dopaminergic products—the exact combination would be a work in progress and be adjusted and nuanced dynamically based on Maria's individual response to these medications. For her sleep disorder, we pulled from our dopamine-targeted menu options helpful for sleep and sedation (Seroquel, gabapentin). All of these medications would be carefully monitored and often discontinued once Maria had mastered her new self-soothing tools and was active in a relapse prevention program that included 12-step, personal, and family therapy. We also addressed her menopausal issues with her gynecologist.

After fourteen months Maria was off all medications, participating in yoga and meditation classes, maintained a close relationship with two new friends from her recovery program, and rehabilitated her relationship with her colleagues from the produce section. Maria and Vincent regained the connection they had when they were first courting and planned a family ski trip to Whistler for the upcoming winter—Maria's ultimate reward for a job, and lifesaving experience, well-done.

Financial Stre$$

The nest egg principal, as we shall now call it . . . the egg is
a protector, like a God, and we sit under the nest egg . . . and
we're protected by it. Without it, no protection! . . . Want me
to go on? It pours rain, hey—the rain—it drops on the egg,
and it falls off the side . . . without the egg . . . WET! It's over!"
—ALBERT BROOKS AND THE NEST EGG, *Lost in America*

The global financial stress during Covid heightened the arousal we all experienced due to the unknowns of how to protect ourselves, the impact of isolation from everything familiar and comforting, an information stream that was neither consistent nor satisfying, and the real possibility that we or someone we loved could die. How long are we going to wear masks? What would happen to our jobs and how would we be able to afford these dramatic and very real disruptions in our lives with no understanding of when they will end? The upshot in arousal was crippling for Shields and impossible to ignore for Swords. The collective anxiety was further intensified by an unstable and divisive political climate that meshed into a societal level of societal stress we have never experienced.

The anxiety over money handicapped everyone. Swords, whose planning skills were already neurochemically compromised, were less likely to have put away much in the way of rainy-day money. Swords' tendency to manage their arousal is to find a reward, and reckless spending can be an automatic soothing strategy. Chasing risky, get rich quick or investment schemes also scratch that itch. The relentless barrage of bad news and misinformation fed their agitation, which created chasms in close relationships and near-fisticuffs in the vegetable aisle in markets. Strategies for Swords to gain control over these issues was further compromised by their reflex to blame others instead of being responsible for finding solutions to manage their finances. The fear during the pandemic aroused their HPA axis and the ensuing cortisol storm, for many, made controlling the chaos difficult.

Shields also struggled with their now-realistic fears of negative outcomes; their coping skills for self-soothing were also challenged. If their tendency was to avoid harm, this was the perfect time to polish it. Their ability to plan and detail strategies was a benefit but many, so overwhelmed by the cacophony of negatives, were frozen to act. As acute as the financial stress was, it was buried in all the other land mines created by this virus. Shields understood the nest egg principal, were familiar with putting money away, knew the status of their finances, and could keep the long game in perspective much better than their Sword cousins. They would not take risks with their money—especially now—and would in fact adjust their spending habits to help protect the nest. Shields were good at protecting their backsides but vulnerable to stress and anxiety. Too often, their self-soothing strategies included a menu of sedating substances like alcohol and opiates. Alcohol consumption went way up during the lockdown. Sleep patterns for both brain types were disrupted, as were the anxiety-reducing benefits of exercise as people became more couch ridden.

Elliot's life as he knew it was wiped out by the pandemic, and despite his tendency to assign blame over accountability, we now understand that the real story was hidden much deeper in his brain chemistry. Elliot, fifty-two, had a very successful travel agency that serviced professional sports teams and some high-end celebrities. His business was solid, and he indulged in a pricey lifestyle without concern for any possible bumps in the road. He rationalized his extravagance as a means to promote his seemingly fail-safe business. Covid had other ideas, and, like so many other businesses, his enterprise took a nosedive. The professional teams he serviced decided to work in a bubble and not travel, and his few celebrity clients were out of work when all the production companies closed down. Elliot had a slick wardrobe, an executive membership to a high-end gym, and a convertible Maserati—but nowhere to go with the exception of Nick's apartment in Sherman Oaks. Nick was his drug dealer, and no virus was going to shut him down because for a cocaine addict, he was an essential worker. Nick went from Elliot's supplier to his victim when Elliot's temper exploded over the supply-and-demand increase for a gram of cocaine, gifting Nick with a black eye. This was not unusual behavior for Elliot when provoked, and he was lucky that Nick—given his own illegal activities—couldn't call the cops and press charges.

Elliot's life during the lockdown was as disastrous as his coping skills. The cascade of his stress began with an eruption from Cynthia, his wife of twelve years, after watching their business evaporate and her discovering that Elliot had not done any financial planning. Having him now so often at home made it easy to discover his secret pornography stash. But when she found out about his cocaine addiction (which explained why there was so little in their savings account), Cynthia's anger finally reached a breaking point and she filed for divorce. Elliot was forced to sell their home and his beloved sports car. His agitation and hypomania provoked an accelerated abuse of cocaine and repeated mentions of suicide. With an ounce of compassion still left in the well, Cynthia stepped in and solicited our help.

After the initial consultation we developed a plan to get Elliot off of the cocaine and then establish some rebalancing of his neurochemistry to get him healthy. Strategies for behavioral change had to be guided by his underlying chemical imbalance, and Elliot was unmistakably a Sword. Our clues in establishing this diagnosis were not subtle. He *blamed* his collapse on the virus, had *addictions* to porn and cocaine, demonstrated *poor planning* skills, *rewarded himself* with sports cars and fancy clothes, *took extraordinary risks,* and *couldn't control his anger*. His coping skills in response to the avalanche of stressful events clearly needed some fine-tuning. His attempts to soothe his bad feelings with stimulant drugs and behavioral misconduct provided immediate but ephemeral gratification. His cocaine abuse pumped a little extra dopamine into his system, which destroyed his sleep cycle, sabotaged any healthy eating behaviors, prohibited him from being interested in his gym activities, and drove his once supportive wife out of his life.

Elliot's program initially included detoxifying from his stimulants and addressing his suicidal thoughts. When he was stabilized, we added in therapies for behavioral modification, anger management, financial planning, and resurrecting the needed lifestyle changes that would enable him to constructively interact with his reflexive reaction to stress by tolerating a little less arousal.

To detoxify from stimulants, we abruptly stopped the cocaine use. This provoked a compensatory rise in transmitters that are agitating, like glutamate, designed to enlist the sympathetic nervous system to make Elliot uncomfortable enough to arouse his cravings for more dopamine (cocaine). This was how he unconsciously learned to quiet his nervous system, a pattern that resulted in a severe addiction. We mitigated this with medication followed by behavioral therapies. The detoxification process varies depending on the chronicity of the abuse, the dosing levels of the abused substances, and any complicating medical issues. Typically for stimulants, the detoxification takes around one week.

Once Elliot was detoxified, we began to address longer-term stabilizing medications to control his dopamine imbalance. These may have included Lamictal, Abilify, and other stimulants. Given his suicidal ideation a good choice here was lithium, which works quickly and mitigates suicidal thoughts. During this phase, we also began to address the healthy eating and exercising he had abandoned. His behavioral therapies included calming exercises like mindfulness and CBT, both having proven beneficial in his substance and behavioral addictions. A 12-step program was introduced, and we connected him with a sponsor to help build a relationship with a sober community. Personal psychotherapy was suggested. Fundamental to any sobriety program are the relationships within his treatment team, for Elliot personally and for the team of practitioners who must have ongoing regular communication with the patient, and each other, to assess his progress and fine-tune any therapeutics. Also, a thorough medical evaluation was conducted to assess any underlying or complicating issues that would interfere with his general wellness or treatment options.

By the third week his suicidal ideation had faded, and he was sleeping better with only melatonin and gabapentin. He had committed to daily walks and a structured eating program. His addiction to online porn was being addressed in therapy.

Connecting Elliot to a financial planner was our next step. Planning was a complicated problem for Elliot as it is for many Swords. First, the detailed organization involving budgets, engaging and not avoiding creditors, scrutinizing bank and credit card statements, and addressing financial problems in general were all skill sets he didn't have.

A plan for Elliot included setting realistic but draconian goals like remaining accountable to his treatment team, partnering with his wife on related financial decisions, taking a beat before impulsively pulling out his credit card, creating an emergency fund for surprise catastrophes, calendaring his bill payments and switching these to electronic automatic-pay paradigms, and detailing his budget in order to feel in control of and not restricted by these needed changes. We encouraged Elliot to reach out to his debtors to meet with them personally to see if he could restructure his debts. As a charming Sword, he had a slight edge in these discussions.

Once Elliot was detoxified and in a better lifestyle mode and with a plan to manage his finances, we introduced him to anger management. Anger for Swords is expressive and sometimes poorly controlled. Reactive impulses drive the situation, and blame is usually in the mix. The goal here is to slow the response time, search for some level of accountability, and practice constructive ways to regulate his anger. The key is to understand the particular conditions that make getting triggered more likely—being tired, arriving late for an appointment, feeling impatient or already stressed—and to then develop strategies to mitigate their consequences that could become habitual. We taught Elliot to turn his negative reactions into positive responses by pointing out how bad these reflexes made him feel in their aftermath. Knowing he could use these feelings to solve the problem he was facing was a new concept. We had Elliot list the most common irritants that provoked him (traffic jams, lane-changing near collisions, someone at the checkout counter slowing down the line etcetera) and connect his feelings to those moments. We then instructed him to connect each item on this list with a solution that was situation specific and he could accept. He was asked to look over the list each day for one week to imprint some new responses. We then had him prioritize these feelings based on a 1–10 scale with 1 being a minor annoyance and 10 pushing him to pull out his sword. We asked him to impose a one-minute holding pattern for his impulse to respond. Since anger emanates from a specific problem, we asked Elliot to substitute an outburst with a solution. He could create these during his deep breathing or counting down from ten. Practicing this gave him a modicum of control, as opposed to a visceral, unmanageable reaction that often accelerated his anger and made the situation more volatile. We also suggested such options as physically leaving the situation, deep breathing, visualizing himself in the same situation as the person who angered him to create a sense of empathy, removing himself to a quiet area where he could stretch his arms and legs and perhaps even yell or scream if the environment permits. Periodically reviewing these personally triggering incidents might give someone with anger issues the ability to see patterns of these experiences and reinforce those diffusing behaviors.

Stress happens, whether triggered by a divorce, hearing you have cancer, battling your health care system, being worried about money or losing your job, facing retirement, or innumerable other events. The biological response that calls upon our HPA axis dumps cortisol into our system that demands a response. How we respond to these uncomfortable emotional states depends on whether we carry a sword or a shield, and ensuring a healthy response must be tailored to our unique brain types. To make these healthy adjustments to our natural inclinations, new choices and decisions need to be learned, practiced, and perfected.

A Few Final Words

No doubt, you Swords have noticed that you have a little Shield in you at times and vice versa. That's normal and natural. We hope that in your reading you have been able to piece together a detailed understanding of your brain type's strengths as well as its possible weaknesses. That you've noticed how your relationship with arousal shapes some of the decisions you make in your work, your intimate relationships, and lifestyles. And along the way, that you've seen glimpses of your own struggles in the stories we've described of our courageous and determined patients. The strategies, exercises and mental models/tricks we've proposed are not meant to be some sort of panacea. We distrust magic and are skeptical of cure-alls. Our goals are more modest. As humans, we are habit bound and resistant to change, however necessary that shift in our behavior might be. The kind of changes we've suggested aren't easy, take work, and require persistence. But what we've found is that if applied, they can be enormously helpful. Our hope is that we've given you a way in, a lens through which to examine some of the things that you do that don't support the best version of how you would like to be in the world.

Adding degrees of freedom and balance to your life is the bounty of learning to override the self-defeating aspects of your brain type. We hope you'll take on the challenge.

Acknowledgments

This book could only have been written with what we've learned over the years from our patients. We would like to thank Laurie Winer, who was enormously helpful in the preparation of the proposal that led to the birth of the book. We would like to extend our appreciation to Cliff Einstein for his early brainstorming. Thanks goes to our literary agent, Jill Marr, for her deft stewarding of the project to the perfect home. We would also like to give our special thanks to Norman Pearlstine and Albert Brooks, who plowed through a draft and so graciously shared their thoughts and wisdom with us. Thanks go to Susan Sullivan, whose mantra "shorter is better" was always listened to if not always heeded. Our gratitude goes to Denise Silvestro, our editor, for her notes that upped our game and fine-tuned the manuscript, as well as to Sherry Wasserman, who added the final editorial sanding. Our thanks also go out to Mike and Stuart Kipper, Harland Winter, Alan Blaustein, Liz Cole, Val, Denise, Veronica, Aaron, Jim Brooks, Myron Shapero, Peter Tilden, David Kaminsky, Judith Delafield, Daniel Seymour, and John Harwell.

This section wouldn't be complete without acknowledging my collaborator David, who has tolerated our differences with humor and grace and shared this long and winding journey of discovery and puzzle solving with me. It has been an enduring mixture of curiosity and persistence glued together with our friendship. So glad to have had this adventure with you. And my deepest thanks to my dear friend Connell, for bringing to our project his contribution as a gifted wordsmith, his stewardship, his patience with me, and his treasured friendship I have been honored to share for so many years.

Index